MARTIN DIES

A Da Capo Press Reprint Series

CIVIL LIBERTIES IN AMERICAN HISTORY

GENERAL EDITOR: LEONARD W. LEVY

Claremont Graduate School

MARTIN DIES

By
WILLIAM GELLERMANN

DA CAPO PRESS • NEW YORK • 1972

Library of Congress Cataloging in Publication Data

Gellermann, William, 1897-
    Martin Dies.
    (Civil liberties in American history)
    Includes bibliographical references.
    1. Dies, Martin, 1901-   2. U.S. Congress.
House. Special Committee on Un-American Activities
(1938-1944)   I. Series.
E743.5.D55G4 1972   328.73'0924 [B]   77-151620
ISBN 0-306-70200-2

This Da Capo Press edition of *Martin Dies* is an unabridged repub-
lication of the first edition published in New York in 1944. It is
reprinted by special arrangement with The John Day Company.

Published by Da Capo Press, Inc.
A Subsidiary of Plenum Publishing Corporation
227 West 17th Street, New York, New York 10011

Manufactured in the United States of America

MARTIN DIES

MARTIN
DIES

WILLIAM GELLERMANN

Associate Professor of Education,
Northwestern University, Author of
The American Legion as Educator

THE JOHN DAY COMPANY   NEW YORK

Government wartime restrictions on materials have made it
essential that the amount of paper used in each book be
reduced to a minimum. This volume is printed on lighter
paper than would have been used before material limita-
tions became necessary, and the number of words on each
page has been substantially increased. The smaller bulk
in no way indicates that the text has been shortened.

MANUFACTURED IN THE UNITED STATES OF AMERICA

VAN REES PRESS, NEW YORK

To BILL and DIANNE

ACKNOWLEDGMENT

The author wishes to acknowledge the invaluable assistance received from Mr. and Mrs. Ira A. Kipnis. Harriet Brewer Kipnis typed more than a third of the manuscript, and Ira Kipnis read the entire manuscript and made many valuable criticisms and suggestions. The author also wishes to acknowledge considerable help received from Miss Helen Mang in the early phases of the study.

At least one additional word of acknowledgment should be included. Without the incentive and assistance provided by my pal, best friend, and wife, Hyla Jean Akre Gellermann, the present study could not have been completed at this time.

WILLIAM GELLERMANN

April 13, 1944

"Some day we must reckon with this great political truth, that either we must make our economic system conform to our political system or we are going to be compelled to make our political system conform to the economic system. That, to my mind, is the greatest question which the American people must answer, and in my judgment they must answer that question soon." —Martin Dies (1937)

"I am not a maudlin internationalist who believes that I or my Government can go all over the world and make people democratic, whether they want to be democratic or not."
—Martin Dies (1943)

CONTENTS

PART I

MARTIN DIES

1 "AMERICANISM"

MARTIN DIES, TEXAS DEMOCRAT, and Chairman of the House Committee on Un-American Activities, has been fighting the battle of American reaction for more than five years.

There is little evidence in this man's public career to indicate that he either understands or believes in American democracy. On the contrary, the evidence indicates that he is a spearhead of a native American reaction.

The essence of totalitarianism is the conception that there are certain areas of human thought in which there are "right" answers which should be accepted by all as above and beyond criticism. Having dignified his own peculiar social philosophy as "Americanism," Dies demands that all others accept this creed, or be accused of "un-Americanism." This is diametrically opposed to the pluralism of American democracy which recognizes that in the area of social, economic, and political constitution there should be opportunity for wide difference of opinion, and that individuals can hold a variety of views on controversial issues without these variations indicating lack of intelligence or of sincerity or patriotism on the part of those who differ.

Dies has been effective in reducing the limits of American tolerance toward individuals and organizations in America whose opinions and social ideals are out of harmony with the intellectual folkways and economic interests of the dominant groups in American society, which Dies has labeled "American." Thus he has made rapid strides in modifying the conception which the American people have of what things are necessary, possible, and desirable in contemporary America. The threat of Martin Dies lies in his effort to convince a majority of his

3

fellow Americans that there are certain areas of human thought in which there are "right" answers to be accepted by all Americans, and that those who do not conform should be "exposed" as "subversive" and subjected to rigorous governmental publicity at public expense. Martin Dies has taken it upon himself to perform this "patriotic" function.

When in the past minorities have become dogmatic and have attempted to impose their views on others by suppressive means, the majority of Americans have ordinarily been able to protect themselves from these coercive tactics. We have been willing for every man to have his say. There have been instances in which those who at first seemed "wrong" and "foolish" have subsequently been found to be "right" and "enlightened" by a majority of the American people, who have finally come to accept what was at first only a minority point of view. More frequently, minority viewpoints have been partially accepted. Under any circumstance, criticism from minority groups and individuals has been valuable in leading the majority to re-examine its own position and to improve its solutions of current problems.

Power has reposed in the hands of a majority which in varying degrees has been committed to the Bill of Rights with its affirmation of the right of individuals to differ. If, however, Martin Dies should prove able to convince a substantial majority of his fellow countrymen that under his leadership they have gained such a monopoly of the truth that they should impose their majority views on minority groups and individuals, the Bill of Rights will be destroyed and individuals will no longer be free to differ on fundamental matters. And the denial to individuals of the right to disagree on fundamental matters is the very essence of totalitarianism.

There are numerous examples of totalitarianism in the present-day world. In Germany nazism is considered the one and only "right" solution. Anyone who criticizes nazism, or suggests that some other form of government might be better, is considered a traitor. Likewise in Italy fascism was considered the "right" solution, and those who questioned or rejected it were vigorously persecuted as national enemies. Each of these "isms"

4

is a set of doctrines so "right" that its proponents require that these doctrines be accepted by all citizens alike.

Martin Dies seeks to impose a similar "ism" on the American people. He calls it "Americanism." His "Americanism" demands that all Americans accept, among other things, the Christian religion as set forth by the Holy Bible; "the capitalistic system under which we live, which is a very distinct part of our whole system of government"; private property and the right of inheritance; "the American system of checks and balances with its three independent co-ordinate branches of government"; "individualism" as contrasted with "political, economic, or social regimentation based upon a planned economy." The good American rejects, among other things, "absolute social and racial equality"; "abolition of inheritance"; class, religious, and racial hatred and intolerance. Those who disagree are "subversives."

Dies explains that individuals have certain God-given rights and that "the destruction of one fundamental right is always followed by the destruction of all others." The "real answer" is to restore "Christian influence" in America. The teachings of Karl Marx are diametrically opposed to those of Jesus Christ. "Marx represents the lowest forms of materialism; Christ symbolizes the highest and noblest conceptions of the spiritual." The conflict between these two viewpoints seems to Dies to be of paramount importance. As he has said, "This irreconcilable conflict between the teachings of Christ and Marx is the issue upon which the future of Western civilization is staked." [1]

Up to the present time, most Americans have been sufficiently tolerant of differences of opinion to consider an individual a perfectly good American even if he rejected one or more of the Dies "isms." We have considered law-abiding Jews good Americans even though they do not accept the Christian religion of the majority. We have considered that a man might work for a socialistic form of government by constitutional means and yet remain a good American, even though a substantial majority of the American people is in favor of capitalism. Those who rejected most of the "isms" which Dies includes under "Americanism" were viewed askance even before Dies embarked upon his crusade; but they were tolerated. Questioning had not yet become "un-American."

The farther people are apart in their basic beliefs and assumptions, the greater the likelihood that they will question each others' judgment and integrity. In a period of economic depression and world war crisis, when millions of people are overwhelmed with a sense of personal insecurity, differences of opinion about basic social institutions and arrangements are not considered as possible material for the solution of social problems but as attempts to destroy the security which remains. It is in these periods of unrest that the preservation of tolerance becomes most difficult. At such times individuals who appeal to the masses with thought patterns which have proved congenial during periods of greater personal security may give the masses a sense of psychological security through reversion to old and familiar types of thought. That is precisely what Martin Dies has done. America's extremity has been Martin Dies' opportunity.

At a time when American capitalism is torn to shreds by its own contradictions, Dies has given the American people a scapegoat which has diverted their attention from these contradictions. His efforts have been appreciated by those who have been most benefited by the diversion. The hearings before the Dies Committee have been valuable to American capitalism. Through the press these hearings have been heralded throughout the land. The American people, by identifying themsel with Dies as he has pursued so-called "subversive" elem into their hidden lairs, have experienced a catharsis somewhat similar to that enjoyed by Germans who identified themselves with Hitler as he persecuted the Jews. All such persecution is based on the same assumption, that if we can only exterminate an alleged internal enemy, everything will be all right. It is an oversimplification, to be sure; but it is serviceable to those who wish to avoid a thoroughgoing re-examination of the present economic system with its periods of depression and unemployment, or of the prevailing world order with its periods of war, misery, and human anguish.

Raymond Gram Swing has written that "the only real distinction between our present-day capitalist democracy and fascism is that one tolerates the democratic technique of operating the country, and the other does not." [2] Anything which tends to destroy democracy in the United States is a step in the direction of fascism. We know that in those countries in Europe which became fascist between World War I and World War II, fascism resulted in considerable measure from the efforts of those who sought to preserve an unequal distribution of economic power. In order to preserve their own favored position, the privileged were willing to liquidate those agencies of democracy which could be used to promote a larger measure of equality. When the great industrialists of Italy and Germany saw that their special privileges were threatened by the growth of democracy, they were willing to make use of political henchmen to destroy every vestige of political and economic democracy in order to save their own economic autocracy from the egalitarian tendencies which democracy represented. The destruction of democracy did not take place all at once; it was accomplished step by step.

Democracy can be destroyed through the elimination of those rights and agencies by means of which it is maintained and extended. What are some of these agencies? One is freedom of speech. Another is freedom of assembly. Freedom of the press is a third, and religious liberty a fourth. And in a highly integrated and dynamic society such as characterizes the industrialed nations of Western civilization in the twentieth century, 'e great masses of the people must be free to organize and to advocate social changes which seem to them likely to increase economic equality, social security, and individual freedom. Deprive the masses of these agencies of democracy and the fascist forces in society are correspondingly strengthened. Other democratic agencies are the labor unions, the co-operatives, and the minor political parties. Destroy freedom of speech, freedom of the press, freedom of assembly, religious liberty, the right to organize, and the right to advocate social change; destroy labor unions, minor political parties, and co-operatives—the agencies by which democratic equality is maintained and extended—and you destroy democracy. And when you destroy democracy you

7

have fascism. Fascism *is* a reorganization of society in which despotic economic power is no longer restrained by the agencies of democracy. Fascism marks the triumph of economic feudalism over political democracy.

If the American people can be deprived of the right to meet, the right to organize, the right to say what they think, the right to advocate changes which they conceive to be in their interests, the right to write and the right to publish, democracy is well on its way to destruction, and fascism is on its way to triumph.

Starting in 1938 and continuing up to the present time, Dies has challenged all of these rights and has done much to liquidate several of them. Thus by his activities in restraint of these rights Martin Dies has been a spearhead of American reaction.

In many ways his present position is a complete reversal of the one he held prior to 1938 when his committee was first instituted. For example, in 1932 we find Dies declaring that America was in the midst of an economic revolution. He continued, "Although we still retain the external form, the professions and precepts of a democratic Government, there has grown up in our midst an industrial and financial oligarchy as absolute in its sway as ever existed in the heyday of mediaeval feudalism. If the present trend is not checked we will have two systems diametrically opposed to each other but existing side by side," He added this significant statement: "If our economic system is to become monopolistic, then our political system will become monopolistic, because two systems diametrically opposed to each other, as light and darkness, as right and wrong, cannot coexist under the same structure and fabric of government." He realized that "no nation could be free politically that was enslaved industrially," that "economic freedom was essential to political freedom." Nevertheless, he has more recently carried on an aggressive campaign of "exposure" against those of his fellow countrymen who have concerned themselves with the problem of regaining the economic freedom which he himself declared essential to political freedom.

In 1932 Martin Dies saw the conflict between political democracy and economic autocracy, and his sympathies seemed clearly on the side of democracy. Was this no more than the passing

8

idealism of youth? On the contrary, Dies saw the conflict not only then but later. For example, in 1937, the year before the launching of his investigation, Dies declared on the floor of the House of Representatives: *"Either we must make our economic system conform to our political system or we are going to be compelled to make our political system conform to the economic system. That, to my mind, is the greatest question which the American people must answer, and in my judgment they must answer that question soon."*

This statement by Dies is genuinely prophetic. It reminds one of the statement which Abraham Lincoln made in a debate with Douglas in 1858. Lincoln said, " 'A house divided against itself cannot stand.' I believe this government cannot endure permanently half slave and half free. I do not expect the house to fall; but I expect it will cease to be divided. It will become all one thing or all the other." William Henry Seward, later Secretary of State under Lincoln, commenting on the same issue and at about the same time, declared, "It is an irrepressible conflict . . . and it means that the United States must, and will, sooner or later, become entirely a slaveholding nation or entirely a free-labor nation."

The interesting contrast between Abraham Lincoln and William Henry Seward, on the one hand, and Martin Dies, on the other, is that whereas Lincoln and Seward stood by their guns and fought for freedom and against slavery until freedom won, Martin Dies, seeing an imminent conflict between political democracy and economic autocracy, turned tail and went over to the side of economic feudalism. In his new role he has rendered great service to the cause of economic autocracy by liquidating the agencies of democracy.

After declaring in 1937 that "we must make our economic system conform to our political system" or suffer the consequences, by 1938 Dies had done a complete about-face. He declared in that year that "the capitalistic system under which we live" is "a very distinct part of our whole system of government" and embarked on a campaign to expose men whose views about our economic system were not different from his own a year before. Let us appeal from Martin Dies drunk with the

9

power and publicity which have come to him as chairman of the House Committee on Un-American Activities, to the earlier Martin Dies sober with the responsibility of being a member of a New Deal Congress under the leadership of President Roosevelt. Let us consider what we mean by democracy and its growth in America.

Democracy is an ethical ideal which recognizes the moral equality of all human beings. Democracy has four principal characteristics.

The first of these is respect for personality. Man is considered to be the measure of all things. Human beings are entitled to be different and to live their own lives as they wish to live them, subject only to the restriction that rights of the individual end when their exercise would deprive others of their rights. Respect for personality finds expression in the Bill of Rights of the American Constitution, which grants each of us the right to freedom of speech, freedom of assembly, trial by jury, freedom of the press, and freedom of religion. Respect for personality is an important attribute of democracy because it recognizes the right of human beings to be different. Religious liberty is not just the right to belong to the Christian (Disciples) Church, as Martin Dies does; it is the right to be a Methodist, or a Catholic. It is the right to be a Jew instead of a Christian, or to be a Buddhist, or to reject all forms of supernaturalism, or to organize a religion of one's own. Respect for personality is an expression of the philosophy of live and let live.

A second characteristic of democracy is shared decisions. To the extent that we have democracy, individuals are permitted to share in decisions which affect their welfare. To the extent that you have equality of power in the reaching of decisions in any social group, to that extent you have democracy. This does not mean that all will be equally influential, but it does mean that when it comes to reaching a decision which concerns the interests of the social group, each individual in the group will have an equal share of power in rendering that decision. To the extent that we have democracy in America, each individual's vote counts for one, and nobody's counts for more than one. Each person, be he man or woman, Jew or Gentile, educated or uneducated, Catholic or Protestant, Negro or white, able to pay a poll tax or not able to pay a poll tax, rich or poor, has one vote, and one vote only, to the extent that we have political democracy in America. Harold Laski pointed out long ago that when you exclude a man from a share in the exercise of power, you are very likely to exclude him also from the benefits which are derived from the exercise of power. There is no better illustration of this in America than the exploitation of the Negroes in Mr. Dies' own section of the country; the Negro is excluded from power, and from the benefits to be derived therefrom.

A third characteristic of democracy is that it recognizes that we live in a changing world, and that social practices and institutions must be modified from time to time. In a democracy nothing is fixed and final; everything is subject to change should the necessity arise. The Constitution of the United States recognizes the `need for change. Time has brought about mighty changes in the Constitution. That being the case, how can anyone of lesser stature than the fathers of our country set himself up to stop the tide of social progress on the supposition that in certain areas perfection has been attained? Inflexible constitutions have been written, adopted, and discarded, but the American Constitution has survived. No doubt its survival is not to be explained in terms of a single factor. But one factor of great importance in its survival has been its inherent recognition of the need for change which symbolizes democracy.

A fourth characteristic of democracy is its use of the method of knowledge and intelligence. Democracy acts on the theory that it is desirable to seek knowledge tending to indicate the social consequences of different proposed courses of action. As John Dewey has pointed out,[3] democracy rejects the method of external authority, dictating conformity to its mandates; the method of custom, demanding conformity to past precedents; the method of routine, which persists in present practice, not caring to ask why, or to consider alternatives; the method of self-interest by an individual or class, pretending to render public service of a superior type if the public will but accept its leadership; and the method of force and violence, whether exercised by force of arms, misrepresentation, or financial power. Democracy itself may have to resort to force in order to protect itself from force, but it always prefers to use the method of knowledge and intelligence. Democracy has no objection to revolution, but anyone favoring revolutionary change must abide by the rules of the game, which provide that he must convince a majority of his fellow countrymen to elect to office men who will enact his proposals into law by strictly constitutional means.

Dies' acts indicate a lack of belief in democracy. He does not respect personality. He does not believe in shared decisions, preferring to decide everything himself, as shown in his arbitrary manner of handling his committee. He does not recognize the fundamental nature of change, believing rather that there are certain things which are fixed and final, right and absolute. He has tried to freeze the status quo, to keep America as it is, instead of working to adjust our social institutions to the requirements of the twentieth century. Finally, he does not believe in the method of knowledge and intelligence, but uses his high office to promote his own political interests rather than the common welfare of the American people. He uses external authority, demanding acceptance of his own ideas as to what is fixed, final, and right; and he uses force and violence to "expose," destroy, embarrass, and terrorize those individuals and organizations whose views are fundamentally different from his own.

Dies gives no evidence of having grasped the dynamic quality of American democracy or of understanding that in the course of American history the common people have gained nothing without struggle. Through organized struggle they have gained national independence, the Bill of Rights, the right to vote, the right to educational opportunity, emancipation from slavery, and freedom from discrimination because of sex. Every time the masses of the people have attempted to move forward in their struggle for equality, there have been those who have tried to tell them that they had already gone far enough, and that to go farther would be sinful, unpatriotic, unnatural, and contrary to the will of God. But such false prophets have always been brushed aside, and progress continued.

Now, as Martin Dies himself implied in 1937, the crucial issue of our time is whether democracy is to be extended to the area of economics. The outcome of the struggle between the masses of the people, who hold the political power, and the few who hold the economic power, is still in doubt. A constructive decision, made with balance and judgment, cannot be reached so long as the scene is clouded by the propaganda of Martin Dies.

In this propaganda Dies uses all of the common devices as defined by the Institute of Propaganda Analysis.[4]

One of his favorite tricks is name-calling by which he causes us to react unfavorably to a person, an organization, or a set of ideas, by associating them with something we already dislike and react against. Consequently, our reaction is controlled by an unfavorable association from the past rather than by a present examination of the facts. A dog can be so thoroughly conditioned by being slapped at the same time that the word "Poison!" is yelled at him, that thereafter he will drop a piece of meat, or leave it alone, if he has not already taken it in his mouth, when the word "Poison!" is yelled at him. In much the same way, humans can be conditioned to come to a dead stop, in their thinking and actions, when certain words are shouted at them. Among such words are "un-Christian," "atheistic," "immoral," "irreligious," "old-fashioned," "radical," "communistic," "reactionary," "fascist," "dishonest," "disloyal," "unpatriotic," "un-American," and, in some parts of the country, "Republican," or "Democratic," depending on the locality. Dies, the propagandist, attempts to get us to reject something without examining it for ourselves on the basis of its merits. His favorite names for organizations have been "Communist," "Communist front," "foreign-controlled," and "un-American"; for individuals, "Communist," "fellow traveler," "crackpot," "subversive," and "agent of Moscow"; for criticism of himself, "abuse," "misrepresentation," and "vilification." Dies seldom bothers to give any proof that the names he attaches are deserved. Nor does he define the opprobrious terms which he applies to individuals and groups; he simply makes the assertion that the individual or organization is a so-and-so and counts on public reaction to bolster his statement.

13

This trick Dies has reinforced with another device, one "by which the propagandist carries over the authority, sanction, and prestige of something we respect and revere to something he would have us accept." [5] Dies has attempted to identify his crusade with the Christian religion, the Declaration of Independence, the Constitution, Americanism, capitalism, and "Congress as an institution." But the principal transfer from which Dies benefits is the prestige which his personal opinions enjoy because the American people transfer to Dies the respect which they rightfully have for Congress and for congressional investigations. Dies is the beneficiary of the reputation for hard work, integrity, and great service which Congress has built up over many years.

Another propaganda technique employed by Dies is the testimonial, which gets us to accept opinions on the recommendation of those whom we admire and respect. For this purpose Dies has called in such witnesses as the comic J. B. Matthews, formerly head of the American League Against War and Fascism, and representatives of the church and patriotic societies to gain testimony in support of his own primary assumptions.

The device, however, which Dies has used more frequently than any other is card-stacking, in which the propagandist, by dodging issues, avoiding facts, overemphasis, underemphasis, and sometimes by downright misrepresentation, leads us to conclusions which we would not reach if we had all the available facts. Anyone who has read the hearings of the Dies Committee, particularly when Dies himself was directing the questioning, realizes that witnesses were often prevented from presenting evidence which ran counter to the things which the committee wanted to prove. Witnesses were denied the right to be cross-examined at equal length by their own attorneys to bring out relevant matters not covered in the examination. Witnesses were summoned who seemed likely to support Dies' position; often others opposed thereto were given no opportunity to be heard. And unfavorable witnesses were sometimes heard only in executive session and their testimony was not included in the published hearings.

Dies uses the glittering generalities device by associating

14

his activities with such color words as "impartial," "nonpartisan," "investigation," "scientific," "our form of government," "American," and "Christian" so as to dignify, add weight to, and gain acceptance for his own position. He uses the bandwagon device, by claiming that practically everybody thinks as he does. He claims that 131,000,000 out of 132,000,000 Americans, including babes in arms, illiterates, and millions who have never heard of Dies support his committee, whereas only a few "subversives" oppose it. Finally, he uses the "plain folks" device to ingratiate himself with the common people, making it appear that he is "an humble Member of this great body [Congress]," a relatively poor man continually conscious of the hardships of the poor farmers in his home district, a father of three sons one of whom is in the military service, a man who constantly recalls and seeks to emulate the pattern set for him by a great and illustrious father.

This is the man and these are the techniques which we shall examine.

2 LIKE FATHER: LIKE SON

THE PRESENT MARTIN DIES is not the first person by that name to enter Congress from the Second Congressional District of Texas, for his father represented the same district from 1909 to 1919. The *Congressional Record* shows similarity in the legislative careers of father and son. An examination of the father's views, expressed in Congress, throws light on how Martin Dies became the kind of person he is. The record shows that Martin Dies, Senior, was a man of unusual ability, keen political insight, and decided views on many of the same social, political, and economic issues on which his son has spoken since he became a member of Congress in 1931.

Born in Louisiana in 1870, Martin Dies, Senior, was reared on a farm and educated in the public schools of Texas. As a young man he was a newspaper printer's devil, and later, newspaper editor. Admitted to the bar in 1892, he practiced law until elected county judge of Tyler County, Texas, in 1894. In 1898 he became district attorney of the First Judicial District of Texas. He entered Congress in 1909 and served until 1919. During the time that Martin Dies, Senior, was in Congress, Martin Dies, Junior, born in Texas on November 5, 1901, was spending an impressionable period of his life in Washington, D. C., where he attended Custer Springs Military Academy and, later, National University.[1]

The elder Dies made his first speech in Congress on March 25, 1909, on tariff legislation. "What I lack ... in a comprehensive knowledge of the details of the tariff bill," he declared, "I hope to make up by the candor and sincerity with which I express myself." Condemning the protective tariff bill then pending before the House as discriminatory against the South, he declared the Payne tariff "just what the country had a right to expect at the hands of the Republican party." He informed the Republicans that if they hoped to gain the support of the South and West they would have to repeal "odious sectional tariff laws," like the one then under consideration, and also "make haste to declare for the white man's domination of this Government and integrity of the Caucasian race." [2] The following day Dies drew applause from the Republican side of the House by supporting a tariff on lumber which, though contrary to the principles in the platform of the Democratic party, was favored by the lumber manufacturers of his own district. When this contradiction was called to his attention, Dies declared that although he would be pleased if men and conditions were perfect, he did not find them so, and consequently, to avoid daydreams and folly he dealt with conditions as he found them.[3]

His discussion of the tariff in which Dies referred to his own candor and sincerity, to the supremacy of the white race, and to certain political and philosophical conclusions which did not immediately concern the tariff shows the discursive trait so characteristic of his speeches. Seldom did he deal exclusively with any topic, but used the one under consideration as a point of departure for comment on whatever subjects happened to be within the realm of his interest at the time. As often as not he spoke on subjects not before the House. He was, however, an interesting, entertaining speaker, and his remarks, no matter how discursive they might be, were usually well received by his fellow congressmen.

Speaking in 1910 on a favorite subject of his early Congressional career—the dangers of foreign immigration—he said, "I love this great Republic of free men, and I pray the God of nations that free government may not perish from this land . . . I am not an alarmist, Mr. Chairman, but it is my deliberate conviction that our free institutions are in danger." In his opinion illiterate immigrants from despotic foreign nations might undermine the foundations of free government here. Patriotism and intelligence were both necessary to effective citizenship in a self-governing nation; neither prerequisite was sufficient without the other. Illiterates from abroad were "incompetent and incapable of arbitrating the destiny of this one remaining Republic on the face of God's earth." Therefore he sought to "quarantine" the United States against illiteracy as "against the bubonic plague." Although not defending the illiteracy which existed among the native population of America, he felt that native-born Americans, reared in the traditions of a free country, did not threaten the American form of government as did foreign-born illiterates who, early in life, had been habituated to despotism in their native lands.

In the same speech he typically expressed convictions on a number of other subjects: he felt that "the selfish rich" were as great a danger to the republic as "the ignorant poor"; that incipient American imperialism and "entangling alliances" might involve the United States in foreign affairs; that opposition to the growth of militarism in the United States was imperative; and that it was more important that "all" Americans be "happy" than that "a few" be "illustrious." Throughout the speech Dies quoted and referred to authorities such as the Holy Bible, Marcus Aurelius, Shakespeare, Montesquieu, De Tocqueville, Lord Bryce, and others.

As he reached the final section of his address, he shouted:

Oh, for a revival of the old time religions of Democracy...
It is easier to drift with the current than to swim up the stream.
It is safer to fall in with popular error than to fall out with it and hazard a battle.

Those who clamor at the door of Congress for private advantage are ever awake and alert. They are quick to reward those who help and punish those who hinder their spoliation of the people.

The representative who combats the selfish schemes of the vigilant few in the interests of the indifferent many may soon find that when election days roll around the plundered, like Grouchy, come up too late to save the day. [Applause] ...

This is my country; this Capitol is the citadel of my liberties... and while I live and occupy a seat in this Chamber no man's derision, and no man's power shall make me ashamed or afraid to combat the wrong, to defend the right. [Applause] ...

Let us hope that the giant of public opinion will awaken from his slumbers in time to throw off the narcotic which deadens the sense of danger. Let us watch by day and pray by night that this Government shall, under the Providence of God, remain a land of freedom to brighten the hopes and encourage the aspirations of mankind. [Applause] [4]

The elder Dies was deeply opposed to the development of militarism in the United States. Except during America's participation in the World War, he was an outspoken opponent of every extension of the military department, such as locating the American flag 8,000 miles out in the Pacific Ocean "to lord it over an inferior people," and building an army organized "to oppress our neighbors" that might "return to oppress our own people," in lieu of encouraging ordinary domestic pursuits. As early as 1911 he urged the United States to "attend to its own business" and stop "meddling" in "the politics of Europe." [5]

On January 22, 1915, Dies declared that the country was in no danger of invasion,[6] and the following year asserted that there was even "less cause for hysteria than there had been a year earlier." He considered it "the lesson of all history that the spirit of liberty, equality, and free government could not live in the military atmosphere." America's best defense, he felt, would be an army of volunteers rather than an overgrown military establishment which might easily prove greater as an internal danger than as a defense against foreign invasion.[7] On January 28, 1916, he warned against a war scare produced by munition dealers, sensational newspaper and magazine stories, inflammatory moving pictures, military men, and "the Teddy Roosevelts, who are never truly happy unless they can see blood and bellow like a bull in a slaughter pen." Urging people to quit talking about and prophesying war,[8] he thought the preparedness parades in Washington were "ridiculous" and amounted to nothing "except to further gum-fuzz and confuse the American people." [9] He proposed that taxes for army and navy appropriations be levied in proportion to wealth rather than on the basis of consumption, since in that way profit-makers might be made less anxious to embark on war.[10] Although always opposed to government ownership, during the war he was "prepared to make an exception in the building of a navy and the manufacture of munitions of war. We will never get rid of the war cry until we take the profits out of making and building for war. ... The Government must make its own instruments of preparedness." [11]

As early as June 7, 1916, he recognized the tendencies leading the country toward compulsory military service and American participation in the war. "If there is anything in this world that will produce war in this country," he declared, "it is the intemperate and idiotic talk going forth from public men in the public press." No nation on earth had "a war grievance" against America, and he predicted that "unless we threaten and bully and fan the smoldering embers of hate into war and alarm the American people into the belief that the country is to be invaded, we will have no war." Amplifying this, he said:

The one thing doing more to drive this country today in the direction of war than any other combination of causes is the simple statement that we are going to have a war, and putting a pistol in our pocket for a war. That has produced many a corpse and funeral out in the western part of Texas where I was raised. A fellow gets a few drinks in him, puts a pistol in his pocket and says, "I know I am going to have a fight with Tom Jones." Tom hears about it, puts a pistol in one pocket and a dirk in another and says, "I am ready." Then if Tom carelessly starts to get his tobacco out of his hip pocket, the fellow shoots him. That is precisely what we are doing today. What do they say? We are going to have a war; we are going to be invaded; we are going into a war with Europe. Let us get ready. Let us arm, let us equip, let us be ready so that at the drop of the hat or the pop of the match we are ready to go off. How many of you want your sons to go into the standing army today? Cry patriotism! How many sons of Members of Congress are serving as private soldiers in the standing army? Mr. Chairman and gentlemen of the House, no nation at any time was ever able to have a standing army without military compulsion. Why do you not tell the American people the plain, unvarnished truth, that you are heading toward compulsory service? The time is coming, if the American people do not right about face and stem this awful cry of fanaticism and hysteria, when you will be sending the corporals and colonels around to put the handcuffs on the young men of America and putting them into a standing army as in Europe they are doing today. This country had better stop and think. Nowhere in all the annals of the world has a republic grown so great, is a people so happy and so prosperous and free. We began it without these doctrines of organized, high military preparedness, and all the years we have grown with the wisdom of the fathers. I appeal to you as representatives of the people of this country, think you well before you set your face against these great traditions upon which we are builded and turn back to the theories of the old blood-soaked soil of Europe. [Great applause] [12]

When the crisis actually came, Dies voted for the declaration of war against Germany, and for conscription.[13] Once America was in the war, he spoke in behalf of "a baptism of spiritual patriotism" which would lead America to victory.[14] He wanted all Americans solidly behind the President for the duration.[15] But when the war was over, he urged that the army be demobilized and the boys be permitted to return to their homes.[16] Then, too, he had harsh words for "the people who wear the stars and garters and the epaulettes of military power," and "want men to command, and power, and more power." [17] Speaking against the President's trip to Europe, Dies urged him to stay out of a "card game where there are more kings and queens than there are presidents." [18]

Unlike his son, Martin Dies, Senior, had little use for Congressional investigations. When an investigation of the legislative lobbies in Washington was being considered, the elder Dies declared, "You know we are doing a whole lot of investigating, and I have never found any good that has come of it, so far as my observation has been concerned." Referring to the investigation of the money trust by Samuel Untermyer, Dies said, "Speaking of the Money Trust and the fifteen-odd thousand dollars paid to our Hebrew brother, Mr. Untermyer, by the parties engaged in conducting the investigation, I want to ask the gentleman [Mr. Cox] this question: Does he know anything more about the Money Trust than he knew and everybody else knew before that investigation?" He was of the opinion that an investigation of the Washington lobbies would "turn out" as the Untermyer investigation had, that is, "not worth a penny"

21

although it would "cost the Government almost a quarter of a million dollars." He urged Congressmen to go back to their legislative work "instead of running around . . . like scared rats in a barn talking about lobbies that do not exist and lobbyists that do not exist." He recommended impeachment of the guilty persons, if there had been dishonesty on the part of Congressmen, rather than "a long-winded investigation," but expressed as his personal conviction that Congress was "pure," "honest," and "incorruptible." [19] When an appropriation of $400,000 was proposed to carry on a federal food investigation, he took the position that there was no reason to spend $400,000 "to find out something which every honest and intelligent one of you already knows." [20] Dies' views on this subject, as on others, were very consistent throughout his entire ten-year term in Congress. He seldom, if ever, changed his mind.

Periodically the elder Dies was alarmed over the "ultraradicalism of the country." [21] He described himself as a "reformer" and "progressive" but declared that progress suffered from "recent converts" who felt "called upon to advocate radical and extreme measures." [22] He contrasted "the steady pull" of the "true reformer" with the "fitful jerks of insurgents," who kick "when honest horses pull" and want "to run away the moment the load begins to move." These insurgents, he felt, were as great an obstacle to true progress as standpatters who refused to move at all.[23] In view of his description of himself as a "progressive" and "reformer" it is interesting to note these statements: "there have been no new lessons in free government since the Constitution was written" in 1787; [24] "human nature is just now what it always has been, and will probably remain so until the end of time." [25]

Dies wanted helpless minorities protected against unrestrained majority rule and domination. He thought that minority sections, classes, and creeds would remain safe in America only as long as America had "a written constitution and an independent judiciary to enforce it." Without minority protection from an "unrestrained majority," white supremacy in the South could not have become as "secure and unshakeable as the eternal hills." [26] Not only did he believe in a written constitution

22

to protect minorities, but he considered the system of checks and balances indispensable to free government. He declared once that President Wilson believed in neither of these two basic principles of free government.[27] Dies thanked God that he himself had "an unshakeable faith in the judiciary." [28]

Speaking against the conservation movement, he said: "The great resources of this country...are for the American people. ...I am not for reservations and parks. I would have the great timber and mineral and coal resources of this country opened to the people.... God Almighty has located the resources of this country in such a form as that His children will not use them in disproportion, and your Pinchots will not be able to controvert and circumvent the laws of God Almighty." The *Congressional Record* shows that to this appeal there was applause and also cries of "Vote! Vote!" in the House.[29]

"I believe...that a little innocent demagoguery," Dies said on January 27, 1915, "is a good thing in Congress, but we are carrying it too far.... I wish the American people to know that all the Government can do is to give them a fair and equal chance in the race of life. Let the farmer alone, to stand upon his manhood, to work out his destiny in his fields, and stop teaching him that it is the duty of this Government to buy his produce or lend him money upon it. Let those who want to escape the ills of poverty learn the truth...that they must labor and practice economy if they would escape poverty." [30]

Discussing the Forest Service, he said, "The people never get anything where the Government manages the business, except the privilege of paying the bills.... The Government as a manager of business...is a failure." [31] In another connection he said, "If I am earnest about anything in this world, if I am wrought up over any public question, it is this cry of having the Government of the United States take over the activities of individuals and putting the Government into Government ownership." [32]

Woman suffrage Dies opposed because "it would thrust the ballot into the hands of millions of ignorant negro women of the South and force unsought political burdens, upon millions of home makers throughout the land who are at present more

23

profitably employed than in running after politics." Fearing that "a race of manly women [would] call forth a race of womanly men," he declared that God had "purposely" made men and women "for different lines of activity":

He gave strength and courage to man and upon woman He bestowed grace and beauty. To man He gave strong reasoning powers and a keen sense of justice; to woman He gave unfailing intuition and kindly sympathies. He fortified man with courage to go into the frontier forest and hew down trees and subdue savage beasts and men; He fitted the woman to preside over the home and sanctify it with motherhood. This same wise Father gave man to the world to write her laws and fight her battles, and by the side of this thundering Mars he placed gentle Venus to bind up his wounds and kiss away his sorrows. *

He considered votes for women not "a great boon" but "a burdensome responsibility," and saw no reason why, in order to please a few women who wanted the ballot, it should be thrust on the vast majority of women, who neither desired to vote nor would avail themselves of the opportunity: "Women are already fully engaged in the world's most important work." Moreover:

The mind of man rather runs to prosaic reasoning, while the mind of woman is given to poetical idealism. It is inevitable that woman's natural bent of mind should incline her to socialism, and nothing would set socialism up in business as quickly as woman suffrage. The Socialist Party recognizes this, and as a result are almost to a man for woman suffrage. And I can think of nothing worse that could happen to this Republic than a reign of socialism, unless it would be woman's abdication of her crown as queen of the American home. . . .

Men have the ballot, and are they better off? Thousands of men are constantly without work, and many stalk empty handed to the bread line. Men, too, are underpaid. . . . If voting would cure the evils of poverty or mollify the exactions of the taskmaster, why do not men vote themselves into Utopian bliss. . . . In good truth we cannot banish the troubles of the world by statute. . . .

In good truth, my dear sisters, you cannot better serve your Government than by keeping to the tasks nature has fitted you for, and in the discharge of which you have been splendidly successful. Incidentally, you can also promote the cause of good government by not interfering with your brothers in the discharge of the task which God and immemorial custom seem to have appointed them to.

Dies warned the mothers of the country to "turn a deaf ear" to the "shouts" of suffragette "agitators" because "their song is that of the siren to tempt you from your homes and God-appointed spheres of life." [33]

Two major agencies Dies saw working toward socialism in the United States: first, the millionaires, who aroused discontent and lack of confidence on the part of the masses of the people; second, the ignorant foreign laborer, "who has been told by a lot of flannel-mouthed politicians that he has a right to quit his job and then shoot the man who tries to take the job." [34]

Dies' ideas on socialism were brought into sharpest relief in a discussion he had with Representative Meyer London of New York on February 22 and 23, 1918. In discussing federal control of railroads Representative London had said:

When you repudiate the idea that public utilities are ultimately to be owned and controlled and managed by the people in their collective capacity you deny the very essence of democracy. . . .

Within a country priding itself on its democratic ideals organized wealth establishes an empire of its own, a dominion of its own. . . . To say that you are opposed to public ownership . . . means to deny the essential principles of democracy, which means self-rule, self-rule industrially, self-rule in economic relations. What good is it if a man has the right to vote if there are within his own country powers which determine how much of his wages shall be taken away from him for bread, how much for meat, how much for sugar, how much for transportation, so that at the end of a day's work or at the end of a year's work he finds the result of his labor taken away from him by some power outside of himself?

The value of political democracy lies in the opportunity it offers to the people to evolve into an industrial democracy.

Otherwise democracy would be a mere myth. Is not self-rule the very essence of democracy? Henry Ward Beecher, in defining slavery, said, "Slavery is a state of affairs where the individual's life is controlled by powers outside of himself". . . .[35]

Calling London's speech "Bolsheviki," the elder Dies under-took to answer it. He considered it "incongruous" that a man like London, who "thinks Washington one of the worst enemies that democracy ever had," should be allowed, as London appar-ently had been, "to occupy the Speaker's chair [Applause] under the flag of our country." Dies declared:

Ours has been a political democracy under Washington and Jeffer-son and Madison and Hamilton, a democracy that guaranteed prop-erty rights and the rights of life and liberty and the pursuit of happiness. He [Mr. London] says that it is a right to evolute into a Bolsheviki industrial democracy, the like of which is now seen in Russia, where we have a demonstration of the efficacy of the Bolshe-viki democracy. Nowhere, my friends, under a canopy of heaven has mankind been vouchsafed so great a Government as this which our fathers instituted and perpetuated up to this time. [Applause] Wherever in all the annals of history has religion been so free to worship God under the dictates of its own conscience as America? Wherever have the portals of home and opportunity been so wide open as in this our free land of liberty in America? And yet this man comes and says he wants it to evolute, "evolute," into an indus-trial democracy, the like that Lenine and Trotsky are practicing in Russia today.

What is that democracy? It is to go into the stable of your neigh-bor and take his horse, to go into his fields and take his plow, to go into the highway and, as you go, take his property, and he calls that industrial democracy.... In the name of God, democracy, Washington, Jefferson, and Hamilton we shall have none of that in our country. [Applause]....

I have become thoroughly disgusted.... Let the gentleman from New York [Mr. London] rise before this majestic Congress, the greatest representative body on earth, and let him tell—or anyone who ever lived on this earth—of any country that has had as much in its life of hope and liberty and justice as the American republic has had for the last hundred years. And yet he says we can make it better.... Will you turn it over to him? No, no. My friends, this question needs to be aired before the American people.... Are you going to let a lot of ignorant-headed Socialists try an experiment on you? You have had your rail-splitting Lincoln, you have had your Grover Cleveland sweeping the office, you have the greatest railroad system in the world and the greatest system of government in the world, and yet you let a Socialist from New York stand up there under the flag of our Country, and say that this country has been the greatest failure in the world! In the name of God it has been the greatest Republic in the world. . . .

A man in the ditches digging can become president. . . . Without honesty in the state there can be no liberty; without property rights and the respect of property rights there can be no liberty. . . . Suppose you steal the railroads; suppose you take them, and if you take the farms and the banks and the factories from those who toil and who by thrift and self-denial have accumulated the property of the country, you will have a national dishonesty in feeling; and, in addition to that, the old earth will never give her fruit except to those who bud and bloom and make the bread of the world, except that labor go into the fields and strive and struggle for it; and I commend to socialism these words—honesty, thrift, and toil. [Applause]. . . .

The gentleman from New York [Mr. London], my Socialist friend, can not find in all the history of the world a government he would prefer to this. Where would he go to seek it? . . . When did it come to pass that you and I should sit under the drippings of the fountain of the gentleman from New York [Mr. London], who follows Lenine and Trotsky, who backed off before the German machine today. You have got to meet power with power. . . .

And do not you think we will tolerate socialism and the arguments of socialism in this national emergency. . . . When this war is over . . . we are not going to have any of your socialism, your Lenines and Trotskys, men who want to put women in the trenches. . . . I have not any sympathy with your Lenines and Trotskys. I have no sympathy with Russian socialism that is ground in the dust. They are getting what is coming to them. They imagine it is Russian socialism if you steal land or steal a plow or steal the fodder or steal a mule or steal horses. You think that means democracy? Democracy means law and order; democracy means property rights guaranteed to those who sow the seed that they shall reap the harvest; it guarantees to those who build the houses that they shall live in the houses they have built. Liberty without property rights is nothing, worthless, and you find it so now. . . .

There is not going to be any socialism here; no socialism. We are honest. My dollar is my dollar, and when a man works a day and gets $2 and saves a dollar that he puts aside that is his money; that belongs to him to shelter him in his old age; it is his home, his bulwark, his place of refuge. We are not going to have socialism here my friends. Your dream of socialism is a nightmare in Russia today. . . . Do not ask a Republic, the democracy of Hamilton and Jefferson, of Lee and Grant and Lincoln, to subscribe to your theory of demoralized socialism because the laborer is worthy of his hire and the man who struggles to win property, sweats for it and denies himself to be something, he is not entitled to be shattered by the dream of socialism. . . .

Here is liberty; here is security of property and life; here is a great Republic, the like of which the world never saw, and men sit down and doze while men like the gentleman from New York fiddle while republics disintegrate. [Applause]. . . . Let this be a free Republic, secure in property rights and secure in individual rights, where in the name of God the blighting shadow of Bolsheviki socialism may come to haunt our dreams no more. [Applause]

Martin Dies, Senior, made his farewell address to the House of Representatives on March 4, 1919:

I was raised on a farm, and all my life . . . my dream has been that I might amass a competency and go back to the country and follow the plow, feed the pigs, pick up the fresh eggs, and live in the fresh air of the open country in which I was born. [Applause] . . .

I had dreams that some day I might become a Member of Congress. . . . But, you know, I never had much ambition to be a rubber stamp. [Laughter and applause] . . .

We are wonderfully anxious to mix up with Europe, Asia, and Africa; we are wonderfully anxious to entangle ourselves in the hopes and destiny, with the broils, distractions, and feuds of the animosities of Europe.

You know, as God shall judge me when I stand before Him, and I believe He lives, the best hope of this great Government, the best hope of this great people, and the children yet to be born from the loins of men and the wombs of women, is to live on this hemisphere and attend to our own business, and not mix up in European politics. [Applause] . . .

They say this is provincialism. In my judgment, when the history of this world shall be written in the years yet to come, it may be said truly, as it is said now, that the best example of free Government the world has ever known was between the signing of the Constitution of the United States and the good year 1912. A hundred years, two hundred, and history will write it down that this Republic, these United States, afforded the best opportunity to mankind for liberty, for hope, opened widest the door of opportunity, of any Government that ever existed in the world from the day the Constitution was made to the fateful days of the present.

The future is not given to mortal man to know. That we are departing rapidly from all of the spirit and traditions of this Republic is apparent to every man with an iota of sense.... I only wish, Mr. Chairman, and gentlemen of the Congress, that we might have a return to the spirit of democracy and republicanism. I only wish that the truly great men who have lived on this earth might send their spirits to guide us now. He is a great man who is content to abide the law, who is not concerned with his own egotism and self-importance that he wants to change the law in order that he may make the change. Washington, Jefferson, Lincoln, Cleveland, Taft, were willing to live under the Constitution and bow in obedience to its mandates and its precepts. A wonderfully good thing it would be for this country, a wonderfully good thing it would be for the parties on both sides of the aisle if they might learn to respect the ancient landmarks which our fathers have set. ...

I love this Republic. . . . It is the best that ever existed. I believe yet the old ship of state will right herself, but these be big times in this world, these be times when men ought to be brave. I am almost tempted to say something now that will displease you. You will send your boys out to fight for the flag, you will send your boys to die for the flag of their country on the fields of France, but you Congressmen, will you die politically for your convictions? [Applause] What sort of courage is it in this America, what is the article of men's courage who will send their sons to the trenches to have their bodies mangled with shells of the enemy, and yet who are not willing to vote their honest convictions as Members of Congress? That is what is the matter with the Congress of the United States today. It is not that you are not intelligent, for you are; it is not that you do not love your country, for you do. The great bane of this body today is the want of that courage to take your political lives in your hands and do your duty as God Almighty gives you the vision to see it. [Applause] [36]

If he was "a demagogue," he was at least "an honest demagogue"—so Martin Dies, Senior, stated his own position. He declared the "abuses of government" in Washington so "universal" and "respectable" that anyone who had had the temerity to attack them, as he had, must of necessity find himself "in bad odor." He asserted that men who wanted "to be on the front pages of the newspapers and in the good graces of the Government" had to "pursue a course directly contrary" to the one which he had set himself.

3   PRE-COMMITTEE DAYS

T HE YOUNGER MARTIN DIES was in many ways "a chip off the old block." It was as if the father after hibernating for twelve years had returned to his old haunts at the Capitol with the same views but with renewed vigor and increased zeal.

A brief survey of the Congressional picture at the beginning of the legislative careers of father and son respectively throws light on the quick prominence and rise of Martin Dies, Junior. The elder Dies was first elected to the House in 1909, two years before Woodrow Wilson became President. There were in the House at that time 172 Democrats and 219 Republicans; two years later there were 228 Democrats and 152 Republicans. The younger Dies, elected to the House in 1931 when he was thirty, two years before Franklin D. Roosevelt became President, entered a House composed of 219 Democrats, 207 Republicans, and 1 Independent; two years later there were 311 Democrats, 117 Republicans, and 5 Independents. The only Democrat from Texas in the House at the beginning of the Congressional careers of both father and son was John Nance Garner, who had entered the House in 1903 and was to serve fifteen successive terms before his election to the Vice-Presidency in 1932. Garner was elected Speaker of the House the year Martin Dies, Junior, became a member of that body.[1] Thanks to Garner, Dies was appointed to numerous important committees, including the very influential Rules Committee.[2]

Martin Dies was not averse to having his Congressional career viewed from the background of his father's legislative experience and ideals. In concluding his first speech in the House he said:

As I stand here this afternoon in this historic Chamber and before the greatest legislative body in the world, I am reminded of one now gone, whose voice is still, whose lips are mute, and whose soul has long since flown to the great beyond. The presence of many of his loyal and devoted friends in this hall evokes the memory of his life, and though I know his body is molding in the silent dust, yet it seems to me that his spirit pervades the Capitol, where he labored for many years for the interests of his people and during one of the greatest crises that ever confronted this Nation. My father was a true son of east Texas. Brave and courageous, he never bent the pregnant hinges of his knee that thrift might follow fawning.

Kind and gentle, he was always tolerant of the faults and frailties of mankind. By his brave and courageous public service, by his fearless expressions of convictions, by his unfailing loyalty and devotion to his friends, and by the profound love that he had for his country he left the world better than he found it. Because he thought he was right he took issue with a Democratic President at a time when public feelings were worked to the highest pitch, and when it meant political suicide. But the people had an abiding faith in the rugged honesty of his character and convictions, and he was returned to Congress by a substantial majority. He had a profound respect and love for this great legislative body, and he believed that it was the bulwark of the people's liberty and the safeguard of their rights. He would never tolerate unjust and careless criticism of the Congress of the United States; and whenever it was attacked, he was always ready to break a lance in its behalf.

Mr. Chairman, I do not know how long I shall be permitted to serve this great body, but whether my services be long or short, distinguished or obscure, it is my fervent hope and sincere wish that I, like my father, may earn the esteem, friendship, and love of the membership of this House.[3]

Like his father, Martin Dies was no conformist in Congress. He preferred those of his associates who were "courageous" and "sincere"—even when he did not agree with them completely— to the "pussy-footing, weak-kneed, trembling, shaking politician" type of legislator who was willing to "barter away our liberties to secure an easy re-election."

How account for the mixture of radicalism and conservatism which characterizes Dies' early views expressed in Congress? There was an intellectual contradiction between wanting the "giants of concentrated wealth" controlled for fear that the weak might be deprived of economic opportunity and political democracy, and believing at the same moment that the use of labor-saving devices should be curtailed; immigration prohibited, and that "artificial laws" should not be permitted to interfere with regular "economic laws." Yet there was actual consistency in Dies' position in the sense that in each instance he was giving expression to what the small farmers who elected him to Congress considered to be their interests. These small farmers were opposed to big business and financial interests. They wanted those groups controlled in the common interest. They did not wish large-scale production to be extended to the land for fear that labor-saving devices might deprive them of their livelihood. They opposed government interference with their right to produce as much as they could, and to sell it for as much as they could get. Tariffs were "artificial laws" by which the few raised the prices which the many had to pay. Dies' views were in fact consistently in harmony with what his constituents conceived to be their economic interests.

So contradictory have been the views expressed by Martin Dies from one time to another in his career that a young woman who first encountered Dies' views in all their glorious multiplicity remarked: "In the course of his career, Martin Dies seems to have expressed almost every point of view at least once."

His statement of what he thought to be the fundamental issue in January, 1932, was as follows:

We are in the midst of the most far-reaching and important economic revolution the world has ever witnessed. This revolution threatens the destruction of the individualism of the American people. During the past decade a radical change has taken place in our economic life. Although we still retain the external form, the professions and precepts of a democratic Government, there has grown up in our midst an industrial and financial oligarchy as absolute in its sway as ever existed in the heyday of mediaeval feudalism. If the present trend is not checked we will have two systems diametrically opposed to each other but existing side by side under the same laws and institutions of government. . . . Despite the fundamental principles of equal and exact justice to all, and equality of opportunity for every man, woman, and child [of our political creed], an industrial and financial feudalism has arisen in the United States that threatens to nullify the intentions and ideas of the founders of this Republic and stultify in letter and spirit the Constitution of the United States and the Declaration of Independence . . .

Jefferson realized that no democracy could long survive the ravages of time and the wreck of ages, whose economic organization became monopolistic as to the few and competitive as to the many. He realized that economic freedom was essential to political freedom, and that no nation could be free politically that was enslaved industrially. . . . If our economic system is to become monopolistic, then our political system will become monopolistic, because two systems diametrically opposed to each other, as light and darkness, as right and wrong, cannot coexist under the same structure and fabric of government.[4]

In June, 1937, he said, *"Some day we must reckon with this great political truth, that either we must make our economic system conform to our political system or we are going to be compelled to make our political system conform to the economic system. That, to my mind, is the greatest question which the American people must answer, and in my judgment they must answer that question soon."* [5] (Italics mine. This is clearly a Marxian interpretation of the relationship of things political and economic. W. G.)

"THE GIANTS OF CONCENTRATED WEALTH"

In 1931 he declared the "giants" of concentrated wealth so dominant in the political, industrial, and financial life of the nation that few men dared "challenge their right to trample underneath mailed fist and iron heel the individualism and economic freedom of the American people," and cited the fact that 85 per cent of the factories in the United States employed less than 20 per cent of the factory workers.

He cited figures by Gardiner C. Means, of Columbia University, showing that the 200 largest nonfinancial corporations in the United States controlled in 1927 more than 40 per cent of the corporate income, more than 35 per cent of the business wealth, and between 15 and 20 per cent of all national wealth. The assets of these 200 largest corporations increased more than twice as rapidly as the assets of other nonfinancial corporations. If their growth continued at the same rate, these 200 corporations would by 1950 control 80 per cent of the nonfinancial corporate wealth in the United States.[6]

As a means to "decentralize some of the enormous wealth" of the country, Dies suggested the advisability of increasing gift and inheritance taxes to take the place of the so-called nuisance taxes.[7] He favored a graduated tax which would make the owners of large apartment houses and hotels pay much more heavily than the owners of small homes.[8] In fact, he desired that all homes occupied by their owners be exempted from taxation up to $5,000 valuation. He wanted small farms also exempted, and favored tax differentials which would favor the independent merchant over the chain store. If we are "to prevent an ever-increasing centralization of wealth in this country," he asserted, "we must decentralize the vast ownership of land in the United States by a few." [9]

Dies felt that certain legislative policies had aggravated the concentration of wealth instead of mitigating it. "Today there are in the United States gigantic monopolies and corporate interests spreading from coast to coast," practically impossible to regulate because "by their tremendous wealth and shrewd manipulation some of them are able to evade the letter and spirit of the law."

The origin of these corporations Dies considered "one of the strangest things in our economic history," and explained:

They did not exist to any extent at all prior to the War between the States. After the War between the States, when the fourteenth amendment was placed in the Constitution for the purpose of protecting the negroes from enforced slavery, the Supreme Court of the United States interpreted that provision to mean corporations, so that we have had a situation in the United States for half a century under which two or three men can go into the State of Delaware, which is smaller than my congressional district, and secure a corporation charter.

They are able to escape personal liability by reason of that transaction. They are able to perpetuate their business for a hundred years or sometimes hundreds of years. They are able to protect themselves even as a person or citizen of the United States can protect himself. Then, having been created under the laws of the State of Delaware, that corporation is able to go into the great State of Texas and when we undertake to properly regulate them we are told that under the Constitution we can do nothing to abridge the immunities and privileges given that corporation in the State of Delaware.

So, by all these fictions, by all of these schemes and devices, we have built up in the United States a class that is not subject to the laws of competition, and we have a nation half competitive, or competitive as to the many and monopolistic as to the few.[10]

Tendencies at work in America, Dies felt, were "creating two extreme classes in the United States, the ultrarich and the ultrapoor," and "destroying the middle class" which had "always formed the backbone of our civilization and society." [11]

INDIVIDUALISM THREATENED

Individualism, which Dies considered basic to America's political and economic systems, he felt was being destroyed, and therefore the major problem of America was how to protect individualism from the inroads of organized minorities, how to "place labor, agriculture, and independent business upon the same plane of economic equality with the more favored groups in our economic life." He saw the solution in increased competition and in safeguards against monopoly. The "dangerous trend toward concentration" would, he feared, lead to the complete establishment of "an economic feudalism" in the United States. He wondered whether the United States would preserve its earlier individualism or "relapse into the tyranny of an enthroned and governing minority, whether that minority be the Communist of Russia, the Fascist of Italy, or the great industrial and financial lords who are seeking control of the wealth, the resources, and the industrial power of this country." [12]

"American individualism" did not mean "the establishment of an industrial and financial feudalism controlled by a few

36

men or interests." This "unrestrained individualism" did not "conform to the spirit of American institutions of government." "There are some who construe American individualism to mean the concentration of wealth and power into the hands of a few. This is the European idea, and never was American in origin or principle." Americans favored a government which was "the servant of the people and not the master." [13]

Individualism could be preserved even in large industrial operations if employers would share with their employees the benefits of large-scale production and provide them with protection in periods of unemployment. Capitalists must use their money "for social betterment."

Dies was "old-fashioned enough still [to] believe in individualism in politics and in business." Under such a system worthy employees were rewarded and ultimately might become employers in their own right. Moreover, independent farmers and businessmen could be counted on to "dispense charity with a generous hand and a kindly smile." They were the men who supported the churches, the schools, and the other civic enterprises of the community. Dies pledged himself to do what he could to protect these independent groups in American economic life. [14]

Dies' position on the way to avoid both monopoly and bureaucracy was not clear. While opposing monopoly, centralization, and bureaucracy, and favoring unhampered individualism, decentralization, and rigorous economy, he did not explain how he would curtail nation-wide monopolies without developing the centralized, bureaucratic control he so vigorously condemned. "I think the greatest evil which confronts this democracy," he said in 1937, "is the trend toward bureaucratic government." [15]

Early in his career he favored government regulation of banks, railroads, and industrial managements, and all industries and businesses which affected the public interest. [16] At the same time he dreaded the consequences of centralized power and control "in the hands of a few." In his opinion "the science of government ... [was] separate and apart from the science of business": "a politician is no more qualified to run business than business is to run the government."

As early as 1932 Dies spoke in behalf of a reduction in governmental expenditures and, criticizing item after item in the federal budget, recommended the abolition of useless commissions in order to effect greater economy.[17] On the other hand he wanted no reduction in the appropriation for the improvement and maintenance of rivers and harbors, on the ground that the work was valuable and necessary and provided employment for men who might otherwise be unemployed. Like his father, Dies missed no opportunity to promote the development of the Sabine-Neches ports in his own Congressional district.[18]

In 1937 he declared, "Now that the emergency is over, it is time to retrench and economize." It was time for people to get over the notion that whenever they were able to think of worthy projects, they could choose to have "this great Santa Claus of the Federal Government send down 5,000 bureaucrats with an unlimited travel expense account, with a lot of theories and no practical sense" to do the job for them. Who, Dies queried, was going to pay for all these projects? He saw two roads ahead for the government—

One road is rocky but leads upward toward the summit of permanent recovery. It is the road of economy, of balanced budgets, of constitutional government, and of common sense. It is the road that does not appeal to unthinking people, nor to the people who have been led to believe that they can get something for nothing, but it is the only road that we can ever take to achieve any degree of normal and permanent recovery in this country, regardless of what anyone may say about it. [Applause] The other road is the well-paved road that leads ever downward. It is the road of extravagance, of loose financing policies, of crackpot schemes and ideas, and at the bottom of this road is the mailed fist and iron heel of a Mussolini, a Hitler, or a Stalin. [Applause]

Dies wanted "an end to fruitless experimentation and the ever-increasing desire on the part of many ... to have the Federal Government act as a wet nurse for every local community and State in the United States ... [Applause]"

Thus the country was "ceasing to be a constitutional democracy," because through the setting up of bureaus Congress had voluntarily decreased its own power much more than it had decreased judicial interpretations, with the result that bureaucrats were actually running the government of the United States.[19] The steady day-by-day tendency to throw "one restriction after another around the freedom and independence of the American people" was leading to "fascism" in the United States; for "when men are compelled to constantly comply with innumerable rules and regulations of some board, when they are compelled to watch every step and every move for the mere right, a right which our fathers fought and died for, to engage in business without being continually hamstrung by the Government or by boards, or by bureaus, they become discontented." The establishment of boards, controlled by politics or by the occupational group to be regulated, tended, in his opinion, to narrow the field of competition.

In Washington, he found, "a bunch of bureaucrats," "self-perpetuating" and "self-governing," many of them "engaged day and night . . . in trying to expand their functions . . . and constantly . . . finding new means and new schemes . . . to superimpose upon our political institutions a gigantic bureaucracy, a bureaucracy which will be just as dictatorial, just as destructive of liberty as the Fascist government of Italy or the Nazi government in Germany." If such a tendency continued, he warned, the American people would find themselves in a situation comparable to that existing in Germany and in Italy. Fascism, he said, was fundamentally "government by men . . . not responsible or responsive to the will of the country," and when legislative bodies shifted their responsibilities to the shoulders of others and sought to administer the affairs of the nation "by the creation of innumerable boards, bureaus, and commissions," there followed inevitably "an army of paid parasites, swooping down on the country like the locusts in the east, eating away all the vitality and creative energy of the people." [20]

The *Congressional Record* shows Dies keenly interested in the problem of unemployment. On September 24, 1931, he and Congressman F. B. Swank submitted to President Hoover a program for the relief of unemployment. The first item was the calling of a special session of Congress to "devise ways and means of forever preventing a recurrence of the ridiculous spectacle of widespread unemployment, want, and suffering in a land of plenty." The plan outlined the following points: an extended program of public works with "labor-saving devices and machines . . . dispensed with, so far as possible"; conferences with industrialists to secure shorter working hours to offset the displacement of men by machines; increased use of cotton at higher prices; a one-year moratorium on mortgage foreclosures; prohibition of immigration for a five-year period: the primary cause of all unemployment here; deportation of "the several million foreigners" who were in America "illegally," as well as those here legally who had committed criminal offenses; prevention of "wild speculation on the stock exchange"; regulation of the "greed" of bank, railroad, and industrial management.

Dies favored no program which would injure "legitimate business," that is, business which had provided employment during the period of depression. In his opinion, however, mass production was impossible without mass consumption, and mass consumption could only be maintained when the purchasing power which resulted from large-scale production was "distributed in fair proportion to capital, labor, and agriculture." Continuing his speech, Dies summarized what he called the problems that now confront us. These were "the problems that now confront us":

1. Preserve "true" competition; prevent "cutthroat" competition.
2. Government regulation in industries in which competition is nonexistent.
3. Prevent monopoly.
4. Do not "discourage or penalize legitimate business."

5. Regulate the stock exchange to prevent "wild speculation."

6. Prohibit all immigration to the United States for five years.

7. An enlarged program of public works.

8. Revise the tariff to restore America's world trade, but prohibit foreign nations from dumping the products of cheap labor in America.

9. Reorganization of government to effect economies and reduce the tax burden.[21]

What Dies actually did was not to state problems but to give his own formulae for solving the unemployment problem.

ON LABOR

At the time of the sit-down strike in 1937 the country, he said, was "faced with lawlessness from another source and in another form, but lawlessness just as reprehensible and indefensible as that which disgraced the world of high finance and industry [Applause]." The sit-down strike was "an open challenge to law and order and a bold threat to that stability without which no nation can long survive," a "menace" which the government should not "condone by inaction"; moreover, in the presence of such a "menace" the government should not "remain discreetly silent."

He recognized the right of labor to bargain collectively, to picket, to strike for higher wages; but he denied that labor had any right to "seize possession of other people's property and to refuse to give up possession until their demands were met":

I denounce this lawlessness as un-American and inimical to the best interests of our country. I yield to no man in my loyalty to the cause of honest and deserving labor, but I do know and I do declare that if sit-down strikes succeed America will fail. If there ever was a time when those in places of authority, whether under municipal, State, or Federal government, should speak out in clear and unmistakable language, it is now. Let those who are responsible for this form of lawlessness realize that they stand before the bar of public opinion with the condemnation and disapproval of every thinking

41

American citizen and of every public official who has the true cause of labor at heart. [Applause] [22]

During the debate on wage-hour legislation Dies insisted that if minimum wages were established for industrial workers it would be only just to establish comparable price standards for the farmers' products, for the farmer, too, was entitled to a fair return from his labor and investment, "a minimum living wage." [23]

The wage and hour bill he found contrary to the platform of the Democratic party in that it repudiated the pledge of the President that "no government could be administered wisely and properly when Congress delegates its constitutional functions to bureaucratic boards or to dictatorial administrators"; the measure created a centralized national board to administer the wage and hour law, with full discretionary powers. [24]

Dies objected to the "vicious principle of vesting wide discriminatory power in a nonelective Cabinet member," and called such a proposal a "stubborn and persistent attempt . . . to bring about a dangerous and unnecessary delegation of power to the Secretary of Labor." Industry, Dies felt, was entitled to appeal to a State agency which would "understand the needs and circumstances of each particular case better than some Federal Bureau." State agencies would forestall any undue concentration of power in Washington and provide "the necessary checks and balances." The proposed measure, Dies declared, would bring about "inequalities" and "injustices"; hence he could not condemn too strongly "the unfair procedure" of those supporting the measure. Since the bill was said to be "unconstitutional," "full of obvious loopholes," "ineffective," and contrary to the pledges of the President and the Democratic party, he could not understand why the sponsors of the bill did not join "in a sincere attempt to write a workable and valid law." [25]

MONETARY LEGISLATION

Martin Dies had no kind words for the Republicans who had exploited the farmers and wage workers by means of tariff and taxation. He opposed the Reconstruction Finance Corporation

42

because it would increase the national debt, bolster up the prices of watered securities, further increase the bureaucracy, and be unfavorable to the interests of the American farmer as compared to American business interests.[26] He favored an estate tax as high as that imposed in England.[27] He advocated either the remonetization of silver or a reduction in the gold content of the American dollar.[28] In 1934 he urged the exchange of American agricultural surpluses for foreign silver. He insisted that protective tariffs on American agricultural products were "a subterfuge" and in no sense a real benefit to American agriculture. Only "an idiotic and fatal fascination for Europe" had led us to "neglect" the potentialities of "our natural trade territories" in the East. By accepting silver for our agricultural surplus we could achieve "a tremendous trade with the Orient." To adopt this exchange for our farm surplus was better than "the present crude method" of destroying the surplus or reducing production.[29]

The Dies Farm-Silver Bill passed the House of Representatives by a vote of 258 to 112 on March 19, 1934. The first silver bill to pass either House of Congress since 1893, it provided for the exchange of farm surpluses for silver on the basis of which additional monetary stock silver certificates were to be issued to American agricultural producers. President Roosevelt seems to have resisted this extensive program of "remonetization" with the result that Dies introduced a less ambitious measure providing for the purchase by the Treasury Department of silver to an amount equal to one-fourth the value of the monetary stock of the United States, and for the issuance of currency based on the silver purchased.[30]

In 1937 Dies moved that the enormous gold and silver stores in the United States Treasury be used to finance the relief program. He saw no reason why the nation should pile up approximately six or seven billion dollars which were not used for currency. Why, he asked, with this gold and silver lying idle in the Government vaults should the Government issue tax-exempt securities to raise $1,500,000 for relief purposes? To issue tax-exempt bonds under such circumstances was to provide "comfort and ease" for bankers without compelling them to run the risks involved in ordinary private business.[31] It was absurd, Dies thought, to acquire gold from foreign countries through "the sweat of the brow of the average man and woman in the United States" just to hoard it, not to put it into circulation. Why operate the United States, he inquired, on a credit economy when it could be run on a cash basis? In his opinion the depressions in this country were caused by permitting bankers to manipulate the credit system through the creation and withdrawal of fiat money.[32]

CONSERVATION

Dies did not have as much confidence as his father had had in the capacity of God Almighty to look after America's natural resources without legislative assistance from Washington. He wanted investigations to determine means of conserving and preventing the collapse of one of the country's great natural resources, oil, of which there had been "wanton and ruthless waste." [33]

Likewise he advocated conservation of timber resources:

You gentlemen who live in east Texas will remember in your youth seeing our virgin pine timbers, the pride of the State of Texas, the most beautiful on the face of the earth, wasted and ruined in many instances. You saw the sawmills in east Texas exhaust the priceless resource. Not only was 60% of it wasted in the ruthless process of exploitation, but many of our own people who live there today are deprived of their former occupation. Had there been the crudest form of conservation in east Texas there would have been timber sufficient to supply the people of east Texas and other parts of the United States for many years.[34]

ISOLATION AND NATIONAL DEFENSE

Martin Dies continued the isolationist sentiment so frequently expressed by his father. Disgusted with "that maudlin sentiment that is continually urging us to save Europe," the younger Dies recommended (December 18, 1931) that Americans save America first and that the President focus attention on the United States instead of on Europe. Cancellation or reduction of European war debts Dies opposed because these debtor na-

44

tions were spending $1,500,000,000 per year for armaments.[35] He ridiculed the suggestion that America go to "the rescue of Germany to prevent Adolf Hitler from seizing the reins of government," and added:

> In the name of common sense, have we reached that point in the affairs of this country that we must dictate to foreign nations the character of government that they must set up to administer their affairs? If we have come to this point, then we may as well prepare ourselves for endless wars in the future. Our best contribution to the general stability and happiness of mankind is to make our own country the shining example of peace, liberty, and happiness, and prosperity. If the majority of the German people want Adolph Hitler, it is none of our business, and we should be content to administer our own affairs without interfering with those of other countries. This is the course recommended by the great men who founded this Nation. It is the only road that will lead to peace, liberty, and safety. [Applause] [36]

Dies felt aliens in the United States were not only the primary source of communistic and fascist doctrine but also an agency trying to involve America in European affairs. At a time when Europe was preparing for another war, Dies saw these different alien groups urging this country to champion their particular national causes in the European struggle. That the founding fathers of the United States had come to this country "to escape that very thing" meant nothing to such groups. The last war had proved "almost disastrous" for the United States and was responsible for many of the subsequent hardships the nation had to face.[37]

Those favoring war were the "profit-seeking interests, meddling internationalists, and alien-minded groups. . . . To the predatory interests war holds out its filthy promise of enormous profits, gained at the expense of orphaned children, forlorn widows, and maimed soldiers. To the internationalists it presents the lure of meddling with the affairs of Europe. To the alien-minded groups it affords an opportunity to promote foreign interests to the detriment of America, and to gratify prejudices and hates imported from native lands." Consequently, Dies thought all Americans should unite to promote

45

strict neutrality, except when it was necessary to defend America itself.

While favoring the cultivation of good will between the United States and all other nations, Dies opposed alliances in any form. He felt the greatest contribution which the United States could make to the world would be to stay at home, tend to its own business, and work out its own salvation. It was for this country to keep "the torch of freedom and peace burning ... so that the battle-scarred and unhappy children of men may see and take heart." God had been good to the United States in providing her with great natural resources and oceans which separated her from Europe and Asia. Therefore, there was no reason whatever for the United States to participate in a foreign war.[38]

He felt the United States had a definite obligation to defend the coast line of the Western Hemisphere, and considered the question of national defense "a nonpartisan issue." His own foreign policy, he stated, "would simply be to stay on our own shores, to mind our own business, and to be prepared to defend our integrity and our institutions."

He much preferred a large navy to a large standing army for the United States, as a strong navy would be able to meet the enemy outside of the country. While "alarmed" over the growth of dictatorship all over the world, he did not think the greatest threat to the nation came from any foreign power. In the interests of democracy the United States "must impose upon itself self-restraint and moderation"; for "democracy is a growth in the individual. It is something in the heart and soul and mind of a people. It cannot be achieved by militarism. Democracy, if I might so express it, is only possible among a people who are capable of restraining their emotions, their feeling, a people sufficiently intelligent and patient to work out their problems in a sane and practical way, who refuse to yield to the excesses of the many or the selfishness of the few [Applause]." [39]

Dies opposed "isms" from the very outset of his legislative career. Fascism, communism, and socialism alike destroyed free thought, free speech, free worship, and considered that the individual exists for the sake of the state. The American system of government, on the other hand, was based on the belief that the state exists for the individual, and "on the active growth and moral value of . . . individuals, without whom the state is a fiction or a monster." All over the entire world there was a "titanic struggle" between individualism and collectivism. Dies urged for the United States a middle road with no resort to extremes.[40]

Speaking on June 6, 1932, in behalf of his bill to exclude and expel alien communists from the United States, Dies set forth every major conclusion to be enunciated later by the House Committee to Investigate Un-American Activities under his chairmanship. He was "convinced" that "the American communist movement" was "directed and controlled by Moscow," that "the ultimate objective" of the Communist party in America was "the seizure of governmental power by an armed uprising led by the Communist party and the establishment, under a regime termed 'the dictatorship of the proletariat,' of a soviet republic which will be a member of a world union of soviet republics." The first step toward communism, he declared, was the development among the laboring classes of the United States of "class consciousness." He listed fourteen "means" by which the communists fostered "class consciousness" in the United States. These were:

First—Promotion of general discontent and hatred for the existing order in the United States, and of a corresponding admiration of the present regime in Russia and all of its policies and activities.

Second—Promotion of strikes and of unrest among the unemployed, and the organization of communist labor unions.

Third—Promotion of unrest and disloyalty in armed forces of the United States.

Fourth—Promotion of discontent among the Negroes.

Fifth—Promotion of discontent among alien elements in the United States.

Sixth—Promotion of discontent and disregard for authority among the children.

Seventh—Promotion among the intelligentsia of discontent with the existing order in the United States.

Eighth—Promotion of discontent among the farmers.

Ninth—Promotion of contempt for religion, especially among the children.

Tenth—Opposition to the deportation of aliens.

Eleventh—Opposition to the restriction of immigration.

Twelfth—Demonstrations and resolutions protesting against governmental action, federal and state, against individuals. (The so-called Scottsboro case is the best current instance of this. The Sacco-Vanzetti case is the most celebrated one that has been so used in the past.)

Thirteenth—Opposition to American "imperialistic domination" of China and Latin America.

Fourteenth—Opposition to and ridicule of the politics of the United States government toward the present regime in Russia.

Dies declared that communists ran for political office not to be elected but to gain publicity. When they took part in strikes their primary purpose was not to win material benefits but to contribute to the development of a revolutionary situation. Moreover, there were "created under communist inspiration a large number of so-called 'united front' organizations ... to carry on, under the direction of the party leaders various activities to further the communist movement in this country." These united front organizations attracted members who were not Communists, and gained the co-operation of "liberal and radical groups or individuals" to promote certain limited parts of the Communist program on which there was general agreement. Through the instrumentality of the Communist International the Communist party of the United States was controlled by Moscow, and this control of the Communist party of the United States from Moscow has been continuous and unabating. Declaring that his bill to exclude immigrants was opposed by "the communistic organizations" and favored by the patriotic, civic, and fraternal organizations in the country, Dies said he felt "confident" that it was also supported by "the great majority of American citizens."

In this same speech in 1932 Dies discussed the "best way to combat communism":

The most effective way to combat communism and to preserve individualism is to evolve and put in practice humane policies in industrial enterprises, give remunerative employment to the largest possible number of people under working conditions which give full opportunity to ability and likewise satisfy the requirements of human dignity and self-respect, eliminate or reduce to a minimum that insecurity of unemployment which is the haunting specter in the workingman's vision of the future, offset the displacing power of the machine by shortening the hours and days of work so as to give to labor the benefit of improved technique and machinery, and emancipating agriculture from the octopus of taxation and tariff which is sucking its life blood and bringing about wholesale bankruptcy and ruin. By concentrating the genius of American inventive mind and capacity to the accomplishment of these noble ends, we can erect the surest bulwark against the waves of collectivism that is sweeping down upon the civilized world. But in the meantime, Mr. Speaker, we are certainly justified and obligated to protect American ideals, traditions, and institutions by providing, as this bill does, for some effective machinery whereby those aliens who come to our shores as guests shall not be allowed to bite the hand that is feeding them.[41]

IMMIGRATION AND THE "ALIEN MENACE"

On the very day after he entered Congress in 1931, Dies introduced his first bill, which provided for the suspension of general immigration into the United States for a period of five years.[42] This was the first of many bills introduced by Dies to restrict immigration.[43] Such suspension of immigration, Dies declared, would contribute to the solution of the unemployment problem.[44] Speaking in behalf of deporting alien seamen (March 5, 1934), Dies indicated that the bill had for many years been sponsored by the American Federation of Labor, but

49

had been vigorously opposed by "certain shipping interests" which had "conducted a well-organized and highly financed lobbying activity against the bill because it would prevent them from employing Oriental labor instead of American labor as a substantial part of their crews." Dies said that his bill was to protect American labor as well as Asiatic laborers "from being exploited and enslaved by greedy shipowners." [45]

Dies did not want Secretary of Labor Perkins to have the discretionary power to deport "habitual criminals," for he did not wish "to continue to give vast discretionary powers to bureaucrats and to officials of this Government, especially in cases of this kind." Declaring Secretary Perkins "a liberal on the immigration question," he found her views not in harmony with his own. The bill to grant her discretionary power was "not right" and "not the proper procedure." [46]

Writing in the *Saturday Evening Post* of April 20, 1935, Dies urged that we "relieve the unemployment in our midst" by deporting the 3,500,000 foreigners who, he asserted, were in America unlawfully. He wanted "relentless war without quarter and without cessation . . . waged upon them until the last one is driven from our shores." In his eyes there was "no middle ground or compromise" in the matter. "Either we are for or against our country." [47]

Later, speaking over the radio, Dies argued that although there were many secondary causes of unemployment, "the primary cause was immigration. If we had not permitted millions of aliens to enter, the secondary causes . . . would not have been sufficient to produce any serious unemployment in this country." The United States, he said, contained 16,500,000 foreign-born, 7,500,000 aliens, and approximately 10,000,000 unemployed. "If we had refused admission to the 16,500,000 foreign born who are living in this country today, we would have no unemployment problem to distress and harass us. . . . From any angle of approach it must be evident to every thinking American citizen that the unemployment problem was transferred to America from foreign lands." And America would "continue to struggle with unemployment" as long as it permitted itself to be "the dumping ground for Europe." [48]

In Congressional discussion (May 20, 1935) Dies expressed the belief that 1,500,000 aliens were on relief in the United States while 6,000,000 other aliens were holding jobs that could be held by American citizens. "I submit that if we are going to use public funds to undertake to put 3,500,000 people to work, we should deport the 3,500,000 aliens unlawfully in our midst, who are either holding jobs or are on relief." He emphasized that he had "no prejudice against" Americans of "foreign stock," nor were his remarks "in prejudice to the Jew or the Italian or anyone else." He considered it, however, to the interest of the naturalized citizens of the United States to stop all new-seed immigration.[49]

In accord with his opinion that a large part of the aliens in the United States were here illegally, Dies said (May 31, 1935) his study of the alien problem was not finished. His chief concern was "to get the facts regardless of what they show." "In my judgment this is one of the most important questions that confronts the American people. Its proper solution will mean much to the future happiness and well-being of this Republic. I am not actuated by racial and religious prejudice but I do believe that charity begins at home and that self-preservation is the first law of nature."[50]

Consequently, he introduced a bill including the following provisions:

1. Permanently stop all new-seed immigration from every country.

2. Deport all aliens unlawfully in the United States, including alien communists, dope peddlers, gangsters, racketeers, criminals, and other undesirables.

3. Deport all aliens legally here who fail to become American citizens within a reasonable time.

4. Gradually reunite families where the admitted relative is not likely to become a public charge or to take some job away from an American citizen.

5. Register and fingerprint all aliens in the United States.

6. Require every alien to secure from the Department of Labor a permit to work before he can hold any job, with the provision that permits to work will be denied to any alien so

51

long as there is an American citizen able and willing to do the work.[51]

Many of Dies' attacks on aliens in the United States were first published in newspapers and magazines and only later introduced into the *Congressional Record* by Dies himself or by fellow congressmen. He attacked aliens in the United States for sending $100,000 a year to their various homelands, as well as for holding jobs which "rightfully belonged" to American citizens. Other charges against aliens were: that their crime rate was twice that of the remainder of the population; that they had brought in "pauper labor conditions," thereby reducing the living standards of American workers; that they were "the backbone of communism and fascism" in America; and that they brought alien standards and ideas to America and, conversely, tried to get America involved in European affairs. "It is from such as these," he said, "that there arises a considerable proportion of the propaganda and pressure for our entrance into entangling alliances which would involve us in European affairs, at a time when Europe is gathering itself for another suicidal war. Each group wants us to champion the cause of its particular nationality, in Europe's age-old quarrels." [52]

Keeping European immigrants out of America, Dies associated with keeping European ideas out of America.[53] However, when his original anti-immigration measures proved too harsh to be enacted into law, Dies introduced a measure for the "deportation of criminals and certain other aliens," which had been endorsed by William Green, John L. Lewis, the C.I.O., and the American Legion.[54] Particularly disturbed over Senator Reynolds criticism that his bill was "un-American," Dies answered that this was "the most amazing statement . . . ever uttered by anyone. Here is a bill which will rid this country of a large group of vicious criminals and yet it is denounced as un-American."

In a letter to Secretary of State Cordell Hull (March 26, 1938) Dies discussed the relief of political refugees from Europe. The solution of this problem, he wrote, was "the colonization of unemployed and persecuted aliens in Paraguay." [55] On March

52

9, 1939, Dies introduced a resolution to exclude alien Fascists and Communists from the United States.[56]

DIES AND THE PRESIDENT

Prior to 1936 Dies had on occasion been critical of the President. But as late as April 24, 1936, he spoke in praise of the New Deal administration. He said that at the outset of his term President Roosevelt had faced a people "on the verge of economic collapse," and with "a smile" and "cheerfulness" had "melted the icy fear that had paralyzed the hearts of a stricken people." Admitting that the Democrats had departed somewhat from their platform and had made mistakes, Dies insisted, nevertheless, that in the presence of an unparalleled emergency Roosevelt had provided the nation "with the highest type of honest and fearless leadership" and had shown courageous, sincere statesmanship. Condemning those who had conducted "a whispering campaign against the President and his family," Dies continued:

Mud slinging should not be tolerated in a political campaign. No one but political scavengers seek to besmirch with their filth the fair name of an opponent. When candidates or their friends resort to mud slinging and personalities they immediately confess the weakness of their cause, the poverty of their thoughts, and the rottenness of their characters. . . . These vile creatures of the sewer who seek to defame the reputation of faithful and honest public servants should be avoided by all honest men and branded for what they are.
No man has ever demonstrated more completely his independence and honesty than Franklin D. Roosevelt. . . . No one can deny that the President's program is in every respect free from the influence or dictation of big business or self-seeking interests. . . . In short, my friends, let us keep in the White House that great leader of the plain people, the Jefferson and Jackson of the twentieth century, our present and our future President, Franklin D. Roosevelt.[57]

Speaking against concentration of power in the hands of the President, on April 1, 1938, Dies said he believed that the President entertained not "the slightest idea" or aspiration to become a dictator; yet, recognizing "an instinctive fear" on the the part of the American people against encroachment by the

Chief Executive on the legislative branch, and considering the way in which "the rights of the people are being destroyed in the name of liberalism, in the name of the common man and under all sorts of pretexts," Dies considered it "nothing but wholesome and right that the American people should jealously guard the liberties and rights which were purchased by the blood of their heroic ancestors." Accordingly, he emphasized that Congress should reserve its right to overrule executive orders which the President might issue in connection with the Government Reorganization Bill.[58] He did not propose, he said, to support the Administration when it was "clearly wrong"; on the other hand, he would not oppose a bill "simply because the President wants it." His support or opposition to any measure he based solely on "the merits of each proposal. . . . If Roosevelt is right we have no right to oppose legislation simply because members have fallen out with the President. [Applause.] "[59]

President Roosevelt's worst enemies were those who advocated that "to be a good Democrat" one must "swallow everything and blindly follow the leadership of someone else," while his best friends were actually those who had "the courage to tell him the truth."

INVESTIGATIONS

In 1932 when it was suggested that a commission be appointed to reconsider the question of European war debts, Dies declared the American people "weary of commissions" and suggested the matter be handled "through the regular channels." [60] This statement sounded like those made by his father. As time went by, however, Dies began to show he had none of his father's oft-expressed dread of investigations.

The next year he proposed his first congressional investigation. Initially he wanted "to investigate the activities of Ogden Mills and the other lobbyists who [were] exerting their influence for the purpose of defeating constructive legislation that [would] restore this country to a normal condition." He also wanted an investigation of "the activities and plans of foreign governments and international bankers to propagandize the country with a view of seeking to cancel the war debts and maintaining the abnormal value of our currency at home and abroad to the detriment of American labor, agriculture, and industry." [61]

In 1935 Dies called for an investigation of the possibility of the shackling of the press by the administration.[62] The following year, as a member of the Rules Committee, he had occasion to investigate lobbying and found "a vicious condition in respect to professional lobbying" by the utility holding companies which were spending money very freely and using questionable methods. Considering it "unwholesome and inimical to the public interest" to "unloose upon Congress a highly charged avalanche of propaganda," he sought means to prevent its recurrence. The Rules Committee decided to introduce legislation requiring all individuals and organizations receiving money for lobbying activities to file their names, receipts, and expenditures with the Clerk of the House and the Secretary of the Senate. In this way it was hoped the "lobbying racket" might be stopped. "Anything that is right," Dies explained, "can survive the sunlight of exposure. It is only shady transactions and questionable practices that must seek refuge behind the cloak of secrecy." [63]

In March, 1937, Dies presented a resolution providing for a House committee to investigate sit-down strikes.[64] To those who asked, "What will you find out as a result of the investigation that you do not now know?" Dies answered that although it had been established already "beyond the peradventure of a doubt" that sit-down strikes were illegal, the cause of the strikes and responsibility for them would have to be determined by "an impartial inquiry" before Congress could formulate legislation suitable to the situation. He himself, he said, would "be the last man to conduct a prejudiced inquiry for the purposes of fixing the responsibility upon the labor side to the controversy." It was "ridiculous" for opponents of this resolution to "contend that the personnel of this committee will be biased in their conduct of the inquiry and in the conclusions they reach." [65]

Throughout 1937 and 1938 Dies presented a series of bills and resolutions calling for various governmental investigations

—"to define conspiracy and combination under section 1, act of July 2, 1890, dealing with monopolies and combinations in restraint of trade, so as to include employees who refuse to vacate the plant, mill, business, or industry of their employer"; "to investigate the motion-picture industry"; to investigate monopolies; "to investigate propaganda"; and others.[66]

As previously mentioned, Dies had introduced a resolution providing for a House investigation of the sit-down strikes (March 23, 1937).[67] Although this resolution seemed to be favored by the Republicans and insurgent Democrats, it lost in a test vote by 150 to 236. The relationship between this resolution and the adoption by the House a year later of the Dies resolution directing an investigation of un-American activities has been noted by M. Nelson McGeary, in a study entitled *The Development of Congressional Investigative Power*. McGeary also notes that when the House Committee on Un-American Activities was finally appointed, with Mr. Dies as chairman, a portion of its attention was promptly directed to the sit-down strikes.[68]

On the basis of the evidence it might seem that Martin Dies considered that anyone who fundamentally disagreed with him ought to be driven out of the Capitol or investigated, possibly both. Yet he objected in Congress to what he called a "scurrilous" editorial in the *New York Tribune* "imputing improper motives" to members of the House who had voted against a certain measure. Although he himself had voted for this bill, he considered it "the most despicable thing in the world . . . for any newspaper, or any member of Congress, or anyone else to say that because a man votes 'yea' or 'nay,' he is thereby betraying his country." This statement was applauded in the House of Representatives.[69]

It annoyed Dies, in 1937, that "certain so-called liberal" members of the House classified themselves as "liberals" and "the rest of us as reactionaries"; but, he explained, "it has always been that way; man loves to adorn himself with terms and phrases that flatter his vanity." "No man can arrogate to himself the label of liberalism who is so intolerant and so bigoted in his views and his conduct that he questions the sincerity of the motives which actuate others, who have minds of their own and have the same right to reach their own conclusions." Moreover, he hoped the day would never come in his own career when he would "become so intolerant and so illiberal" that he would "cast insinuations upon the motives and conduct of [his] colleagues because [he happened] to disagree with them." [70]

This plea for tolerance and for the right of individuals to have differences of opinion without being accused of disloyalty is of great interest in light of subsequent developments in the career of Martin Dies. So also is his attack upon the extraordinary discretionary powers granted to the President in the period of national emergency. Dies wanted Congress to reassume these powers at once because he was convinced that "the processes by which people lose their liberties are not sudden: they are gradual, they are insidious, they work slowly through increasing delegation of power on the part of legislative assemblies to executive departments." Through an extension of emergency powers, he feared the President of the United States might come to have more power than the rulers of Europe. Therefore, Dies did not propose to lend his vote "to clothe with such imperial powers Franklin D. Roosevelt or any other man, be he the wisest man in the Republic, the most popular man, or the wisest —I do not propose to transfer the rights of my people to one man, whether he be benevolent or otherwise. [Applause.] " [71]

PART II
THE COMMITTEE

4 THE INVESTIGATORS

O N JULY 21, 1937, Dies introduced in the House of Representatives his resolution providing for a special committee to investigate un-American propaganda. In obtaining the passage of the resolution it was no doubt of advantage to Dies that he himself was a member of the Rules Committee and submitted the resolution to the House of Representatives as a report made by that committee "without amendment." [1]

When Dies called for the immediate consideration of House Resolution 282 ten months later, it read as follows:

Resolved, that the Speaker of the House of Representatives be, and he is hereby, authorized to appoint a special committee to be composed of seven members for the purpose of conducting an investigation of (1) the extent, character, and objects of un-American propaganda activities in the United States, (2) the diffusion within the United States of subversive and un-American propaganda that is instigated from foreign countries or of a domestic origin and attacks the principle of the form of government as guaranteed by our Constitution, and (3) all other questions in relation thereto that would aid Congress in any necessary remedial legislation.

That said special committee, or any subcommittee thereof is hereby authorized to sit and act during the present Congress at such times and places within the United States, whether or not the House is sitting, has recessed, or has adjourned, to hold such hearings, to require the attendance of such witnessses and the production of such books, papers, and documents, by subpena or otherwise, and to take such testimony as it deems necessary. Subpenas shall be issued under the signature of the chairman and shall be served by any person designated by him. The chairman of the committee or any

61

member thereof may administer oaths to witnesses. Every person who, having been summoned as a witness by authority of said committee, or any subcommittee thereof, willfully makes default, or who, having appeared, refuses to answer any question pertinent to the investigation heretofore authorized, shall be held to the penalties provided by section 102 of the Revised Statutes of the United States (U. S. C., title 2, sec. 192).[2]

In his speech Dies insisted that the measure was not directed against any race. Americans might disagree on economic questions and the methods whereby certain social objectives could best be achieved, but all Americans, he thought, should be able to agree on "those inherent and fundamental rights that distinguish this country from all foreign nations." In his opinion this basic distinction was "the conception we have in America that we derive fundamental and inherent rights not from society, not from government, but from Almighty God, and having derived those fundamental rights from God, no man or no majority of men can deprive us of the inherent right to worship God according to the dictates of our conscience or to speak our opinions and our convictions as we feel them." He assured the House that if he had anything to do with the investigation, there would be no abridgment of "the undisputed right of every citizen in the United States to express his convictions and enjoy freedom of speech."

Although he was not "inclined to be an alarmist," Dies said he had shocking information on the extent in the United States of communistic and fascist activities which deserved investigation. To the question how long the investigation would continue, he answered that the committee "ought to" conclude its hearings within a period of seven months. (It has actually lasted five years.) Dies said he believed in every man's right to express his economic, political, and religious views, and thought the success of the committee would depend upon the way the investigation was conducted. He could conceive, he said, of a committee made up of men whose object it was "to gain publicity . . . to arouse hatred against some race or creed, or to do things of that sort" which "might do more harm than good." The value of an investigation would lie in an exposure of subversive activities, such exposure being, he thought, one of the most effective weapons with which to fight them in a democracy. He emphasized that a legislative investigation "might jeopardize fundamental rights far more important" than the objective of preventing un-American activities which such an investigation sought to promote. There was "no one," he said, who detested "more sincerely and more deeply" than he "any attempt to inflame the American people against any group without our boundaries." On the other hand, it was his opinion that if un-American activities could be brought out into the light, public sentiment could be trusted in this country "to do the rest." He promised that if he were appointed to the committee he would insist upon "an economical investigation with sufficient funds to do the work." He refused to estimate how much the investigation would actually cost. (It has cost so far more than $500,000.)

The American Legion had endorsed Dies' resolution, and Mr. Dies entered in the record a letter from John Thomas Taylor, director of the American Legion's National Legislative Committee, to that effect. The following organizations also, Dies stated, had endorsed the investigation of un-American activities: the American League for Peace and Democracy; the Allied Organization of the Grand Army of the Republic; the Committee for Industrial Organization of Newark, N. J.; the Democratic Central Committee of Indiana; the Daughters of America; the German-American League for Culture; the Farmers' Educational and Co-operative Union, Local No. 68, of Pennsylvania; the Federal Council of Churches of Christ in America; the Fraternal Patriotic Americans, Inc.; the Disabled American Veterans of the World War; the General Executive Board, State Councils of Junior Order of United American Mechanics, Inc.; the House of Representatives of the State of Indiana; the Heights Jewish Club, Inc., of New York City; the International Workers Order; the International Typographical Union; the Jewish War Veterans of the United States; the Ladies of the Grand Army of the Republic; the New York City Federation of Women's Clubs, Inc.; the Non-Sectarian Anti-Nazi League; the Non-Partisan League of Massachusetts; the

Senate of the General Assembly of the State of Indiana; the Toby Edison Memorial Club of Newark, N. J.; the United Spanish War Veterans; the United War Veterans Council; and the Veterans of Foreign Wars of the United States.

Dies suggested that the committee might well investigate among other things the amount of money spent by foreign nations for propaganda in the United States.[3]

Opposition to the adoption of the resolution was voiced by Maverick of Texas, who considered investigation no substitute for appropriate legislation, and felt the resolution would lead to a great deal of "publicity." He predicted that the word "un-American," which he defined as "simply something that somebody else does not agree to," would be applied inquisitionally against the advocacy of such things as freedom of speech, the wage and hour bill, and a fair living wage. "Nobody knows what is un-American," but "goose-step" was the very essence of it. Another who saw no need for the investigation was Representative Starnes, who was later to serve on the committee.

Representative Boileau predicted that if Representative Thomas of New Jersey, who had argued for the investigation, were appointed to the committee, there would likely be "an effort to investigate the New Deal, as he claims it to be un-American," and that if Dies were appointed to the committee, Dies would "think that those of us who advocated the wage and hour bill are un-American." Boileau foresaw that the passage of the resolution would warn American citizens to be careful with whom they associated and where they went, because otherwise they would be labeled "enemies of our great democracy" and called unpatriotic. Further, he warned, individuals thus labeled might have to spend the rest of their lives trying to convince the American people that they were "really patriotic."

Representative Coffee of Washington called the resolution "a disguise for a smelling expedition aimed at liberal organizations in the United States" and said it was designed to undermine and sterilize free speech in the United States. He was worried as to who was going to define the word "un-American" and decide its economic and political connotations, and where the committee would stop in its "snooping, punitive expedition." "Inveighing against communism per se" is "a puerile pastime"; but "eliminating the social injustices which breed discontent" is "a laudable objective."

However, the resolution passed by a vote of 181 to 41.[4] On June 7, 1938, the Speaker of the House appointed the following members to the Special Committee to Investigate Un-American Activities:

Messrs. Martin Dies, Texas, chairman;
Arthur D. Healey, Massachusetts;
John J. Dempsey, New Mexico;
Joe Starnes, Alabama;
Harold G. Mosier, Ohio;
Noah M. Mason, Illinois;
J. Parnell Thomas, New Jersey.[5]

Who are the four men who made up a majority of the Dies committee from 1938 to 1943? These four were Dies of Texas, chairman, and Starnes of Alabama, both Democrats, and Mason of Illinois and Thomas of New Jersey, Republicans. Other committee members have come and gone but these four have served continuously. Until the number of committee members was increased from 7 to 8 in 1943, these four made up a majority.

The committee was under the control of two Republicans and two Democrats. Therefore, it was under bipartisan control from the standpoint of party membership. However, all four of these men were clearly anti-New Deal; all four were conservative. In other words, the committee majority was in no sense nonpartisan in so far as major matters of social policy were concerned; the majority was definitely anti-Roosevelt in orientation. As long as these four were in the saddle, as they were before the committee membership was increased in 1943, Dies was free to be himself—whatever he did to embarrass the President was sure to be acceptable. For as long as that purpose was served, it did not make much difference what Dies said; he could safely count on majority support.

Consulting *Who's Who in America,* we find that Martin Dies was born in Texas in 1901, was graduated from the University of Texas, and later attended National (Catholic) University in Washington, D. C. He married at the age of nineteen and has three children. He was elected to Congress at the age of twenty-eight and has been there ever since. He is the senior member of the law firm Dies, Stephenson and Dies, in Orange, Texas, which is his home. He is a member of the Christian (Disciples) Church.[6]

Congressman Joe Starnes, the number two man on the Dies committee, was born in Alabama in 1895 and was graduated from the University of Alabama. Starnes married at the age of twenty-six and has two children. He was elected to Congress in 1936 and has been there since. He taught in Alabama schools from 1912 to 1917, was a second lieutenant in World War I, and is a lieutenant colonel in the National Guard. Starnes was admitted to the bar in 1921 and practiced law before entering Congress. He is a Methodist, and a member of the American Legion, the Veterans of Foreign Wars, and the Masonic and Shrine Lodges.[7]

John Parnell Thomas was born in New Jersey in 1895 and attended the University of Pennsylvania. He married at the age of twenty-six and has two children. He was elected to Congress in 1936 and has served since. He has been a bond salesman and bond department manager in New York City and is now a member of Thomas and Godfrey, insurance brokers, New York City. He became a captain in World War I. He has been mayor of Allendale, New Jersey, and served as a member of the New Jersey Assembly, has been a trustee of the Allendale Public Library, and is a director of the Allendale Building and Loan Association. He is a Mason; no religious denomination is mentioned.[8]

Noah Morgan Mason was born in Wales in 1882. He graduated from the Southern Illinois Normal University in 1925. He married at the age of twenty-one and has three children. He started teaching school at Oglesby, Illinois, in 1902, and became superintendent there in 1908, a position which he held until 1936 when he was elected to Congress, where he has served since. Mason served as city commissioner in Oglesby from 1918 to 1926 and as state senator from 1930 to 1936. He is a Mason, a member of the Rotary Club and of the Union Church of Oglesby.[9]

Selected passages from the hearings, which fill more than 10,000 printed pages, bear testimony to the social philosophy which permeated these four men. The hearings had hardly gotten under way when, on August 22, 1938, Committeeman Mason remarked: "I want to interject this thought before you go any further. It seems to me this strategy of frightening critics of communism by crying red-baiting or Fascist is duplicated to a great extent by the New Deal; that whenever anyone criticizes that, they are economic royalists or reactionists or other such names."[10] In other words, Mr. Mason could not resist the temptation to use the hearings as a sounding board for his own opposition to the New Deal.

Three days earlier, when the committee was examining Mrs. Hallie Flanagan and Mrs. Ellen Woodward, executives of the Federal Theater Project, Representative Mason, seeking to discredit that project, made the following contribution to the hearings:

MR. MASON. Right in that connection, if I may, I have here a picture of Congressman Sirovich and Mrs. Hallie Flanagan and Mrs. Ellen Woodward in conference with him at the time they tried to get the bill passed to make permanent this unsavory mess. It seems to me that this picture, taken at that time, should be a part of the record.

THE CHAIRMAN. There is no evidence that that picture was taken at that time.

MR. STARNES. Or that it was taken in connection with that campaign.

MR. THOMAS. I agree that there is no evidence to show that.

MR. MASON. Well, it is evidence enough for me.[11]

Congressman Starnes is the committee member who blushes whenever he recalls that at one time he read part of Voltaire's *Candide*.[12] He is also the statesman who asked one of the witnesses whether Christopher Marlowe, contemporary of William Shakespeare, was a Communist.[13] Mr. Starnes is no lover of the New Deal. When Mrs. Ellen Woodward was testifying before the committee, she brought out that one of the previous witnesses heard by the committee had been in the hospital on account of his "physical and mental condition." This led to the following choice passage of testimony:

MR. STARNES. And Mr. Harry Hopkins has been in the hospital, too, hasn't he?
MRS. WOODWARD. Yes. But it was for no mental difficulty.
MR. STARNES. That might be a matter of opinion.[14]

Representative J. Parnell Thomas could not "see very much difference between a person...sympathetic to the communist cause, and a member of the Communist Party." [15] Related to this statement is another he made later in the hearings, that "it seems as though the New Deal was hand in glove with the Communist Party." [16] Whereupon Dies asked Committeeman Thomas a question which led him to state his position in even more unmistakable terms.

THE CHAIRMAN. Is this a speech or a question?
MR. THOMAS. No; it is not a speech. I just want to say this now, that it seems that the New Deal is working along hand and glove with the Communist Party. The New Deal is either for the Communist Party, or is playing into the hands of the Communist Party.
THE CHAIRMAN. Let us confine ourselves to the subject under consideration.
MR. DEMPSEY. They would not play along with the Republican Party, because it has practically gone out of existence.
MR. THOMAS. No Republican would want to play with them.[17]

While Thomas was very outspoken in defense of the Grand Old Party, often differing with his fellow committeemen along old-fashioned political lines,[18] he was not the least averse to co-operating with anyone, even with Southern Democrats, like Dies and Starnes, when an opportunity presented itself to attack the so-called New Deal.[19] He often attempted to criticize the Administration when others wanted to proceed with the investigation.

On one thing, therefore, there was complete agreement among these four men—the New Deal was bad and should be stopped. In one of its important aspects the Dies committee was virtually a Republican anti-New Deal campaign committee, supported in its activities by the taxpayers of the United States. The fact that there were so-called Democrats on the committee only added to its effectiveness. While ostensibly investigating un-American activities the Dies group was actually seeking to discredit a popularly elected administration. In the eyes of the American people the Dies committee was associated with the investigation of un-American activities; consequently, whenever the committee concerned itself with a criticism of the Roosevelt administration, the general impression was created that the Roosevelt administration was to that extent "un-American." The committee consistently failed to distinguish between the investigation of un-American activities and of New Deal practices. Thus the committee became an agency whereby the transfer device of propaganda dissemination was continually operative against the Administration.

The transfer device was employed by the committee throughout its hearings in the following manner:

An admitted Communist was shown to be a member of a progressive organization. If the progressive organization had several Communists in it and favored certain policies which were also favored by the Communists, the organization was dubbed "a Communist front organization." Then if it could be shown that federal employees were members of the same group, the "odium" of Communist control was transferred to the federal government. This line of argument was used over and over again, and before long the committee had labeled almost every progressive group in America a front organization. Once the American people had been sold this bill of goods, the rest was easy. Every time the committee showed that a Communist had made a trip to Russia, it was a reflection on the New Deal. If members of the Communist party belonged to progressive groups and worked for such a cause as the defeat of General Franco in Spain or for the relief of Spanish refugees through these progressive organizations, the committee concluded that any such organization was a Communist front. Then, if there were federal employees who belonged to an organization opposed to war and fascism, or in favor of peace and democracy, they, too, were allegedly contaminated by Communist influence. These people were part of the New Deal administration and carried the virus with them. Before long the New Deal "is either for the Communist Party, or is playing into the hands of the Communist Party." [20] The whole process is utterly fantastic. But it is surprising what can be accomplished by a propaganda agency which has $500,000 at its disposal, plus free publicity from reactionary newspapers, free printing at government expense, and the prestige of a Congressional "investigating" committee. Having continually painted the New Deal with the communist brush, with every attack the committee made on communists it cast an added reflection on the New Deal.

Reading the published hearings of the Dies committee, one observes that there were 3,138 pages of testimony in 1938, 4,061 pages in 1939, 1,278 pages in 1940, 354 pages in 1941, none in 1942, and 922 pages in 1943. Of appendix materials, 1,382 pages were published in 1940, 339 pages in 1941, 285 pages in 1942, and 98 pages in 1943. As the hearings progressed from year to year, the role of the chairman in the hearings became less and less predominant as more of the questioning of witnesses was done by committee employees and less by Dies.

From the beginning of the hearings an occasional committeeman dragged his feet, but the majority of four (Dies, Starnes, Thomas, and Mason) invariably emerged triumphant.

Among those who dissented was John J. Dempsey of New Mexico, who occasionally objected to conclusions reached by Dies and associates on the basis of their presuppositions, without regard to the evidence. Principal objector, however, was Jerry Voorhis of California, who served on the committee from 1939 to 1943, when he resigned in protest over irregularities in Dies' committee procedures.

Jerry Voorhis was born in Kansas in 1901 and graduated from Yale in 1923. He married in 1924 and has three children. He has served in Congress since 1936 and is a Democrat from California. He has traveled, and taught school; was headmaster of the Voorhis School for Boys from 1928 to 1938, and lectured at Pomona College from 1930 to 1935. He is a member of the

Episcopalian Church, Phi Beta Kappa, Phi Delta Kappa, and the American Federation of Teachers.[21] While Voorhis was on the committee, his influence was invariably exercised on the side of moderation, as is clearly indicated in the minority reports he made to Congress and in his periodic participation in the hearings.

5 THE COMMITTEE IN ACTION

L ET US ATTEND A HEARING of the Dies committee. Its meetings are held in an air-cooled caucus room on the second floor of the old House office building in Washington. Hearings before the Dies committee began here on August 12, 1938, and have been held periodically since.

In the center of the room are four tables thrown together to form a large rectangular table. On one side of the rectangle are seated members of the committee. Two committee members are talking together. Starnes is looking over some papers. Dies leans on the table, resting his head on one hand and doodling with the other. Dempsey, Mason, and Thomas are waiting for the meeting to get under way. On the other side of the table are witnesses, and behind the witnesses are uniformed policemen. At the ends of the table are committee attorneys and other employees, including court reporters to take down the proceedings. In this group we notice J. B. Matthews, a former teacher, later ousted from the Fellowship of Reconcilation on the ground that he advocated class warfare, still later head of the American League for Peace and Democracy. Matthews is now research director for the Dies committee. Also in the room are more than a score of newspaper reporters, and a number of photographers with flash bulbs, cameras, and motion picture machines. And there are other visitors like ourselves, who want to know what is going on and are all eyes and ears.

At the moment Dies is not smoking one of the eight cigars which he allows himself daily but is chewing gum leisurely. He sits there with a gavel before him, waiting to call the meeting to order at approximately 10 A.M. Committee members and witnesses are restless, some squirming in their chairs, some sprawled out, all waiting. Then Dies stands to his full height of six feet three inches, assembles his 203 pounds in a semidignified manner, and raps the gavel on the table, calling for order in what seems a very loud voice. A witness is sworn by the chairman, and the day's hearing is under way, to last until four or five in the afternoon with a brief interval for lunch.[1]

Most of the questioning is tedious, but by no means all of it. The witnesses are usually questioned at great length. But let us read in full the testimony of one sample witness. This will indicate the pattern of the Dies committee investigation.

Dies questions the witness as follows:

THE CHAIRMAN. Before you testify, Miss Saunders, let me say we are not interested, as a committee, in the racial question, except only insofar as it forms a vital part of communistic teachings, practices, and doctrines. Later on it will be developed that Communists are working among the Negroes in certain sections of the country, and that their appeal is racial equality.

MISS SAUNDERS. That is right.

THE CHAIRMAN. Only as we link that in with Communist practices, doctrines, and methods—only to that extent, we are concerned with your testimony.

MISS SAUNDERS. And only to that extent can I testify.

THE CHAIRMAN. In your testimony I will ask certain questions, because we do not want to do anything that will stir up or increase any hatreds.

MISS SAUNDERS. It has much to do with racial hatreds, if it is explained clearly.

THE CHAIRMAN. That is true. I will ask some questions, and you will limit yourself to answering the questions. This is a delicate matter, and I would like for you to answer the questions rather than make voluntary statements or get into a discussion of the fifteenth amendment, or something else than we have before us. I will ask certain pertinent questions, and I know you will cooperate in giving the material facts we want to develop by your testimony.

MISS SAUNDERS. I will be glad to, Congressman Dies, but I feel very strongly about the fifteenth amendment.

THE CHAIRMAN. But this is not the place nor the time to discuss the fifteenth amendment.

73

MISS SAUNDERS. That is exactly the point the Communists are making.

THE CHAIRMAN. We will reach that. Where were you from originally?

MISS SAUNDERS. Originally from Vienna, Austria.

THE CHAIRMAN. Are you a citizen of the United States?

MISS SAUNDERS. Yes, sir; since 1920. I believe my father took out citizenship papers then.

THE CHAIRMAN. How long have you been in New York?

MISS SAUNDERS. Since 1930.

THE CHAIRMAN. You have been employed by the Federal Theater Project; is that true?

MISS SAUNDERS. Yes, sir.

THE CHAIRMAN. When were you first employed?

MISS SAUNDERS. March 3, 1936.

THE CHAIRMAN. How long did you remain with the project?

MISS SAUNDERS. Until October 8, 1937, when I took 90 days leave of absence for private industry. I returned to the project January 7, 1938.

THE CHAIRMAN. You are on the project now?

MISS SAUNDERS. Yes, sir.

THE CHAIRMAN. What is the work that you are doing now?

MISS SAUNDERS. As an actress.

THE CHAIRMAN. Have you seen with your eyes evidence of communistic or subversive activities on this particular project?

MISS SAUNDERS. I can only say that literature has been sent around to me personally.

THE CHAIRMAN. Do you know that Communist literature has been distributed on the premises?

MISS SAUNDERS. Surely.

THE CHAIRMAN. On one occasion you were called on the telephone. Will you go into the details of that without going too much into it?

MISS SAUNDERS. Yes, sir. On Decoration Day I received a phone call from Mr. Van Cleave.

THE CHAIRMAN. This year?

MISS SAUNDERS. Yes, sir; and he asked me for a date. I lived at the Fraternity Club, and there are a great many men there. I thought it was someone I met at the Fraternity Club. I said, "Mr. Van Cleave, I do not remember you; when did I meet you?" He said, "I was the gentleman who sketched you in Sing for Your

74

Supper." I said, "There were 289 people down there, and I do not know more than 25 of them." He said, "I am the fellow who was sketching you." The day before I had noticed a Negro making a sketch of me as I was dancing. He shoved the sketch in my face. I did not know his name, and did not know anything about him. All I knew was that a Negro had sketched me. I signed out and left the building. At first I thought it was someone trying to play a joke on me, and I became very angry about it and asked how he got my telephone number. He said that he took it from a petition blank or a petition to President Roosevelt, which we all signed regarding the $1,000 pay cut. He took my name and address from that petition.

MR. MOSIER. How did he know that was your address?

MISS SAUNDERS. He was one of the committee passing it around.

THE CHAIRMAN. After that time when he asked permission to make a date with you, did you report it to the supervisor?

MISS SAUNDERS. I reported it to Mr. Hecht.

THE CHAIRMAN. What did Mr. Hecht say to you?

MISS SAUNDERS. He said, "Sallie, I am surprised at you. He has just as much right to life, liberty, and pursuit of happiness as you have." He said, "It is in the Constitution." I said, "Mr. Hecht, that happens to be in the preamble to the Constitution."

THE CHAIRMAN. Let us not go into that. We know there is feeling in the matter, and we have to be very cautious about race feeling. You reported it to him, and he advised you, in effect, that he was in favor of social equality?

MISS SAUNDERS. According to the Constitution, and there was some press clipping about equal social rights.

THE CHAIRMAN. Did you report it to anyone else?

MISS SAUNDERS. I talked it over with Miss Coonan, and she was appalled. I requested for an immediate transfer, which was granted. I then reported the matter through a personal friend to Senator Pat Harrison.

THE CHAIRMAN. Who was Mr. Hecht?

MISS SAUNDERS. Mr. Hecht is in Sing for Your Supper.

THE CHAIRMAN. An employee of the Federal project?

MISS SAUNDERS. Yes, sir.

THE CHAIRMAN. I think that is far enough. Is he connected with the Workers Alliance?

MISS SAUNDERS. Mr. Hecht is of split nationality. He has a card in every organization which has the most power at the moment.

Mr. Mosier. What is his full name?

Miss Saunders. Harold Hecht.

The Chairman. Did you report it to Trudy Goodrich?

Miss Saunders. She is a secretary of a Workers Alliance division, and she came to me of her own accord. She said she felt very sorry that I felt that way about it, because she personally encouraged Negro attention on all occasions and went out with them or with any Negro who asked her to.

Mr. Starnes. Did she say that it was the policy of the Workers Alliance to do that?

Miss Saunders. She did not say that; but she is a representative of that party, and they hobnob indiscriminately with them, throwing parties with them right and left.

Mr. Starnes. Is that a part of the Communist program?

Miss Saunders. Yes, sir; social equality and race merging.

The Chairman. I think that is all. I thank you for your testimony.[2]

At the conclusion of this testimony, several of the reporters rush from the committee room to report to their newspapers. And this testimony may prove of interest to some newspaper readers. But is it evidence? Evidence of what? The testimony gives us insight into the racial views of Martin Dies but it tells us little, if anything, about un-American activities in the United States. Nevertheless, there is much more testimony of this sort in the hearings than of the kind which we shall cite in the remainder of this chapter. Later, when Jerry Voorhis joined the committee, it is clear that the intellectual level of its proceedings was raised appreciably.

An interesting passage in the hearings is one in which Representative Starnes (presiding in place of Dies) carried on the following discourse with Joseph P. Lash, national secretary of the American Student Union, about intelligence and the capitalistic system:

Mr. Starnes. Now, Mr. Witness, that is one of the most important points of this investigation. You can understand that; you are an intelligent man. You can understand that if we change from our present capitalistic system of government to one in which there is no profit that we have brought about a complete change in our whole system of living in this country.

76

MR. LASH. Mr. Voorhis, would you say, or do you think the profit system has been—

MR. STARNES (interposing). Mr. Lash, you are not permitted to ask questions of the members of the committee.

MR. LASH. Well—

MR. STARNES (interposing). Mr. Lash, you are not permitted to interrogate members of this committee, to address interrogations to them. If you have any statement address it to the Chair or to the counsel. Now, proceed, Dr. Matthews.

MR. VOORHIS. I will be very glad to answer the question.

MR. STARNES. I am willing to rule, Mr. Voorhis, that that is improper.

MR. LASH. Mr. Chairman, I want to explain my purpose in that. I think that a good many of the difficulties and of the problems of America inhere in problems growing out of the profit system. I believe that today, and I believed it at that time.

MR. STARNES. In other words, you do not believe in the profit system?

MR. LASH. But I do not think that is incompatible with loyalty to the American Government or with loyalty to the framework, the laws and the Constitution and the Bill of Rights under which we operate, and I do not believe that anywhere in the Bill of Rights is the profit system incorporated or in the Constitution.

MR. VOORHIS. I would like to comment on that statement, Mr. Chairman.

MR. STARNES. Just a moment. As an American citizen you are entitled to that belief, but, at the same time, I think as an intelligent man you will admit that it is absolutely in contradistinction with what this Government has believed in as a nation since its inception.

MR. LASH. Mr. Chairman, I cannot believe that—

MR. VOORHIS. Well, Mr. Lash—

MR. LASH (interposing). I just cannot believe that Americanism is incompatible with disbelief in some of the elements of the profit system.

MR. VOORHIS. Just let me make one suggestion, Mr. Lash. I do not believe that the American constitutional democracy presupposes any particular economic structure of the country. Neither do I believe that it is the job of this committee to inquire into people's views, but I do believe there is an essential and a deep difference between people who are willing to abide by the methods of con-

77

stitutional democracy in trying to arrive at what they believe in and people who are not trying to do that.

MR. LASH. Isn't that a job for the Supreme Court, Mr. Voorhis?

MR. STARNES. Proceed, Dr. Matthews.[3]

The Dies committee has always had a very difficult time distinguishing between "liberals" and "radicals." For example, after the committee hearings had been going on for over a year, we find the following discussion taking place between members of the committee over the meaning of the word "liberal":

MR. STARNES. There is one thing that I think should be clarified for the record, and that is this very loose term or designation of liberals. If by being a liberal a man must believe in State socialism or be opposed to capitalism in any form or against the profit motive, and must be against everything except certain of what I call a species of intellectual idiocy in the form of certain movements, then I think some line ought to be drawn by people who are genuinely liberal against the use of that term.

In other words, this morning I noticed one statement of yours which impressed me very much. You spoke of the gullibility of liberals. I think that is one of the outstanding characteristics of a lot of people who call themselves liberal; that is, their gullibility.

MR. HENSON. Of course, many of these terms are likely to be redefined and misused.

MR. STARNES. Why, certainly.

MR. HENSON. Stuart Chase has written a book, the Tyranny of Words, which shows how words are inadequate weapons and tools to make ourselves understood. But "liberals," of course, is an unusually flexible term.

MR. STARNES. I am finding that out in these hearings.

THE CHAIRMAN. Is it not a fact, Mr. Henson, for years that the word "liberal," being derived from the word "liberty," was taken simply to mean those who are in favor of the fundamental principles of liberty? That could include both the conservative and the progressive or anyone else.

If this committee were to define that term in its report, as I think it should; that is, what a liberal is, it would be the greatest service that could be performed in this country; because the idea of dividing people along economic lines is a folly.

MR. HENSON. But I doubt if you can adequately define it.

MR. STARNES. I would not want to undertake the job, as a member of the committee, I will say that much.

MR. VOORHIS. Mr. Chairman, I would like to point out, apropos of what Mr. Starnes said, that conversely neither is it necessary, in my opinion, if a person is completely sincere in his belief in democracy—it does not necessarily follow that he has to be opposed to any modification of the full expression of finance capitalism. What I mean is, I believe a person can be the most earnest adherent of American constitutional democracy and still believe in the T.V.A. and believe that progressive measures, bringing about a greater real democracy among the people, are not only consistent with that but are a necessary part of the preservation of the basic structure of constitutional democracy.

You do not need to answer that, Mr. Henson.

MR. HENSON. I do not want to settle intra-Democratic Party political difficulties.

MR. STARNES. It is nothing like that, Mr. Henson. I was just trying to get a definition of the term, "liberal." I have been listening here for a period of 15 months and most of those who denominate themselves as liberals, as they have impressed me, are this kind of people. I admit that they are very liberal. They are liberal in several ways. They are liberal in the use of the English language. They are liberal in the use of refined invective. They are liberal in the use of other people's money. They are very liberal in taking care of themselves at the expense of somebody else. But they do not seem to be so liberal in according to other people a right to a conscientious opinion about a matter and place some sort of a stigmatizing label upon a man if they do not agree with him.

I have been very much impressed with this term, "liberal." I am just trying to get a real definition of it.

MR. MASON. Mr. Chairman, it seems to me that we are just degenerating into giving our own opinions, instead of getting a statement from the witness.

MR. STARNES. I think so, myself.

THE CHAIRMAN. Let us proceed, gentlemen. We have clarified this issue, something that has been vexing the people for many generations. Having decided that, let us proceed.

MR. MATTHEWS. Would you say that an additional criterion to be used in conjunction with these other criteria, before identifying one who follows the Communist Party line, would be refraining from any criticism over a period of years of the Soviet Union or actually approving everything that occurs in the Soviet Union? [4]

79

In investigating witnesses, the Dies committee had certain test questions which were supposed to indicate whether a person was a Communist or not. Although the Communist party is a legal organization, men were asked if they belonged to it. If they said they did, they were then asked to name their associates; this most of them refused to do on the ground that the Dies committee was assembling a black list which would make it impossible for individuals identified as Communists to secure employment. If a suspected Communist denied membership in the Communist party, he was asked if he were a member of certain of the groups which Dies had designated as "front" organizations. If he belonged to them, that fact led the committee to assume that he was actually a member of the Communist party. Sooner or later Dies got around to the question which he considered to be the crucial one: "In the event of a war between the United States and the Soviet Union, which side would you support?" Any evasion on the part of a witness in answering this question indicated that the witness was either a communist or a fellow traveler.

Now, Dies had previously insisted that a genuine Communist was not bound by ordinary moral codes; he had said that communists continually perjured themselves. If so, what difference did it make what a witness said under oath? A genuine Communist as free of moral restrictions as Dies insists, would certainly lie and shout "I would support the United States! To hell with Russia!"

But the witnesses did not do that. They objected to being required to answer a question which seemed to them to be utterly hypothetical, and certainly not within the scope of an investigation of "un-American activities." These witnesses were almost invariably people of pride and integrity. It is evident that the question offended their self-respect; they therefore refused to answer it unequivocally as Dies wished. Their answers were couched in terms which indicated resentment at being required to respond in a categorical manner to such a question.

Here are some of the questions which were addressed to a witness called before the committee on "un-American activities" on April 12, 1940. This witness, Milton Wolff, an American citizen born in Brooklyn on October 8, 1915, was asked, among other things:

MR. MATTHEWS [asking questions for the committee]. Are you a member of the Communist Party?

MR. WOLFF. I am not.

MR. MATTHEWS. Have you ever been a member of the Communist Party?

MR. WOLFF. I have not.

MR. MATTHEWS. Have you ever been a member of the Young Communist League?

MR. WOLFF. I have not....

MR. MATTHEWS. And what types of work had you done before you went to Spain?

MR. WOLFF. I was an art student. I was in a C.C.C. camp and I worked in—as a shipping clerk at one time.

MR. MATTHEWS. And you had been in Spain approximately a year and a half when you say you were made commander of the Lincoln Battalion?

(No answer.)

MR. MATTHEWS. Now, how did you happen to join the Loyalist Army?

MR. WOLFF. When the war broke out in Spain I recognized it, or it was my opinion at least, that it was a war of democracy against fascism. I understood that the regularly elected republican government of Spain was under attack by a rebellious army, much the same as the Southern Army attacked the regularly elected Government of the North during the Civil War.

I also realized that Italy and Germany had a very strong hand in on the Fascist side as against that of Republican Spain.

At that time in America we were already beginning to feel and see the actions of our democratic breed of fascism—I am Jewish, and knowing that as a Jew we are the first to suffer when fascism does come, I went to Spain to fight against it. There was a chance to fight on the front—

THE CHAIRMAN [Martin Dies]. Isn't it true that you also suffer under communism?

MR. WOLFF. I have no idea of that at all. As far as my knowledge —as far as my knowledge goes, I know of no instances where Jews have suffered under communism.

THE CHAIRMAN. Didn't you know that the Government of Soviet

Russia was under a Communist dictatorship just as bad as a Fascist dictatorship?

MR. WOLFF. I knew the Government of the Soviet Union, as far as I knew, was elected by the people. I knew that there was a strong Communist Party in the Soviet Union. I was not aware of the existence of any dictatorship in the Soviet Union.

THE CHAIRMAN. Didn't you regard Stalin as a dictator just like Mussolini and Hitler?

MR. WOLFF. Did I record him?

THE CHAIRMAN. Didn't you regard him as a dictator like you did Mussolini as a dictator?

MR. WOLFF. No; I did not.

THE CHAIRMAN. You do now?

MR. WOLFF. I do not.

THE CHAIRMAN. You don't think he is a dictator?

MR. WOLFF. I do not.

THE CHAIRMAN. You don't think they have a dictatorship in Russia?

MR. WOLFF. I do not.

THE CHAIRMAN. Do you think that is a democracy?

MR. WOLFF. I don't know what type of government it is, but I do know it is my opinion that it is not a dictatorship.

THE CHAIRMAN. Do you think it is a democracy?

MR. WOLFF. No; I don't think it is a democracy—I don't think it is a democracy, for instance, similar to—I imagine that you are referring to and your standard is based on American democracy. I don't think it is that type of democracy.

THE CHAIRMAN. Is it any type of democracy?

MR. WOLFF. I don't know.

MR. VOORHIS. What do you think of the support of Germany by Russia?

MR. WOLFF. What is that?

MR. VOORHIS. What do you think of the support of Germany by Russia?

MR. WOLFF. At this time I would like to ask the committee a question. I received a subpena in court last week asking me to appear before the House Committee Investigating Un-American Activities, headed by Martin Dies, of Texas. I would like to know what my opinion of Soviet support of Germany or alleged support of Germany has to do with the subpena that was served on me.

THE CHAIRMAN. Well, you gave your opinion with reference to

the democracy in Spain. I was trying to get your idea of what you meant by democracy.

MR. WOLFF. I was more familiar with democracy in Spain than I was either in the Soviet Union, since I had never been there.

THE CHAIRMAN. You had never been to Spain either.

MR. WOLFF. When I got to Spain I was aware of it.

THE CHAIRMAN. But at the time you joined—

MR. WOLFF. There was no need for me to go to the Soviet Union to defend anything there. There was no struggle. All I knew there was in Spain a regularly elected government.

THE CHAIRMAN. Let us proceed.

MR. MATTHEWS. In the event of a war between the United States and the Soviet Union, which side would you support?

MR. WOLFF. Is there such a war today?

THE CHAIRMAN. You certainly would know. You went over and fought in Spain.

MR. WOLFF. Is there such a war today?

THE CHAIRMAN. If there were such a war.

MR. WOLFF. Is there a war today between the United States and Soviet Russia?

THE CHAIRMAN. If war should break out between the United States and the Soviet Union, would you support this Government?

MR. WOLFF. If war should break out between the United States and the Soviet Government, I would be glad to give my answer.[5]

On April 23, 1940, the committee addressed the same question to Andrew R. Onda, who gave his occupation as county secretary of the Communist party in Cleveland, Ohio:

THE CHAIRMAN. Would you support the United States in case of war between the United States and Russia?

MR. ONDA. Is there such a war?

THE CHAIRMAN. Well, in the event there were such a war where would your allegiance lie? With the United States or Russia?

MR. FLEISCHER [Mr. Onda's lawyer]. Ask him if there was a war between the North and South what he would do?

MR. ONDA. If there was a war between the North and South what would you do?

THE CHAIRMAN. I am the one that is doing the asking of the questions. I am asking you the question whether or not in the event of war between the United States and Russia whether you would support the United States? Now, do you decline to answer?

Mr. Onda. I answered that question for you.

The Chairman. What is the answer?

Mr. Onda. I said there is no such war.

The Chairman. Well, if there was such a war?

Mr. Onda. And as far as the people of America are concerned I am sure the people will not have such a war.

The Chairman. Would you support the country in such a war?

Mr. Onda. When that time comes you call me back and I will give you the answer.

Mr. Thomas. In other words, you are dodging the question?

Mr. Onda. And I asked the question whether Mr. Dies would support the North in a war against the South.

The Chairman. Mr. Dies, would support the United States.

Mr. Thomas. You have dodged the same question the same as any other Communist dodges the question.

Mr. Onda. What do you mean "dodge"?

Mr. Thomas. You know what the word means.

Mr. Onda. You are screwy.

Mr. Voorhis. Can you conceive of a situation of international conflict in which you would feel called upon to give aid and comfort to an enemy of the United States?

Mr. Fleischer. Mr. Chairman, may I object to this type of question on the ground it is highly speculative and hypothetical? This witness is to be examined as to what he knows or specific acts or functions he has done. Any questions to disclose the operation of his mind is outside the scope of the committee. I except to Mr. Voorhis' question.

Mr. Thomas. I don't think you can get anything from this type of witness.

Mr. Fleischer. I object to that remark by Mr. Thomas and ask it to be stricken.

The Chairman. The witness is dismissed.[6]

Michael J. Quill, president of the Transport Workers of America, affiliated with the Congress for Industrial Organizations, testifying before the Dies committee on May 8, 1940, objected to the committee's refusal to grant him an opportunity to answer charges made by other witnesses against the transport workers; instead, the committee asked him numerous questions seeking to prove that he was subversive. For example:

Mr. Thomas. I would like to ask Mr. Quill a question.

Mr. Quill, if this country should get into a war with Soviet Russia, and I hope that never comes about, but if it should get into a war with Soviet Russia, would you be willing to take up arms for this country against Soviet Russia?

Mr. Quill. Sir, I am an American citizen and if this country was invaded by any country—

Mr. Thomas. That is not the question. It is a very simple question. It is a question that we have asked many other witnesses and some of them have been very free in their answers. My question is: If this country should ever get into a war with Soviet Russia, would you be willing to take up arms in defense of this country against Soviet Russia?

Mr. Quill. And my answer is very direct, Mr. Chairman, or Mr. Parnell Thomas Feeney—

The Chairman. Wait just a minute.

Mr. Quill. If this country should ever get into a war with Soviet Russia or any other country, I am first of all an American citizen and would defend this country's flag.

Mr. Thomas. Then you would be very willing to join the Army of this country against Soviet Russia even though we had to go over there to fight on their soil?

Mr. Quill. I am opposed to going overseas and leaving America. And I believe that this is what is being done here under your leadership, Mr. Chairman. You are trying to bring about a war hysteria to stampede the American people into war.

The Chairman. I think the witness should be held in contempt for that statement.

Mr. Quill. You are not frightening me. You can put me in jail but the cause will go on. You are not frightening me.

Mr. Voorhis. Well, Mr. Quill—

Mr. Thomas. Let us go into executive session.

Mr. Voorhis. Just a minute. Mr. Quill, you answered the question and made your statement. Now, do you want to insist upon making that additional statement about the committee?

Mr. Quill. What is that?

Mr. Voorhis. What good is it going to do you? I say, do you insist upon making that additional statement about the committee?

Mr. Quill. Mr. Chairman, I came here with evidence to clear my union, and I want to produce it, and the chairman is not giving me a chance to do it.

Mr. VOORHIS. That is a different matter. We are going to get to that.

Mr. QUILL. Because you are afraid to hear the truth from me. I want to clear my union. I brought evidence here of sabotage in the New York subways and I want to present it here.

THE CHAIRMAN. So far as the Chair is concerned, we are not going to proceed any further. This witness has deliberately come here for the purpose of insulting this committee. You are not going to get by with that insofar as this Chair is concerned. You have been treated courteously and you have been warned. I think the committee should determine whether it will hear this witness.

Mr. QUILL. I want to be heard and you are afraid to hear the truth.

THE CHAIRMAN. You will be in order.

Mr. VOORHIS. Mr. Quill, I think perhaps all the members of the committee—I know I speak for myself when I say this, that I am anxious to hear you on these points, but you are making it difficult because of the fact that it is not an explanation of your answer to a question, but you are gratuitously adding things about the work of the committee that I don't think have anything to do with either the defense of the Transport Workers Union or the answers to the question. It will make it that much easier if you don't do that.

THE CHAIRMAN. The question is now whether the committee will go into executive session and determine what we shall do about this matter.

Mr. QUILL. I want to get this in the record.

THE CHAIRMAN. The committee is going into executive session.

Mr. QUILL. You are afraid to hear the defense of our union. Our union is not controlled by the Communist Party and I am going to put this in the record.

THE CHAIRMAN. You are going to have some respect for a congressional committee. You are not going to come here and insult it.

Mr. QUILL. You are afraid to hear the truth, but the labor movement will live.

THE CHAIRMAN. Clear the room.[7]

This testimony brings out another propaganda technique employed by the Dies committee, namely, the card-stacking device. When witnesses who are sympathetic with the committee's red-baiting policies appear, their testimony has been practically unrestricted, and has readily been given credence by committee members.[8] But after charges have been made against individuals or groups and those accused wish to be heard in their own defense, the committee refuses them the right to make statements in their own behalf and insists that they answer questions asked by the committee, without giving them an opportunity to be heard in cross-examination to correct misapprehensions created by the restricted range and implication of guilt implied in the committee's questions.[9] Harry F. Ward, chairman of the American League for Peace and Democracy, after denying that he was a Communist, admitted that he belonged to a large number of organizations which the committee regarded as Communist-controlled. This line of questioning, implying communism by association, ran as follows, in discussing the American League for Peace and Democracy:

THE CHAIRMAN. Your position is that the league was never controlled by Communists; that is your position?

MR. WARD. No; I am not in a position to say at that time, under Mr. Matthews' administration, not at all. I am only in a position to discuss it after I came in.

THE CHAIRMAN. Now, he is not contesting that.

MR. WARD. This does not refer to my period.

THE CHAIRMAN. You are not contesting the issue then as to whether or not it was controlled by Communists prior to the time you got in?

MR. WARD. I know nothing about that, sir.

THE CHAIRMAN. But, how do you explain certain remarks of yours that are very much in line with the whole program of the Communists? I mean that last statement that he read there, Doctor.

MR. WARD. Which one?

THE CHAIRMAN. The one in which you say that you put out trial balloons.

MR. WARD. The one against capitalism.

THE CHAIRMAN. Yes.

MR. WARD. Why, Mr. Dies, you certainly know, sir, that there are lots of people in this country who are against capitalism who are also very strongly anti-Communists.

THE CHAIRMAN. You are speaking about socialists.

MR. WARD. Yes; and there are lots of other people too. There are

87

lots of economists on technical and practical grounds. You can be against capitalism on moral grounds as I am and practical grounds, as I am. That does not make you a Communist by a long shot.

THE CHAIRMAN. All right.

MR. MATTHEWS. Do you classify yourself, Dr. Ward, as an anti-Communist?

MR. WARD. I do not classify myself at all under those categories, because they are entirely misleading. I am not a Communist.

MR. MATTHEWS. You do not disassociate yourself—

MR. WARD (interposing). Certainly.

THE CHAIRMAN. But, you are not an anti-Communist?

MR. WARD. My position on communism is that of a critical student, sir.

THE CHAIRMAN. Critical student?

MR. WARD. Critical student, as anybody must be in professional work as I am.

MR. STARNES. What is your attitude toward democracy?

MR. WARD. Democracy?

MR. STARNES. Yes.

MR. WARD. I am a believer in—

MR. STARNES. I am talking now about the type of democracy we have in this country.

MR. WARD. I am talking about American democracy, sir. I am talking about that, because I came to this country when I became old enough to choose for myself, because it was here, I believe, sir; in the basic principles of American democracy. I believe that is the only way mankind is ever going to be saved from the perils that now confront him, is by the perpetuation and extension of those principles to every area of human life.[10]

The disposition of the committee to accept the testimony of red-baiting witnesses without much actual evidence and then using such inadequate testimony as an excuse to dub an organization "Communist-controlled" is revealed in the unrefuted testimony of Mr. McMichael, chairman, and Mr. Cadden, executive secretary, of the American Youth Congress (November 30, 1939):

MR. STARNES. . . . If any other organization in the whole United States of America feels that it has been placed in an unjust position by statements of witnesses before this committee—not by committee members—we will be happy to afford them an opportunity of coming here and stating under oath what their real position is. I want to state once and for all to you gentlemen, that there is absolutely no disposition here at all to suppress the truth, no disposition here to malign anyone. There is a disposition only to find out what the truth is with reference to subversive and un-American activities.

MR. McMICHAEL. If that is so, I think you will be glad to have me speak to that point.

MR. STARNES. That is all we are interested in on that line.

MR. McMICHAEL. Some 15 months ago—

MR. STARNES. Mr. Counsel, are you ready to proceed?

MR. McMICHAEL. I am responding to his question in the light of what you have said. Some 15 months ago we sent a request to the Dies committee for an opportunity to have people who had been working with the Youth Congress as friends who helped the youth movement in this country, appear before this committee and answer certain charges that had been made against the American Youth Congress by people who were not friends of the youth movement, and who were not making any real contribution to youth problems. We have been continually asking for that opportunity from that time until now, and now we have it for the first time.

MR. STARNES. And I was glad to afford you that opportunity, let me tell you.

MR. McMICHAEL. Thank you. I just wish you had been a little speedier about it, because you have slandered the American Youth Congress.

MR. STARNES. I have just been in a position where I could do it for you, and I did it as quickly as I could. I invited you to appear—

MR. McMICHAEL. I am glad you take that point of view. Evidently the controlling force in the committee did not take that point of view for 15 months. Now that you have given us an opportunity to come here, let me say that what we were talking to was not what certain people had said at this hearing, but what Mr. Dies, the chairman of this committee, had reported to the Congress as a representative of the American people, using American taxes to unearth supposedly un-American activities. He made a report to Congress without giving the people who had worked in the Youth congress an opportunity to appear before this committee and answer.

I will cite you from the congressional hearings of this particular committee. When Mr. Dies outlined the work of the committee, he said it was not the purpose to slander any organization, and when any individual or organization is slandered, or anything bad is said about any individual or organization, he said you were going to give that individual or organization a full opportunity to appear and speak. We have waited 15 months. Then you let "Bill" Hinckley know he was to testify—was it November 15?

MR. STARNES. There is no quarrel about that. Suppose we proceed in an orderly manner, and you may make any statement you wish. . . .

MR. CADDEN. But the first report that was made about the American Youth Congress was made in January 1939, and up to that time there were three witnesses who had been heard by the committee. The first one that was heard was Mr. Matthews. Before he became connected with the committee he was a witness. He was a witness in August 1938. He said at that time he had a connection with the American Youth Congress at its beginning, and we have tried very hard to discover what that connection was. We have never been able to discover any connection whatsoever between Mr. Matthews and the American Youth Congress. He was the only one who testified before the committee made its report that he had a connection with the Congress. The others who testified—Chaillaux, of the Amercan Legion, and Walter Steele, the editor of some small magazine—did not even pretend to have any first-hand knowledge or connection with the American Youth Congress, but reported on the hearsay that had been passed along to them about us and about the work of the Communists and the communistic nature, as they called it, of the American Youth Congress. These people had no first-hand information.

It was on the testimony of these three witnesses that the committee made its original report to Congress, and I think just any sensible objective look at the type of witnesses that they are, and the fact that they are repeating hearsay and are not even attempting to give evidence, shows how weak the kind of charge that was placed against the Youth Congress has been, because Homer Chaillaux—I know him—if he could get one shred of evidence on me or on the American Youth Congress, or Bill Hinckley, or anybody else in the Congress, he would have done it years ago, and would have made it public and we would have had photostatic copies in every newspaper in this country, because that is his job. But he has not been able to do that. All he has been able to do is to make accusations.[11]

In other words, the Dies committee seems to have classified the American Youth Congress as Communist-controlled on the testimony of three "hearsay" witnesses who had had no direct association with the organization itself. This is typical, as is evident to anyone who has read all of the hearings. Dies requires little or no actual evidence to "find" what he already "knows."

Special supplements to the hearings were prepared in the form of appendix volumes. Part I, 938 pages, is entitled *A Compilation of Original Sources Used As Exhibits to Show the Nature and Aims of the Communist Party, Its Connections with the U.S.S.R. and Its Advocacy of Force and Violence*. An examination of this volume proves the determination of Dies and associates not to weigh the evidence on both sides but to pull together every available document, regardless of its antiquity, allegedly showing that communists have been a revolutionary party in certain Western nations during the last one hundred years. The evidence is definitely *ex parte* and, as assembled by the committee, has no probative value. Clearly, it does not prove either that the Communist party of the United States is under the control of the U.S.S.R. or that it favors the forceful overthrow of the United States government. It may prove these things to Dies, but he was convinced before the hearings began; the evidence, however, fails to substantiate Dies' presuppositions in a manner which would convince a court of law or a jury of scholars. The same is true of the other appendix volumes.

Part II of the Appendix is 413 pages long and is entitled *A Preliminary Digest and Report on the Un-American Activities of Various Nazi Organizations and Individuals in the United States, Including Diplomatic and Consular Agents of the German Government*. Although there was undoubtedly abundant evidence to prove the existence of such activities, Mr. Dies uncovered practically nothing not already known. Part III of the Appendix is a *Preliminary Report on Totalitarian Propaganda in the United States* and is 59 pages long. Part IV, 177 pages, is entitled *German-American Bund;* Part V, 100 pages, is entitled *Transport Workers Union;* Part VI, a *Report on Japanese Activities,* was published after Pearl Harbor and was

285 pages long; and in 1943 the committee finally published a *Report on the Axis Front Movement in the United States; First Section—Nazi Activities* of 98 pages.

An indication of how little evidence is required by the committee to prove what it already believes is found on pages 1622 and 1624 of the appendix on the Transport Workers Union. On page 1622 we read:

O'Shea testified that he had been asked to step out of the presidency of the union by the Communist Party in order that Quill might be elected in his place. This was partially confirmed by Quill, who declared that he had been unopposed for the office at the time of his election in December 1935.[12]

On page 1624, without any futher relative evidence having been introduced, we read:

Michael Quill was elected president of the Transport Workers Union in December 1935 after O'Shea had been instructed by the Communist Party leaders to withdraw in order that Quill might be chosen head· of the union without opposition. Quill has remained in the presidency of the union until the present time.[13]

Thus on page 1622 we find that O'Shea *testified* that the Communist party had requested his withdrawal from the presidency of the Transport Workers Union and by page 1624 what two pages before had been merely the testimony of one witness has already been accepted as a statement of "fact" to be used in support of equally unreliable evidence. No consideration is given to the apparent bias on the part of a witness obviously disgruntled over the loss of his position as head of the union. Nor is any attempt made to procure evidence either for or against this statement or to permit testimony to the contrary.[14] The fact that Quill had been unopposed at the time of his election to the presidency in 1935 is taken as partial confirmation of O'Shea's testimony; yet there is no evidence, other than O'Shea's assertion to that effect, to indicate that the Communists were in any way responsible for placing O'Shea in the presidency, or for his removal from that position, or for securing the subsequent election of Michael Quill to that post. To submit such testimony, unaccompanied by any type of critical analysis, as conclusive proof of Communist control of the leadership of the Transport Workers Union is to violate all the rules of sufficient evidence. Yet on just such flimsy "proof" as this the Dies committee built its entire superstructure of alleged Communist control of the Transport Workers Union. Moreover, the supposed Communist control of one union is then taken as evidence of Communist infiltration in many unions.

It is on the results obtained from such "witchcraft" that the committee's conclusions have been based. No impartial observer can accept findings which are grounded in presuppositions, unsupported hypotheses, statements by biased witnesses, and interpolations by the investigators. Little credence, therefore, can be given to the startling discoveries made by the Committee to Investigate Un-American Activities.

Dies showed his hand unmistakably in his book *The Trojan Horse in America—A Report to the Nation* published before the 1940 presidential election. This book devoted over 300 pages to the alleged threat of communism, and less than 50 to the alleged threat of fascism. An anti-New Deal campaign document, it included such sentences as "Stalin baited his hook with a 'progressive' worm, and New Deal suckers swallowed bait, hook, line, and sinker"; [15] "The First Lady of the Land has been one of the most valuable assets which the Trojan Horse organizations of the Communist Party have possessed, due to the immense prestige which her sponsorship has conferred upon them"; [16] and "Following the lead of the White House, cabinet officers have done their part to add to the influence of some of the Communist Trojan Horses." [17]

Illustrative of this last statement were cited an address by Secretary Ickes to the National Negro Congress, an endorsement of a parade of the American League for Peace and Democracy by Attorney-General Jackson, and endorsements of the American Committee for the Protection of the Foreign Born by Secretary Wallace and Attorney-General Murphy. [18] "Even the President of the United States joked at one time about [the committee's] revelations," said Mr. Dies, but the President had subsequently changed his opinion. [19] Dies said, "The President cannot supply the leadership on which our national security rests until he inaugurates a thorough and genuine house-cleaning in government service." [20] This was virtually a recommendation by Dies that the American people clean house in the 1940 election. Dies repeated his charge, unsupported by any real evidence presented at the hearings, that the American Student Union was "under the leadership of Stalin's Trojan Horse organization," [21] and proclaimed that hundreds of college professors are teaching "the doctrine of loyalty to the Soviet Union." [22] The viciousness of Dies' attack and its clear political purpose can be fully appreciated only by reading the entire book; throughout, assertion and malice take the place of evidence and objectivity, which 10,000 pages of hearings testimony fail to substantiate.

In brief, Dies has used the hearings, the reports, his press releases, speeches, radio addresses, and his book to red-bait the Roosevelt administration and all progressive organizations. He has capitalized throughout on the popular conception that Congressional committees are fact-finding, when, as a matter of fact, the Dies committee has done little more than to declare its own basic prejudices as if they were "facts" revealed by careful investigation.

6 THE DIES COMMITTEE HEARS DIES

THE CAREFUL SELECTION of witnesses permitted to appear before the Dies committee probably tells us more about the views of Martin Dies than the statements which he himself made during the committee sessions.

But let us examine the views which he expressed, as they are found in the published record of the hearings.

Among his statements none has been made more frequently than the assertion that the committee intended to be "absolutely fair and impartial." He has also frequently stated that the committee is not interested in "opinions or conclusions," but simply in "the facts." However, in the course of the hearings, Dies has not been averse to expressing his own "opinions and conclusions."

At the outset of the investigation, on August 12, 1938, Dies said that the committee would permit no character assassinations or smearing of innocent people, for the public would have no confidence in the findings of the committee if it showed partisanship. He warned against the tendency to call un-American those opinions with which we ourselves do not agree, and noted a common practice on the part of both conservatives and liberals of referring to their opponents' views as "communistic" or "fascistic" when "unable to refute their arguments with facts and logic." Dies wanted the utmost care to be exercised to distinguish between what was "obviously un-American" and what was "no more or less than an honest difference of opinion with respect to some economic, political, or social question." The committee, he said, was more interested in facts and specific proof than in opinions and generalities. Moreover, opinions and general statements had "no probative force in any court of justice," he said, and could not be made the basis of any findings on the part of his committee.[1]

On the second day of the investigation Dies declared that his committee was "not after any labor organization." He promised that when charges were made against labor organizations before the committee, an opportunity would be granted the groups thus attacked to answer the charges.[2] The committee's interest in the internal affairs of the labor movement was solely concerned with such instances of internal strife as gave definite evidence of "communistic influence or control." He explained that the inquiry into the sit-down strike, for example, was undertaken to determine the extent to which communists had instigated or were responsible for such strikes. The committee could not "predicate a finding upon something that is not established as being thoroughly authentic." For example, when a group like the Communists endorsed a political party or candidate, that endorsement did not indicate that the political party or candidate shared the views of the endorsing group.[3] Dies later altered his opinion as to the rights of those against whom false charges were made before his committee. Sometimes he said that everyone against whom charges were made would be given an opportunity to answer such charges. At other times he pointed out that the committee had so many witnesses on hand who had been subpenaed to testify that it could not hear many organizations which had asked to be heard.[4] Early in the hearings Dies acknowledged that when witnesses before the committee made false charges against individuals and organizations, merely permitting those individuals and organizations to answer such charges did not necessarily repair the damage which had been done.[5]

It was easy, he said, to make general charges; what the committee wanted was "definite proof." The committee was anxious to conduct the investigation "in a judicial way"; otherwise, it could do a great deal of injury. Dies recalled that only a decade before people who had "advanced views" concerning social and economic problems were often called Communists.[6]

In contrast to this desire for "specific truth" expressed by Dies on August 16, 1938, we find him asking Homer Chaillaux of the American Legion for views concerning the Soviet Union, in support of which the latter provided little more than assertions. Dies called attention to many groups who were "anxious to expose" fascism in this country but were "strangely silent on the question of communism." He then asked Mr. Chaillaux, "What does that lead you to believe, when you see so many evidences of that sort?" In response, Mr. Chaillaux expressed opinions, which, it need not be added, were in harmony with those of Dies. The workings of communism, Dies said, could be seen in the resistance to and effort to discredit all inquiry directed toward an exposure of communism. Mr. Chaillaux agreed and added that in their efforts to discredit inquiry in this area, the Communists had discovered a method to gain publicity. This type of friendly exchange of opinion between Chairman Dies and the witness, which was by no means confined to this one instance, was out of harmony with the statement made elsewhere by Dies, that the committee would not "allow a witness to make a statement except where there is absolute proof of the facts." [7]

On September 30, 1938, a month and a half after the investigation began, Dies qualified his earlier statement that those against whom charges had been made by witnesses would be given an opportunity to answer those charges before the committee. Denial was insufficient. Witnesses most come "with clean hands," said Dies: "they must be prepared to bring their books and their records and give [the] committee the benefit of the facts." Thus, while permitting witnesses to make unsubstantiated charges against persons and organizations, Dies insisted that those against whom charges were made must, if they were to appear before his committee, not only make denials under oath but must produce books and records, "real evidence," to disprove such charges. He seems to have taken the position that charges made before his committee stood until those against whom the charges were made were "able to disprove . . . the testimony." Then, Dies said, he would be the first to acknowledge that the original testimony was in error. [8] In taking this position he reversed the usual assumption underlying American legal procedure, namely, that individuals are innocent until evidence is presented which proves them guilty beyond the shadow of a reasonable doubt.

Dies noted the ease with which pro-Communist and pro-Nazi organizations were formed, that they were not restricted in their activities, and that they were able to use their corporate charters "as smoke screens to carry out their activities." Such organizations were required to make no public accounting and were not compelled to provide the public with any information concerning their activities.[9] He noted that fascists who organized in the United States used the excuse that their activities were to combat communism. Those who were opposed to communism "should resort to Americanism and the principles of Americanism to combat it and not resort to some other alien philosophy, which is just as bad," he said.[10]

By Americanism, Dies meant belief in the present form of American government, with the guarantees provided for the protection of minorities. Certain people in America, he observed, welcomed an investigation of communism but were opposed to an investigation of nazism or fascism. On the other hand, there were those who were anxious to have nazism and fascism investigated but who described as "red-hunters" those who investigated communism. The Dies committee had been labeled fascistic and red-baiting in turn. In this one-sidedness on the part of certain people in America, Dies saw "the beginning of some sort of cleavage in the United States along European lines, which is a bad and unwholesome condition." [11] Dies declared it part of the communistic strategy to "organize front organizations with high-sounding titles and names for the purpose of luring people into their ranks"; he noted, however, that the Communists were careful to retain control of these organizations.[12] Another article of Communist strategy was "to try to ridicule things, to laugh things off." [13] Communists "ridiculed constantly, and . . . as long as they succeeded in that strategy they were able to prevent a general housecleaning." [14]

In introducing testimony concerning the Bridges case Dies explained that four years previously he had introduced a measure which would have made it possible to deport an alien Communist from the United States on the ground that he was a member of the Communist party, without showing that the Communist party advocated the forceful overthrow of the government. Dies explained, however, that this bill, which the House passed, was defeated in the Senate by means of a filibuster led by Senator Robert M. LaFollette. In the meantime the Circuit Court of Appeals had held, in the Strecker case, that to deport an alien Communist it was not only necessary to show that he was a Communist, but it must also be shown that "he advocated force and violence." [15]

The committee heard protracted testimony by Harper L. Knowles, chairman, and Ray E. Nimmo, counsel, of the Radical Research Committee of the American Legion, Department of California. These gentlemen were allowed unusual freedom in developing their testimony. Chairman Dies commented that although their procedure was somewhat unusual, it was perfectly all right because they were dealing with "such an important matter" in the Harry Bridges case.[16] He asserted that the methods used by Communists in Germany, France, and Italy were identical to those used in the sit-down strikes in the East and in the general strike on the West Coast.[17] He noted that both in Michigan and on the West Coast it was part of Communist party strategy in a strike to bring in members from outside the strike area for reinforcements.[18]

Chairman Dies insisted that the Bridges case was "entirely different" from the Strecker case, in that the government had more evidence against Bridges. He charged that by its own negligence or omission the Labor Department had not used the best available evidence in the Strecker case and had refused to act against Bridges.[19] The Strecker case, he asserted, "had absolutely nothing in the world to do with the Bridges case" but had been seized upon by the government "as a welcome opportunity to suspend deportation proceedings against Harry Bridges." He was sure that the Labor Department had all the evidence needed "to justify the deportation of Harry Bridges." At this point in the so-called investigation Dies deserted the role of investigator, became a virtual witness, expressed his own opinions and grievances,[20] and energetically argued that Bridges should be deported.[21]

On October 26, 1938, Dies voiced resentment of the attitude which the President and his advisers had taken toward the Dies investigation. A campaign against the committee had been aided by Cabinet members, by several departments' refusal to provide the committee with adequate personnel. Dies said that Secretary Perkins, Secretary Ickes, and President Roosevelt had tried to discredit the investigation by using the "Shirley Temple fabrication; . . . conceived by certain radical writers whose sympathies for Soviet Russia are matters of common knowledge." When these and other efforts failed to stifle the investigation, the President was induced "as a last desperate move" to use "the prestige of his great office" in an attempt to discredit it. The President's statement that the committee had not tried to get the truth and "did not call for facts to support personal opinions" convinced Dies that President Roosevelt was "obviously misinformed." Dies asserted that the evidence received by his committee "would be acceptable in any court." By giving all individuals and organizations against whom charges were made an invitation to appear in their own defense the committee had shown that it was "absolutely fair." Dies added:

The testimony with reference to the Michigan situation showed very clearly that well-known Communists instigated and engineered the sit-down strike and the so-called Lansing holiday, when a mob of 15,000 people barricaded the State capitol and 2,000 of them, many of whom were armed with clubs, were ordered to march on the university and to bring part of it back with them. The evidence shows that the State police sat helplessly by for lack of instructions from the Governor in the face of open rebellion, while the Governor looked down upon the scene from a window in the capitol. It cannot be disputed that misdemeanors and felonies were committed on that disgraceful day under the very eyes of the Governor, who had sworn to uphold law and order. If open and undisguised rebellion is to be countenanced in the name of political expediency, then constitutional democracy will perish in America.

The people of this country are entitled to know the truth. As chairman of this committee, I have felt it my duty to conduct a fearless investigation, regardless of political expediency. Under my conception of public duty, it would have been wrong to shield Governor Murphy simply because he was a Democrat and a strong friend of the President. While I deeply regret the President's bitter attack on a congressional committee of an independent department of the Government, and while I regret that the President did not read the testimony before issuing this statement, I wish to make it plain that I shall continue to do my duty undeterred and unafraid.[22]

This statement was made on the eve of the national election of 1938. It is not noticeably "impartial," and it is difficult to see how Dies could make such charges on the basis of the limited evidence presented to his committee concerning the Michigan situation.[23] Clearly the evidence heard did not justify the above charges.

Apparently the word "nonpartisan" has a special meaning. We find, for example, John P. Frey of the American Federation of Labor testifying that he was thoroughly "nonpartisan" on the ground that he was not a member of a political party and would never be as long as he held a position in the American Federation of Labor. Chairman Dies did not challenge this definition of "nonpartisan." [24] In testifying before the committee John M. Barringer, formerly city manager in Flint, Michigan, described the city manager form of government as "purely nonpartisan" because it did not deal with political issues. Again Chairman Dies did not challenge the definition.[25] The meaning of "nonpartisan" was further enunciated when Dies asked Mr. Knowles if the American Legion's investigation of radical activities was "absolutely nonpartisan." Mr. Knowles, in collaboration with Chairman Dies, explained that the American Legion was "not a partisan organization"—"not at all"—it was, as Dies said, "composed of members of every political party, except Communists and other radicals." [26]

In examining a witness on October 26, 1938, Dies asked rhetorically, if it were not true that Communists, along with their long-range program to establish communism in the United States, did not have a short-range program to develop a leaning on the part of as many people as possible toward government control and government ownership. Dies also called attention to communistic agitation against "imperialistic war," combined with lack of agitation on their part against any war in which Russia and the United States would be allies. Communists, in their effort to aid Russia, had seized control of strategic positions in numerous organizations. The most effective way to deal with this situation, Dies thought, was to expose it to the American people. He explained that to get information about Communists it was necessary for certain patriotic citizens to get inside communistic organizations, thus employing "the same tactics that the Communists use so successfully." In this way it had been possible for committee witnesses to show that while Communists had recently laid less stress on their revolutionary intentions, this soft-pedaling was part of their Trojan Horse policy. In their inner meetings the Communists still advocated the forceful overthrow of government.[27]

Dies urged that the way to answer the testimony heard by his committee was not by newspaper attacks, or by ridicule, but by statements made to the committee under oath. He emphasized that the purpose of his committee was to give the American people a picture of "the true situation." He did not "vouch for the accuracy of all testimony" heard by the committee and would not say that the committee was "going to predicate findings upon all of that testimony." The purpose of the investigation was to give "the American people an opportunity to be heard." Through giving all sides an opportunity to be heard, the committee would, Dies thought, be able to base its findings "upon facts and not upon any conclusions or opinions."

Early in the investigation Chairman Dies objected to a statement by Mr. Mason, a member of the committee, that the League for Peace and Democracy was "an adjunct of the American Communist movement." Dies declared that the committee had no proof to support this contention, and that in the absence of proof it would not be fair to make a charge of this kind against an organization to which many government officials belonged; many people might join organizations without knowing that they were communistic. However, by November 4, 1938, Dies was much concerned over evidence indicating that four or five hundred government employees were connected with organizations which had Communists on their boards, organizations which followed "Communist programs to a large extent." Dies expressed the hope that a number of these people might be subpenaed to appear before his committee. It annoyed him that the League Against War and Fascism and other liberal groups cried out loud against fascism while silent about communism. However, at that time Dies recognized that the majority of the members of the American League for Peace and Democracy, the C.I.O., and other "front organizations" were "loyal, patriotic Americans."

The next day Dies argued that many who were champions of racial and religious tolerance were promoters of class hatred, and that in consequence of this divided attitude they brought down upon themselves racial and religious hatred. He argued that Americans must not only fight racial and religious intolerance but must also fight class intolerance.[28] The same thing that had happened across the Atlantic was "about to happen here," and helpless minorities would be subjected to barbaric treatment. We know from the history of foreign countries, said Dies, that "class hatred always precedes racial and religious hatred." Racial, religious, and class hatred propaganda was being disseminated in the United States, and Dies feared a relationship between what was going on here and what was going on in certain foreign nations.[29] He said that Germany and Russia were making the same effort to spread class, religious, and racial hatred in the United States as they had in their own countries.[30]

Introducing into the hearings an article by D. J. Saposs, chief economist of the National Labor Relations Board, which appeared in the December, 1931, issue of *Labor Age*, Dies said on November 19, 1938, that this article revealed Mr. Saposs' "attitude toward the American form of government and the capitalist system under which we live, which is a very distinct part of our whole system of government." [31] This was the first unqualified statement by Dies in the hearings that "the capitalistic system under which we live" is an indispensable part of the American form of government. If that is so, rejection of capitalism would be equivalent to rejecting the American form of government. Americanism thus becomes a much more limited concept than many have imagined. And the Dies committee is "nonpartisan" in the sense that it enjoys the support of reactionaries in both the Republican and Democratic parties. It is a bipartisan agency the major purpose of which is not to protect our form of government (political democracy) but to protect the economic status quo (economic autocracy). It is opposed not only to communism and fascism but also to industrial democracy. By calling those who espouse any major change in our economic system "subversive," "un-American," "crackpot," "communist," or "fascist," it seeks to discredit all those who seek progressive innovation. *This is the heart of the Dies committee; it is a common front of conservatives of both old parties against the New Deal and all those who believe in industrial democracy.*

Chairman Dies expressed the belief that organizations which disseminated class, racial, or religious hatred were "un-American." In cases of such propaganda he felt the question of "un-Americanism" was "raised sufficiently to warrant" investigation of the organizations responsible for such propaganda.[32] He proposed to investigate men like Saposs and other "economic crackpots" employed in Washington, D. C. These people should be exposed because no government official had "the right to live on the taxpayers' money contributed by patriotic people of America, when he does not believe in the Government he is working for." In the views held by certain government employees Dies saw "a very alarming situation" because some of these men made "class hatred their primary tactics." Class hatred was "the motivating force...behind all their activities." [33] Chairman Dies again emphasized that many who talked loudest against religious and racial hatred were "silent" on the subject of class hatred.[34]

Dies was struck with the large number of organizations in the United States which described themselves as "American," "patriotic," and "Christian," and used the existence of communism as the reason for their own existence, in exactly the same way as the Fascist party abroad.[35] In this they were employing the same tactics as the Communists, who used "anti-nazi-ism and anti-fascism as a smokescreen to hide their own activities." [36]

Chairman Dies distinguished between permitting an organization "under the control of a foreign government" to exist in the United States and granting "the right of a man to believe in communism." He explained that "Americanism" is "the only 'ism' that permits people to be un-American." "Americanism" gives people liberty of speech, thought, and action, but Dies distinguished between the right to believe in communism and the right to belong to an organization which was under the control of a foreign government. He had the same reaction to Americans belonging to the German-American Bund.[37] Chairman Dies was annoyed with a statement by Mr. Aubrey Williams that he (Williams) was "not so sure that class warfare is not all right." Dies, saying he had "no doubt" that this class warfare philosophy actuated Mr. Williams, and some others, declared that the same argument could be used with equal force by those who favored the promotion of racial and religious warfare.[38]

Discussing evidence which indicated that Communists had recruited Americans to fight for Loyalist Spain, Dies said the committee was not taking sides in any controversy.[39] He was just interested in "the Communist angle." [40] At one point, however, he tried to lead a witness to say that in Loyalist Spain churches were "demolished," and priests and nuns "butchered." When he found the witness arguing to the contrary, Dies commented that the testimony was "wandering afield" and had introduced "a very controversial subject." [41]

On November 23, 1938, Chairman Dies, after quoting a statement made by Roger Baldwin, executive director of the American Civil Liberties Union in November 1933, to the effect that "communism [was] the goal," called attention to a statement by Secretary Ickes admitting that he was a member of the American Civil Liberties Union. Dies said that in making this statement Secretary Ickes had "engaged in his usual campaign of abuse and vilification." Dies would not enter a contest with the Secretary to determine which could be "most abusive"; he was "willing to award the palm to the Secretary." Dies added that Secretary Ickes would be welcome to appear before the Dies committee at any time.[42]

When Homer Martin, president of the United Automobile Workers, appeared before the committee, he testified that nothing was more important to the preservation of democracy than the protection of the working people of America. He declared the existence of special privilege the greatest danger to America. Chairman Dies asked if this applied "not only to organized money but also to special privileged organized groups." [43] Martin argued that as long as the Communist party was recognized as a legal political party in America, Communists were entitled to "an economic chance for existence" and should be granted the right to belong to labor unions. Dies would not take economic subsistence away from a Communist. In fact, he would "oppose with [his] last breath any attempt to take away [a Communist's] means of subsistence"—but Dies did not think that Communists should be permitted to be members of labor unions. [44]

When Mrs. Ellen S. Woodward of the Works Progress Administration wished to refute charges made against the Federal Writers' Project, Dies insisted that she be given an opportunity to be heard, although Representative Thomas had introduced a motion to the contrary. Mrs. Woodward charged that the Dies committee had accepted reports from others while refusing her the right to report. Chairman Dies explained that although his committee had heard "hearsay testimony and opinion evidence," it would not predicate its findings on such evidence but would be "governed by direct evidence and the very best testimony . . . in the record." [45] Although Dies was anxious to be "fair" with Mrs. Woodward, Mrs. Woodward objected to Dies' procedure and, appealing to Mr. Mosier, pleaded, "Do not let him just ride me." She charged that the committee had not been "fair" and had handled matters in an "un-American" way. [46] When Mrs. Woodward testified that she knew of no communistic activities in federal projects, Chairman Dies asked if she would testify under oath that they were "not being carried on." [47] Mrs. Woodward indicated there was a difference between what she 'and Chairman Dies considered "proof" that people were Communists. Dies indicated that it would be difficult to get their Communist cards; he thought that their communism might be proven by witnesses who had sat in Communist meetings with them. Mrs. Woodward replied that although she attended a number of Republican meetings, she was actually a Democrat.[48]

When Mrs. Woodward said that she had no fear that communism would take root in America, Chairman Dies recalled that France and Russia had not been afraid either "until they had trouble." [49] When Mrs. Woodward referred in her testimony to "the capitalistic press," Representative Thomas wanted to know what that meant. Chairman Dies clarified everything by saying that this was "a communistic term." [50]

As the investigation proceeded, Dies had his troubles. The committee was charged with having accused Shirley Temple of being a Communist, with trying to damage labor, and with having accused Christopher Marlowe of being a Communist. Earl Browder said the committee had given him $9,975,000 worth of publicity.[51] Dr. Howard Stone Anderson was accused of saying objectionable things before the committee about Chicago and Mr. James Roosevelt.[52] A false charge was made to the effect that Gypsy Rose Lee, a strip-tease dancer, had been subpenaed to testify. Dies said that this story appeared to have been "concocted by the Communists for the purpose of discrediting the committee." It might have been done by Communists who were seeking "to ridicule the committee." Chairman Dies explained that the committee had "tried every way in the world to conduct this thing in an unpartisan manner." He did not "think the subject matter of Americanism had anything to do with partisan bias." [53] When witnesses made statements before the committee, it did not follow that the members of the committee shared their views, warned Dies in December, 1938. He complained that whenever a witness made a statement before the committee, the press charged the committee with making the statement. He explained that individuals might read communistic and socialistic literature without sharing the views expressed in such literature. The committee took the same attitude as a court or jury, he said; it listened to all kinds of evidence but would not form its opinions on hearsay or on anything else except competent evidence. "We accord witnesses freedom of speech on these subjects, but that does not mean we accept or that we endorse those views." [54] He explained, further, that Congressional committees were not governed by the rules of evidence, because, unlike the courts, they could not pass judgment or sentence anyone. Dies demanded that anyone who wanted to deny anything stated as fact before his committee should make that denial in the form of an affidavit.[55]

When a Mr. Cooke who appeared before the Dies committee testified that "you could tell that [a certain person] was a little bit prejudiced against the Jews [because] he told me of some things ... the Jews had been engaged in such as caring for a certain number of refugees being sent over, and some of these big department stores firing Americans and hiring Jews, and things of that sort that would more or less indicate to me at any rate that he wouldn't care about sleeping with any of them," Chairman Dies interposed, "That doesn't necessarily show that a man is prejudiced from what you said." This led Committeeman Thomas to remark, "Of course, there might be some other people living in the South that wouldn't care to sleep with them either." After this remark Dies was momentarily silent.[56]

Discussing questions prepared by a witness for "our Dixie friends," Chairman Dies would not permit these questions to be read into the record because they were "too vile for publication." Nevertheless, Dies told the witness "to look at them," and then asked the witness if he thought these questions were "the type of stuff to circulate with reference to the President of the United States and his wife." This question by Chairman Dies became part of the hearings. After he had himself asked the above question, Dies asked the witness if there was not "a way of asking questions" which might "forward a whispering campaign to assassinate someone's reputation and character." [57] Dies said a whispering campaign was a most effective way of disseminating propaganda, and added that the creation of class, religious, and racial hatred in the United States paved the way for dictatorship. When the witness argued that the material which he had distributed had been less harmful than a "state of mind created by this rather strange investigating committee," Dies excused the witness.[58]

Chairman Dies and Representative Thomas occasionally sparred over political issues. On December 5, 1938, when Thomas commented that although people sometimes criticized the Republican party, very few ever resigned from it, Chairman Dies protested that that had not been true either in 1932 or in 1936.[59] On May 22, 1939, Representative Thomas noted "an inclination on the part of the Chair" to make it appear that the Republican party was mixed up in certain improper activities which the committee was investigating.[60]

Dies recommended (May 24, 1939) the use of constitutional democracy rather than hatred of certain people and preparation for armed conflict. He feared that one kind of hatred might lead to another and that the country might finally be divided into armed camps and be destroyed through their hatred of one another. He argued that hatred of one group was as harmful as hatred of another and that to be truly tolerant one must be tolerant "with respect to all groups." In his judgment "there would be no such thing as tolerance in this country unless it is applied impartially with respect to every group." Hatred of a race, a class, or a creed violated the basic principles of the republic, and seemed likely to lead to dictatorship. The promotion of hatred he considered the first step toward dictatorship. Our democratic government rests upon the protection of certain fundamental rights of the individual regardless of race, creed, or economic condition, and when the individual is denied any of these rights, "on any excuse, on any ground whatever" our whole system of government is dealt a serious blow. Although immigrants were not entitled to the protection of the Constitution in the same way as citizens, Dies argued that every American citizen should be "protected in the enjoyment of his fundamental rights" whether he was Jew, Gentile, Catholic, or Protestant. Dies thought it better to judge a man on the basis of his conduct rather than on the basis of the race to which he happened to belong; he considered this "the only American way": "And on any other basis this country will fall." [61] The issue as he saw it was not a choice between fascism and communism, but "between fundamental Americanism, based upon tolerance, and the known principles that have come down to us," on the one hand, and "all other forms," on the other.[62]

Dies commented (August 23, 1939) that the "anti" organizations in the United States, which were hostile to what they referred to as "Jewish communism," were invariably sympathetic to Hitler or Mussolini or some other type of military dictatorship. He also noted that hatred groups directed their hatred against a minority, such as the Jews or the Catholics, and never against a majority; it was easy to hate a minority; it would require "courage" to hate a majority. In a period of crisis men like Deatherage and Pelley, who in ordinary times would be considered "jokes," were more serious because they had developed a racket.[63] Dies considered Pelley a "racketeer" and thought that the government should take steps to protect the American people from him. He also considered Pelley a publicity agent, representing a foreign government, and a man engaged in the "wholesale fleecing" of the American people.[64]

Dies acknowledged that the presence of Communists in labor unions did not imply that the labor leaders were sympathetic with communism.[65] He considered it a fact that many well-intentioned people in the United States had been misled by Communist slogans and had taken part in the Communist movement thinking they were promoting liberty.[66] The Communist party Dies considered a subsidized group in America working to promote the interests of Russia here.[67] In the United States Communists were "masquerading under the name of liberalism," and associated themselves with liberal and democratic groups. On the other hand, Nazis were "masquerading under the name of patriotism." Dies called attention to the way in which Nazi groups in the United States gained force through treating communism and Judaism as if they were synonymous.[68] He saw in the growth of the Communist party an agency for organized espionage and sabotage in case of war.[69]

Dies considered it very serious that Communists held key positions in American labor unions. This was a matter which should be neither ignored nor side-stepped. He felt that the evidence presented before his committee should make any union unwilling to have Communists in key positions in its organization. The time had come for union leaders to take the initiative in this matter; they should make their books and records available to the committee in an effort to determine whether the charges made before the committee were true or untrue.[70] It was the duty of labor organizations to expel Communists, not because they had different political views but because they belonged to an organization which owed obedience to a foreign government ruled by a dictator. Dies felt that this issue must "be met sooner or later." [71] It was evident to him that the "general conviction ... over the country" that certain labor unions were dominated by Communists was harmful to the unions themselves. He considered it very strange that certain union leaders had not co-operated with the committee in clearing up the situation.[72] On the other hand certain "selfish employers" might like to brand all labor unions as "communistic" and thus destroy them or make their work ineffective; there was danger that labor leaders who were not Communists might be accused of being Communists.[73] It was clear to Dies that the Communists in America were seeking dictatorship "regardless of what they may say." [74]

Expressing the belief that a distinction should be drawn between the freedom of speech granted "legitimate organizations" and freedom of speech granted "agencies and agents of foreign powers," Dies declared (September 25, 1939) that the preservation of freedom did not require that we "harbor in our bosom known enemies." Not even the "wildest" interpretation of the Bill of Rights justified either harboring or encouraging such enemies. The first thing was to decide how to deal with foreign agents who were active in government and labor organizations. Dies insisted that both the government and labor organizations should "clean house"; known Communists should be compelled either to get out of labor organizations and government or to renounce the Communist party. The testimony presented to his committee had proved beyond any question that both the German-American Bund and the Communist party of the United States were "agencies of foreign powers," said Dies. As such he saw no reason why they should be permitted to operate in the

United States, or why they should be permitted to collect large sums of money from the American people to carry on their operations, or "to abuse the Bill of Rights for the purpose of building up an espionage or sabotage system in the United States." He felt that this point had been overlooked by many Americans in their effort to preserve the Bill of Rights. He would give American citizens the right to think whatever they chose, no matter how mistaken they might be, but he would not permit individuals to serve the interests of foreign powers in the name of the Bill of Rights.[75]

He thought the great majority of German-Americans were "loyal, patriotic citizens"; there was danger, however, that in consequence of the activities of a few disloyal German-Americans, there might arise in this country a sentiment against German-Americans generally. It was his opinion that in no community were more than 5 per cent of those of German descent in sympathy with the Nazis. Fritz Kuhn had rendered a great disservice to people of German descent in the United States. Dies felt that the German minority in the United States, which had carried on propaganda against the Jewish minority, had done the German minority generally more harm than it had done the Jewish minority.[76]

In the persecution of the Jews in Germany, Dies saw "a symptom" of something much deeper, a device used by Hitler to make it possible for his Nazi minority to gain control of Germany. Both the Nazis and the Communists were "subversive groups" which had been permitted to grow until they were so powerful that the state was no longer able to control them.[77] In the United States, Russia had, in the Communist party, a growing espionage system of 100,000 members, organized in 5,000 branches. If the United States sought to organize a comparable espionage system in a foreign nation it would be impossible for it to hire a comparable group of "trained agents" supplied with equally strategic information.[78]

By September 27, 1939, Dies had reached the conclusion that the Communist party of the United States was "engaged in a racket," was "the agent of a foreign power," had "misappropriated funds," and was "without any moral standard or code of honor." Since that was the case, Dies could not understand why the United States government was unable to deal with the Communists. The issue, as he saw it, was whether Communists like Browder, and fascists like Pelley, should be permitted to "conduct a first-class racket in the United States with impunity." Such people should be dealt with for misappropriation of funds —"no question of democracy [was] involved"; the United States must not harbor such people.[79]

On the whole, Dies' comments decreased as the hearings progressed. The committee, after having "exposed" and "destroyed" by unfavorable publicity most of the organizations which in any way threatened the political and economic status quo, became less active. Fear of the committee's inquisitional methods made "hearings" less necessary than at the outset. Liberal and radical organizations languished, and there was less need either for committee action or for Dies' pronouncements. However, Dies made several interesting comments in October, 1939. In questioning Harry F. Ward, head of the American League Against War and Fascism, he said that there was "no better way of determining what the real purposes of the league" were than by finding out the "views and activities" of the men who ran the American League. Dies said that in such cases "the real purposes" were entirely different from the declared or "spoken" purposes.[80] (Of course, the same thing can be said of the Dies committee. An examination of the "views and activities" of the members of the Dies committee tells us more about the committee than their "prospectus.")

While "a patriotic, loyal American citizen" might have belonged to an organization before Dies had dubbed it a Communist-front organization, it was clear to Dies by the fall of 1939 that the evidence of Communist control had become so "overwhelming" that when people "persist in continuing in such organizations" the committee could "reach no other conclusion than that they are either Communists or definitely fellow travelers of the Communist Party." Dies continued:

We certainly are justified now in laying down and saying definitely that if they continue in these organizations, the country can

113

reach but one conclusion, namely, that they are Communists or fellow travelers. And I can see very little difference between a fellow traveler and a Communist. In fact, I think I think more of the Communist, because he at least has the honesty to say that "I am a Communist."

Very well, gentlemen, let us proceed.[81]

This interesting conclusion by the chairman is in no sense justified on the basis of the testimony heard by the committee. However, if a conclusion of this kind could be broadcast to the American people as if it were a fact based on careful investigation and sufficient evidence, Dies by labeling organizations "Communist-front" could virtually destroy their effectiveness. Possibly all of the major organizations to the left of center had some Communists in them. The fact that there were Communists in them could be used to show that they were foreign-controlled. Once Dies had declared an organization a "Communist-front" organization, if you remained in it you were either a Communist or a fellow traveler. This line of argument is utterly destructive of the law of sufficient reason. But Dies has been successful enough with it to weaken appreciably the New Deal and every organization to the left of center. Yet a minute or so after making a blanket statement like the one above, Dies can turn around and in the next breath say:

There are selfish employers who would be only too happy to use this issue for the purpose of hurting honest laboring people who are not Communists.

We know further that simply because some people have the same views, or have certain views and the Communists coincide with them, does not mean that they are Communists. . . .

The argument is made that Lindbergh is a Fascist because he appears to have certain ideas. That, in my judgment, is absolutely unjustified, just as it is to say that some of the group who wants to revise the neutrality law are pro-English, or anything of that sort. We have got to be careful about that. The committee recognizes that.[82]

But, obviously, Dies does not recognize that, when it comes to organizations which are to the left of center.

About this time, Dies defined a "liberal" as anyone who

believed in "liberty," whether he was a conservative or a progressive. He stated that it would be a great service to the country if the committee would define the word "liberal" in this way "because the idea of dividing the people along economic lines is a folly." [83]

On October 24, 1939, Dies expressed ideas which led to nothing, but which are interesting because of what they tell us about Dies. We conclude with these words:

If the committee is continued next year, as I assume it will be, it will be my purpose to recommend that we go into the question of the causes of communism and nazi-ism. We have dealt heretofore with the manifestations of it, more or less as a disease. We have dealt with the symptoms, but we have not gotten into what is really behind it. What I would like for the committee to do, if it is supplied with ample funds, is to go into the fundamental question or the fundamental causes of communism and nazi-ism. I think if we could give the country a complete picture of what causes people to join these movements, and what is back of them, whether it is poverty, degradation, lack of proper environment, slums, tenement houses, and so forth, we will have done an important work....

We have given the American people a very graphic picture of the situation, but we have not by any means completed the investigation of a number of organizations that should be exposed. We have not gotten around to them, but our jurisdiction extends to all un-American activities, which would include people and organizations that preach radical hatred, religious hatred, and so forth, as well as the question of foreign control. I think it is important, if the committee is to be continued, that the cause of all these things should be investigated, because here is Earl Browder who denies that poverty is the cause of it. In fact, he says that a large number of the members of the Communist Party are regularly employed. He says that a large number of them are skilled workers, and that they are well employed, and that the appeal is intellectual. If he is right about that, then poverty and unemployment have nothing to do with it.[84]

7 THE COMMITTEE INVESTIGATES EDUCATION

ALTHOUGH THE ATTENTION of the Dies committee has not been focused primarily on American education, whenever witnesses have shown any disposition to discuss subversive activities in the schools and colleges, the committee has shown unusual eagerness to listen. For example, on the second day of the investigation (August 13, 1938) Committeeman Starnes said that he was "particularly interested in getting some information" on the educational activities of the Communists. He therefore asked John P. Frey, president of the metal trades department of the American Federation of Labor, to give the names of Communists in control of the Teachers Union in New York City, and for insight into the "methods followed here in obtaining a foothold in the educational system in this country." Mr. Frey explained that because of his interest in un-American activities he occasionally visited universities and discussed economic questions with the students. He declared he had sat with members of Communist cells in the universities and that he knew "something about the extent to which communists have succeeded in winning the most loyal support of the young Americans who are going through our American educational institutions." [1]

Two days later, when Mr. Frey gave the committee his evidence, it was derived from a report by himself and two others, describing a dispute which had arisen in Local No. 5 of the American Federation of Teachers in New York City. Stating that the New York union had come under the control of the Communist party, and that those in the union who opposed communism withdrew and formed another organization, Frey declared that ten members of the executive board of Local No. 5 out of an executive board of thirty-three were members of a Communist group. Although Frey was not able to give the committee a list of New York teachers who were members of the Communist party at the time, he thought he would be able to give the committee such a list later. Meanwhile, he was sure that Communists "controlled the election machinery" of Local No. 5, and that it was because of that control that many teachers had resigned to organize an independent union.

Then Mr. Frey was asked to provide the committee with names of educational institutions in which there were Communist teachers. "Taxpayers ought to have" such information, he declared, and the committee could get the facts from Professor Linville, former president of Local No. 5. Continuing, Frey gave the name of an Englishwoman, who, he asserted, was the wife of a Communist party official in Great Britain, and said, "I have nothing that she has written, and I have no record of anything that she has said. I merely have the record that ... she is a professional exchange student, and attends classes in universities all over the world." Mr. Frey gave no other specific information and no additional proof. Nevertheless, his testimony was gratefully received. It is typical of the superficial quality of much testimony on the same subject which came from later witnesses.[2]

Next to testify on "un-American" activities in American education was Walter S. Steele, who claimed to represent the American Coalition Committee on National Security, of which he was chairman, as well as the *National Republic* magazine, 114 other patriotic organizations which he listed, and also the Veterans of Foreign Wars and the R.O.T.C. Association of the United States.[3] While Mr. Steele gave over four hundred pages of testimony, he did not go into detail concerning the activities of "radicals" in educational institutions because, he said, "the coverage of that activity in completeness would in itself require hundreds of pages of testimony." He added, "I will state with earnestness and could easily prove to this committee the fact that there has possibly been as much if not more 'red' activity in this field than in any other excepting among the working class." While "not attempting to go into...detail about it," Steele showed no hesitation in making broad general charges. He said that "many professors [were] wound up into the machinery of radicalism in the United States"; some were Communists, some were Socialists, some were atheists, many were "on the firing line in co-operating movements." The American Association of University Professors "blacklisted" colleges which dismissed "radicals." The American Federation of Teachers was "honeycombed with radicals of extreme types." In fact, it had carried on a campaign against teachers' loyalty oaths. Jerome Davis, president of the American Federation of Teachers at that time, was "referred to in Communistic circles as a friend of Russia" and was one of the many intellectuals in America who "approved the mass killings—purges—in Russia." Granville Hicks was an example of communistic penetration, as was also the placing of a bust of John Reed, "notorious Bolshevik," in the hall of fame at Harvard University. Mr. Steele warned the committee that "there are many strange things being perpetrated under the protection of so-called academic freedom in our country today." [4] When asked for "evidence" of communistic progress in education, Steele explained that most college teachers would not "admit" they were Communists. Although he had "not counted them," Steele thought there was "a large number" of Communists in American colleges and universities. That Steele had little actual evidence [5] was recognized by Dies himself.[6]

Asked the number of Communist teachers in public schools, colleges, and universities, Homer Chaillaux, director of the National Americanism Commission of the American Legion,[7] said the Legion knew there was "a great deal" of communism in American education. However, he specifically mentioned only the case of Granville Hicks at Harvard University. He said that a number of universities had chapters "raising funds for loyal Spain"; among these were Columbia University, New York University, Harvard University, Northwestern University, and George Washington University. Moreover, the American Student Union had chapters in universities "all over the country." Answering a leading question by Chairman Dies concerning

American Student Union chapters, Chaillaux affirmed that "among other things, they teach pacifism and the students announce that in no event would they fight for their country." [8] Furthermore, the American Student Union "has co-operated directly with communist movements" in the United States; it has favored abolition of military training in schools and colleges. It has also favored the anti-lynching bill, endorsed the C.I.O., denounced "the jailing of labor agitators, and criticized colleges and universities expelling students and discharging professors for radical activities." [9] J. B. Matthews, another witness, said the American Student Union was a "front" organization for communism among American college students, and that its principle activity—promotion of "an anti-war strike" each year—was under the direction of the Communist party. [10] Matthews said the "World Youth Congress" was also a "front" organization, "dedicated to forwarding the aims of the foreign policy of the Soviet Union." Matthews explained: "Anyone who denies this demonstrable fact is either the unfortunate victim of deceit or a willful deceiver." He recognized the World Youth Congress as a "front" for the Communist party by the similarity of its resolutions to the Communist party line. [11] Matthews spoke as an authority, having been the first national chairman of the American League for Peace and Democracy; he asserted that he had worked actively with the American Student Union and other affiliated groups. [12]

One of the funniest sections of the Dies hearings is one which includes the testimony of three professors from Brooklyn College, Brooklyn, N. Y. [13] These men were convinced there was "undoubtedly" communism at Brooklyn College. As proof they cited "an incessant barrage of handbills," promoted in no small part by the Teachers Union, which was "incontestably a pressure group." Professor Fenlon asserted that very many teachers and students could not help but believe the Teachers Union was "linked with communism." He himself thought evidence was ample to prove the American Student Union "bound up with communism." The influence of communism on the campus was attributed less to numbers than "to ceaseless appeals and untiring pressure." Communism had "split" teachers and students; previously there had been peace on the campus. The professor was sure there were at least one thousand Communists on the campus and that their influence was increasing.[14] Professor Earl A. Martin asserted that although the Communist group was in a minority, it was well-organized, articulate, and had influence all out of proportion to its numbers.[15] Professor Martin Meyer saw clear evidence of communism in the fact that at least 150 out of a total of 300 people attending a meeting addressed by representatives of the American Legion had walked out when a young man in the audience got up in the midst of the address and asked everybody to leave who thought the speaker "unfair." [16]

Initiating a series of committee hearings in Detroit, Chester Howe, committee investigator, said (October 11, 1938): "We expect to show, through reputable witnesses, that many school teachers have communist leanings by attending meetings and making contributions to a cause alien to this Nation. The wives of some of the most prominent agitators in the United States are teachers in the Detroit public schools and attend meetings with or without their husbands and at every opportunity forward the cause of un-Americanism to the children of the State." [17]

Sergeant Harry Mikuliak of the Detroit Police Department was asked by Chairman Dies to give the committee "some information on the school-teacher proposition." Mikuliak testified that Professor Walter Bergman, assistant director of research at Wayne University, was alleged to have requested that the "Internationale," official song of Soviet Russia, be sung at the outset of a mass meeting. Bergman was also alleged to have said that the United States was becoming fascist. Mikuliak testified that Phil Raymond, "one of the most active agitators in Detroit," was the husband of Vera Katz, a Detroit school teacher. She drove him to radical meetings and had attended several of them. Mikuliak mentioned several other school teachers who were married to alleged Communists. One of these school teachers had even attended the Third Annual Congress Against War and Fascism; another was a director of the League for Industrial Democracy.[18] Sergeant Mikuliak did not present one shred of evidence to prove that the teachers themselves were Communists; theirs was the sin of association.

Walter S. Reynolds, chairman of a subcommittee on subversive activities of the American Legion in Michigan, testified that numerous professors co-operated with Communists in behalf of Loyalist Spain, scores permitting their names to be included on committees to aid such causes. He mentioned Paul H. Douglas, Jerome Davis, Albert Einstein, and K. F. Mather as professors of this kind. Reynolds added: "Scores of professors with many degrees have made utterances which are not only false and injurious to American prestige abroad, but are repulsive and highly insulting to the intelligence of the average American citizen." [19] He said that Dr. Walter G. Bergman, "a radical professor," hid "his real 'red' color" by being a member of the Socialist party, and running for office on the Socialist ticket. Reynolds said Bergman was president of the Detroit Federation of Teachers and that he was on the executive committee of the League for Industrial Democracy—"a strictly communist organization." In Reynolds' testimony assertion takes the place of specific evidence in practically every instance. Reynolds saw much significance in the fact that, at a mass meeting, Bergman had referred to the Sacco-Vanzetti trials and had affirmed the innocence of Tom Mooney, "whose conviction was recently upheld by the Supreme Court." Reynolds concluded that it was "only too evident that as a professor of a university he belongs perhaps to the most damaging elements to the American institutions, particularly schools in this State." [20]

Vinson L. Fitzgerald, prosecuting attorney of Macomb County, Michigan, testified that the committee possessed a list which, he thought, contained the names of approximately seventy-five Detroit public school teachers, "who, it is alleged, while they might not be actual members of the Communist Party as such, at least are fellow travelers, and have attended, or do attend, Communist meetings." [21] Statements like the above were not exceptional in the testimony heard by Dies concerning un-American activities in American education. These are characteristic of repeated assertions and charges made without any proof whatever. Nevertheless, in spite of there being little or no evidence, Chairman Dies declared that the mayor of Detroit should be congratulated for "following up the testimony taken by our committee in Detroit" and "taking decided steps to clean up the situation in . . . the schools there."

On October 19, 1938, Clyde Morrow, a Ford Motor Company employee connected with the Americanization committee of the American Legion and one time member of the Communist party, named several Detroit teachers as members of what he alleged were Communist-dominated organizations, such as the League for Industrial Democracy, and of the American Federation of Teachers, which he said was used "as a cover up." One of these teachers was accused of hearing a lecture by Anna Louise Strong, editor of the *Moscow Daily News*. This allegedly showed radical inclination on the part of the teacher who heard the lecture. Morrow called the committee's attention to a newspaper story to the effect that Superintendent Cody of the Detroit schools had said he would be satisfied "if he had 10 school teachers who were 'red' and the rest well read"; Superintendent Cody said he knew four or five teachers were Communists and kept them "under constant surveillance." [22]

Herman Luhrs of the American Legion testified that he had a letter which Dr. Goodwin Watson of Columbia University had sent to the school superintendent of Flint, Michigan, inviting him to make a trip to Russia; Luhrs declared that this letter showed that Goodwin Watson was tied up with a "front" organization of the Communist party. [23]

Zygmund Dobrzyniski, a Detroit high school graduate, [24] was asked by Chairman Dies on November 14, 1938 if he had learned anything about the activities of Communists in the Detroit schools. Dobrzyniski said he did not know a great deal about communistic activities in the Detroit schools but thought they were not serious below the university level. [25] Harper L. Knowles, chairman of the Radical Research Committee of the American Legion, Department of California, testified that the American Student Union, the youth section of the American League Against War and Fascism, the American Youth Congress, and the youth section of the Emergency Peace Committee, were closely related, and were all "notoriously communistic."

In the fact that certain "radicals" had previously attended American institutions of higher learning, Knowles saw clear evidence of indoctrination and "proselyting within our educational domains." Professors Max Radin, Harry Conover, G. M. Kefauver, Harold C. Hand, George S. Counts, and Thomas Addis were cited as illustrative of the extent to which American educational institutions have become "impregnated with Marxian philosophies." Knowles charged that these men followed the Communist party line in their school activities.[26]

Knowles said that while most liberal and radical groups in American colleges did not openly advocate communism, "the direct and indirect suggestions to students" from these groups, had an effect much more "deadly" than would their open support of communistic doctrines. Knowles said "Americanism" could not, in most instances, find fault with the specific utterances of instructors, but it did find fault with "the far more insidious method" by which students in elementary schools, high schools, and colleges were led to have "an unhealthy disrespect" for the great patriots of America. It was though "tearing down" American traditions that the adolescent mind was made receptive to doctrines of communism. "The willful tearing down of traditions surrounding the adoption of our Constitution and sincerity of our forefathers in building a democracy, can have but one malignant purpose and that is to inculcate in the minds of the students a disrespect for American traditions which per se almost invariably causes at least a partial acceptance of false ideology." To show the harmful effect of this kind of education, Knowles introduced a letter, written by a Stanford University student, which allegedly showed that although the young man had been brought up by parents who revered America's established institutions, he was leaving college "a cynic as to American ideals."

Knowles named A. S. Kaen, J. L. Kirchen, Haakon Chevalier, T. K. Whipple, Max Radin, G. P. Adams, Ralph Chaney, A. M. Kidd, and Robert A. Brady, teachers at the University of California, who, although they might not be members of the Communist party, were "used as tools" to further the "left-wing" movement. To show that "the left-wing trend" was prevalent on all educational levels, Knowles introduced a newspaper clipping reporting that a conference of the California Federation of Teachers had "unanimously endorsed" the following "Communist Resolutions": repeal of the criminal syndicalism law in California, abolition of military training, freedom for Tom Mooney, and enactment of the Frazier-Lundeen bill. Knowles asserted that junior college students in California had to "run the same gamut" as those in universities "with respect as to the activities of radical instructors." One high school teacher of social studies had been removed by the school board for "communistic activities and teachings." Knowles explained that while it was "commonly reported" that many elementary school teachers "inculcated in the minds of pupils certain radical or liberal teachings," such instances were not "sufficiently overt," and there was not enough available evidence, to justify a detailed report on the subject.[27] On November 5, 1938, James A. Cobb, a Washington, D. C. attorney associated with Howard University as a teacher since 1916, charged that Mordecai W. Johnson, president of Howard University, had advocated doctrines of communism. Cobb asserted that if Dr. Johnson was not "a Communist," he was, at least, "communistic, or certainly was preaching communist doctrines." [28]

Alice Lee Jemison, Washington representative of the national president of the American Indian Federation, another witness before the Dies committee, testified extensively on the subject of education and educators. She testified that, although Willard D. Beatty, director of the Division of Education of the Office of Indian Affairs, was not a member of the American Civil Liberties Union, he was, at the time he was appointed, national president of the Progressive Education Association, "which was founded by John Dewey, who is a well-known radical professor in Columbia University, and who is a member of the American Civil Liberties Union." Moreover, Dr. Beatty had been "closely associated with Dr. George S. Counts, Dr. Carleton Washburne, and Dr. Harold L. Rugg, and other radical professors who are members of the American Civil Liberties Union." [29] Of John Dewey, Miss Jemison said that in addition to being a professor at Columbia University and an honorary president of the Pro-

124

gressive Education Association he was "a member of many radical organizations in the United States, and a member of the American Civil Liberties Union." Moreover, she explained, "John Dewey has been attacked by Matthew Woll, of the American Federation of Labor." (This last was too much, even for Martin Dies; he explained that "the mere fact that somebody denounced him is no particular proof.") But Miss Jemison, to clinch her point, indicated that one Walter Albion Squires, D.D. had written a book called *Educational Movements of Today* in which he had said that in Russia John Dewey "is recognized as an educational guide. In America his influence is a potent force in the progressive secularization of the public-school curriculum. His attitude is distinctly antireligious unless we change our conceptions concerning the nature of religion."

Miss Jemison testified that associated with John Dewey in the reorganization of the educational system in Soviet Russia were Dr. Beatty and Dr. Counts. Chairman Dies inquired if this latter individual was not "the author of several books, including *The Soviet Challenge to America*, and *Dare the School Build a a New Social Order?*" Miss Jemison answered in the affirmative. *New Russia's Primer* by M. Ilin, which Martin Dies said compared the United States and Russia in such a way as to point out the superiority of the latter, had been translated into English by George S. Counts. She explained that in his introduction Dr. Counts said that the book was written for elementary school children and had also stated "that anyone who has read [the book] can never believe in the capitalist system"; nevertheless, Miss Jemison testified that she knew of "one Indian school" in which that book was used.[30]

In an extended statement which Miss Jemison submitted, John Dewey's writings indicated that he was "an atheist." She asserted it to be "a well-known and well-established fact that Professor Counts is completely in sympathy with the communist program of Soviet Russia." Moreover Dr. Frank W. Ballou, director of education for the District of Columbia, who had worked with Dr. Counts on the Commission on the Social Studies of the American Historical Association, was said to have termed him "a radical." Furthermore, Counts had been listed

125

in 1935 as an instructor at the University of Moscow summer session, and "was listed as a radical professor with a record of close association with radicals in the Red Network" written by Mrs. Dilling.[31]

Dr. Harold Rugg, Mr. Arthur E. Morgan, Mr. Alvin S. Johnson, Mr. E. C. Lindeman, and Mr. Carleton Washburne, "all of whom are listed in the Red Network as radical professors," were alleged to be members of the advisory committee of the magazine of the Progressive Education Association. Dr. Walter Albion Squires, D.D. was quoted to prove that the Winnetka system of character education, with which Dr. Washburne was associated, rested on "antireligious assumptions." Dr. Beatty was alleged to have acquired his educational philosophy from Dr. Washburne, and the committee's attention was further directed to "the close association in progressive education of Dr. Beatty and the former Director of Indian Education, Dr. Carson Ryan, Jr." [32]

Sam Baron, an alternate member of the executive committee of the Socialist party of America, said the American Student Union was controlled by Communists, although he made it clear that by this statement he did not imply that all individuals connected with the organization were Communists.[33] George Edward Sullivan, Washington lawyer and antisubversive writer, asserted that American youth was being "constantly kidnaped from the Nation" through having their "minds and morals poisoned by propaganda" and their patriotism destroyed. In many public schools "our Republic" was being compelled "to dig its own grave but at taxpayers' expense." When protests were made to school officials concerning subversive propaganda in textbooks, they became indignant, and "hypocritically" talked of "academic freedom." Under the head of "academic freedom," Sullivan explained, school officials are "exercising for themselves a most pernicious 'academic anarchy.' ".

Mr. Sullivan said that although no one attributed disloyalty to the rank and file of American teachers, there was "good cause for alarm." Thousands of teachers from all over the United States had taken courses at Teachers College, Columbia University, "where they came under the direct influence of Dr.

George S. Counts, professor of education there." After quoting fragments from *Social Frontier,* a magazine edited by Dr. Counts, the testimony continued as follows:

THE CHAIRMAN. Was not that professor discharged from Columbia University recently?

MR. SULLIVAN. Not at all; he is still there.

THE CHAIRMAN. Is he still there?

MR. SULLIVAN. The last I heard, he was still there and makes trips back and forth to Soviet Russia.

THE CHAIRMAN. Proceed.

MR. SULLIVAN. Dr. Counts wrote the Foreword to Stalin's book, the New Russian Policy, published in 1931. In the following year, he wrote a book of his own, Dare the School Build a New Social Order? urging teachers to "positively influence the social attitudes, ideals, and behavior of the coming generation" (p. 29), for "democracy under novel conditions (p. 40), which "should not be identified" with "the Federal Constitution, the popular election of officials, or the practice of universal suffrage" (p. 40), and "finally be prepared as a last resort, in either the defense or the realization of this purpose, to follow the method of revolution (pp. 41-42).

American teachers are further harassed about retention or assertion of 100 percent American ideas and principles by an outrageous "report" of so-called "Commission on the Social Studies," sponsored by an organization named the American Historical Association, published in parts or volumes, commencing in 1932. Dr. Counts served as a member of that commission, as did also Dr. Frank W. Ballou, the superintendent of schools of the Nation's Capital. In part I of said report (published in 1932), page 45, it was pointedly suggested that "enlightened" communities do not expect teachers to denounce communism.

THE CHAIRMAN. Right there: No one accuses Dr. Ballou of being a Communist, do they?

MR. SULLIVAN. I am not charging anyone with being a Communist, but the record shows that his acts have aided Communist propaganda with regard to education.

THE CHAIRMAN. Now is not that a conclusion on your part?

MR. SULLIVAN. A conclusion from facts. This very propaganda, in the form of this report of the Commission on the Social studies, of which he was a member of the committee on direction, was expressly recommended by him on June 5, 1935, to be listed by the

127

board of education for general reference reading by teachers in our public schools. And, upon his recommendation, he having been a member of that commission, the board of education adopted his recommendation and listed it as one of these books.

THE CHAIRMAN. Listed what?

MR. SULLIVAN. Listed this report with his outrageous stuff in it; listed it in Public School Document No. 1, 1936, for the teachers to read.

THE CHAIRMAN. Well, could not teachers be permitted to read reports and could not they read the manifesto of Marx and Lenin, and socialistic and communistic reports, without being subject to the imputation they were in sympathy with the Communists? I mean, in order to be fair about this, you would not advocate that a man should not be permitted to read Communist literature, would you?

MR. SULLIVAN. Not at all, I think everybody should read it, but they should read it as what it is—propaganda.

MR. THOMAS. But they are reading it to school children, are they not?

MR. SULLIVAN. Reading it to those school children without any denunciation of it; therefore, it is given to the school children as though it were factual, instead of propaganda.[34]

On September 11, 1939, Benjamin Gitlow, former general secretary of the Communist party of the United States,[35] testified that the party had in the 1920's organized, at the behest of the Communist International, a delegation of reputedly "impartial" Americans who were not communists, to visit Soviet Russia to investigate conditions and to submit "an impartial, unbiased report to the American people on what were the actual conditions in Soviet Russia." The expenses of the delegation were paid by Moscow. Included on the technical and advisory staff, according to Gitlow, were such men as Carleton Washburne, Jerome Davis, Stuart Chase, Paul H. Douglas, George S. Counts and R. G. Tugwell. Mr. Gitlow asserted that the delegation had been deluged with receptions and banquets and sightseeing tours but "had no time to investigate actual conditions." He referred to the delegation as having "one wild party from the day they landed in Russia to the day they got out of Russia." Their report, which was represented to the American people as the report of "a nonpartisan, unprejudiced commission of workers," was, he said, actually written by a concealed member of the Communist party.[36]

Mr. Gitlow testified that school teachers who joined the Communist party organizations in the United States found it "advisable" to "operate in the party" under assumed rather than under their real names.[37] Gitlow said that in New York City a number of teachers and professors had withdrawn from the Teachers Union because it was dominated by the Communist party and was apparently more interested in promoting the political objectives of the Communist party than in advancing the interests of the teachers. Gitlow knew John Dewey was one of those who had withdrawn from the Teachers Union. He testified, however, that he did not really know enough about what was going on in the American Federation of Teachers to testify under oath about it.[38] He agreed to provide the committee with the names of leading colleges penetrated by the Communist party, and names of professors who had taken part in the Communist movement. If this information was ever provided, it does not appear in the published hearings.[39]

Earl Browder, secretary of the Communist party of the United States, testified that certain teachers made financial contributions to the Communist party.[40] He also testified that some public school teachers attended classes in Communist party schools. He indicated that college and university as well as public school teachers attended these communist schools. Columbia University was mentioned specifically in this connection. Browder said at least twelve universities had sent people to attend "our workers' schools." He mentioned Granville Hicks at Harvard University as "one of our most distinguished Communist educators." Browder thought that in all cities in which the Communist party had workers' schools it would be found that students from universities were attending these schools. This did not mean, however, that faculty members from the university were attending them. Occasionally, faculty members gave lectures, but they never taught regular courses. Browder thought that some of these faculty lecturers were regular members of the staff of Brooklyn College.[41]

Asked if there were college professors and teachers in the United States who were members of the Communist party, and whose membership in the party was a matter of open knowledge, Browder said that he did not know of any. Asked if he knew of teachers who were members of the Communist party, but used one name as teachers and another name in connection with their party activity, Browder said that he did not know of any. Discussing the "moral" aspect of the problem, Browder argued that when a man like Granville Hicks was ousted from an institution of higher learning, those who discharged him alleged other reasons for dismissing him than his political beliefs and affiliations. Browder distinguished between the "moral" precepts of such people and those who would protect workers from dismissal regardless of their political beliefs. Browder insisted that, if a college ousted a man because he was a communist, it "ought to have the courage to say so." Asked if a college teacher who was a Communist "ought to have the courage to say so," he replied that, sometimes, they might be "forced to adopt the morality of those who run the college. [Laughter]" When Browder was asked if "communist morality" was subordinated to the interest of the class struggle, he replied that there was no "such a thing as Communist morality. [Laughter]." Subsequently he explained that what he meant was that, since there were relatively few Communists, they had "no special morality separate from the morality of the great mass of the people." Browder testified that the question of whether Communist professors should or should not conceal the fact they were Communists was a matter which he would leave entirely to the individual professor. Browder said that he "would not try to give any answer for him." [42]

When asked whether the Communist party used schools and colleges as "transmission belts," that is, as "a medium of operation," in the same way that the party used the trade-union movement, Browder replied that the party made use of "any place where people come together" as an opportunity to promote its purposes. He admitted that his party had operated through the medium of schools and colleges, in so far as possible, although the party had made no special effort to place advocates of communism in teaching positions. Nevertheless, Browder thought that the influence of the Communist party on schools and teachers was much greater than might be implied from the relatively small membership of the party. He would not say that the party exerted influence in every college in America, and did not want to mention particular colleges—"I do not like to cause trouble to anybody"—but he affirmed that the Communists had influence at Columbia University, Brooklyn College, City College, and the University of Minnesota. He stated that he had made "special speeches" in approximately twenty-three colleges and universities in America and remarked that he had always received a "very good reception." Browder declared that the Communist party sought to influence every organization and individual in America.[43]

Alexander Trachtenberg, secretary and treasurer of International Publishers and a member of the national committee of the Communist party, testified that he had been a member of the Teachers Union while he was teaching at the Rand School of Social Science in New York City. He denied that the party used schools and colleges as "transmission belts." [44] The Book Union, which shared headquarters with International Publishers, had on its advisory council, he said, such people as Heywood Broun, Kenneth Burke, R. Palme Dutt, Robert Morss Lovett, Lewis Mumford, Clifford Odets, John Strachey, Carl Van Doren, and Bernhard Stern. He testified that Bernhard Stern was a professor at Columbia University.[45] On September 23, 1939, Dr. D. H. Dubrowski, once an official representative of the Soviet government in the United States, testified that Dr. George Hartmann was head of the Friends of Soviet Russia in 1922.[46]

The Dies committee next focused its attention on education when on November 27, 1939, Major Hampden Wilson, a Veterans' Administration investigator assigned to the Dies committee, reported on his investigation of educational institutions. Major Wilson had in a period of approximately eight months visited forty-two states and more than fifty institutions of higher learning, and state and city boards of education. His method of investigation consisted of going to the administrative heads of the institutions involved; he was careful to avoid contacts with "junior professors" or students. Wilson found the administrative heads inclined to minimize the amount of subversive activity in their institutions; on the other hand "many deans, professors, and so forth, have been very definite in pointing out the serious nature of these activities in special institutions." [47]

Wilson found the American Student Union the agency most frequently used "in spreading communism." Professors who sponsored American Student Union groups were "universally ... characterized as ... 'red,' 'pink,' or so-called 'liberal.' " These professors were, according to Wilson, continually striving to get themselves before student bodies in defense of liberty and were also very anxious to be popular. "An alert teacher who is filled with zeal for the spread of communism" could exert immeasurable influence. The activities of these sponsors, while commendable in some ways, "when coupled with the spread of communism ... becomes the basest kind of prostitution." College chapters of the American Federation of Teachers talked a lot about freedom of speech and academic freedom and were "invariably" supporters of the American Student Union. [48] The American Student Union, in addition to sponsoring "red" speakers and "red" movements, "is always a 'noisy' minority wherever it exists." The American Federation of Teachers was important "in the furtherance of Communist aims." When such unions are strong enough, "they assume to exercise a voice in the employment and discharge of professors" and in certain instances "this has caused great strife and a much lowered morale in faculty groups." [49]

Representative Voorhis of the Dies committee asked Major Wilson what he meant when he said that a professor was a "red." To this question Wilson replied, "So characterized by the local authorities and locally informed." He did not mean, he said, that such professors were necessarily members of the Communist party. "In fact they are told that they are much more valuable to the party not to become members of it." Voorhis indicated that Major Wilson had been "fairly general" in his report; Voorhis wanted the report to be more accurate and specific for fear that the general impression might go out that the American educational system is communistic, which Voorhis considered contrary to the facts.[50] Major Wilson stated it "the general consensus of opinion" that from 1 to 5 per cent of faculty members were lending support to communism. Voorhis then asked Wilson if he knew the position of Dr. George S. Counts on the question of foreign isms; Wilson said that he did. Although Voorhis' statement was in the form of a question, it is apparent that he meant to call attention to the effort of Dr. Counts to exclude Communists from the American Federation of Teachers.[51]

We conclude our review of Major Wilson's testimony with a bit of dainty questioning by Representative Starnes:

MR. STARNES. Did you find any evidence of the fact [*sic*] that in their attempt to infiltrate into the schools or colleges or to get their viewpoints expressed before student bodies of our great educational institutions, that the Communists often have some member of the faculty or some front organization on the campus to extend an invitation and then have the school authorities refuse to grant a place for this Communist to speak; then set up the cry of suppression of free speech and the violation of civil liberties? Did you find that to be a technique that is used to a considerable extent?

MAJOR WILSON. That is universally their technique. It is the desire of the American Student Union to present itself to the student body as an active agent to procure advantages for the student body, which of itself is quite commendable. They always, however, antagonize practically everywhere possible the general administration; always agitating some advantage whether deserved or not that the authorities are opposed to granting.

MR. STARNES. In other words, antagonizing, deliberately antagonizing, the authorities and encouraging them to refuse the privilege of the use of the buildings there to Communists in order to set up their cry of suppression of civil liberties and denying free speech.

MAJOR WILSON. And to win favor among certain types of students who think that the organization is thereby increasing its power and influence in the institution.

MR. STARNES. That seems to be a well-established procedure. Of course, there is not any denial of the right of free speech. It is just merely to raise a false issue that that is built up.[52]

This is one of those delightfully revealing passages of testimony which clearly indicate the slant of Dies' number two man.

The Dies committee also heard testimony by George W. Hartmann, associate professor of educational psychology at Teachers College, Columbia University, New York City. Professor Hartmann stated at the outset that his social attitudes overlapped those of Mr. Voorhis of the Dies committee about 95 per cent. It was his opinion that American teachers generally were too conservative rather than vice versa. But Hartmann had no use for the "underground behavior" of the Communists which "takes the form of deception; of lying; of the familiar technique known as character assassination; of behavior which is not only unprofessional, but low and vile in any group, no matter where it may occur." Hartmann stated that Local No. 5 in New York City was Communist-controlled; the tactics of the Stalinist group, he said, made it possible for a small minority to dominate an entire organization. Hartmann stated that "constructive relations with the Communists are absolutely impossible, no matter what the area concerned may be." (One might remark in passing that the war has proved otherwise.) "They have cursed and contaminated every revolutionary reform movement with which they have been associated," said Dr. Hartmann. He declared that "communism cannot stand ventilation." To clarify the point, Mr. Starnes explained: "It is sort of like a skunk. When you ventilate it, it loses its power or force." Hartmann, however, preferred to compare communism to "the pus in a boil."

Hartmann stated that Communists took advantage of a certain "intellectual lag among intellectuals" in that certain "gullible" intellectuals did not realize that "the U.S.S.R. today is neither a workers' republic nor a peasants' government nor a Socialist society." Intellectuals of this type, some of whom were teachers, seemed "unable to make this distinction between a genuine democratic principle and their complete contradiction in behavior and action." Unemployment made people more sensitive to the message of Communists than they would be under other circumstances. Hartmann thought there were "somewhere between two and three thousand" Communists among college teachers in America. The "most damning thing" about the Communists, said Hartmann, is their refusal to admit their identity. Congressman Starnes thanked Dr. Hartmann for the "fine statement" that he had given the committee.[53]

Dr. Henry R. Linville, executive director of the New York Teachers Guild, gave his views and experiences in connection with the American Federation of Teachers. He explained how, in his judgment, the Communists had gained control of the New York and national organizations of the American Federation of Teachers. Although Professor Counts had recently been elected president of the national organization, Dr. Linville was convinced that the executive council was still overwhelmingly under Communist control. Linville did not think it wise for the "liberal group" to "indulge ... this Communist element to the extent that the whole national movement may be discredited." He recommended that the "liberal group" challenge the right of the Communists to be present in the meetings of the organization. Until this was done, the situation facing "liberal" teachers in the American Federation of Teachers would be "a very difficult one." Dr. Linville declared that in the 1935 convention of the organization every one of those, except Dr. Counts, who had "actively opposed the Stalinists" had been defeated in the annual election and his place taken by "a person supposed to be a Stalinist."

(Actually, the "liberals" in the American Federation of Teachers acted along the lines recommended by Dr. Linville and threw out of the organization those locals which they considered "Communist-controlled." Calling their enemies "Communist" or "Communist-controlled," they abridged the constitution of the organization, which provided against any discrimination against any group on account of political belief, by throwing them out of the organization, but were able to secure a majority vote when the action was submitted to the membership in the form of a referendum. The situation was much the same as if in 1933 the Democrats had thrown all Republicans out of Congress and submitted their action to the country for referendum vote. A majority might at that time

135

have upheld the action, but it would nonetheless have been an entirely unconstitutional procedure. The Dies committee has grasped the same general technique: in dealing with a small and unpopular group it is possible to deny them their constitutional rights through appealing to a momentarily intolerant majority. However, it should be noted that all such procedure is basically totalitarian. It accepts the idea that only those who are agreed on the fundamentals are entitled to be protected in the exercises of their constitutional rights, that those who are not in agreement on these fundamentals should be exposed, persecuted, and destroyed because they are "Communist," "reactionary," or "un-American," and therefore beyond the limits of tolerance.)

Dr. Linville recognized that it was not an easy matter to identify Communists. The list of members of the Communist party was not available. He proposed that the test of whether different organizations were or were not under communistic control be determined by the resolutions adopted by their conventions. A convention which adopted resolutions supporting the Loyalist side of the struggle in Spain or expressing pride in the achievements of the Abraham Lincoln Brigade there, indicated thereby that it was a Communist-front organization. Other expressions of agreement with the Communist party line would add further proof of Communist domination.[54]

That the Dies investigation of American education, as evidenced by its published hearings, is indeed a very superficial picture, no one who knows anything about American education will deny. Fortunately, some of the incorrect statements made by early witnesses before the committee were partially corrected by the testimony of Dr. Hartmann and Dr. Linville. For example, the incidental references of each of them to their fellow educators, such as John Dewey, were vastly more accurate and just. But, clearly, the testimony of Hartmann and Linville was itself definitely *ex parte*. It would have been more American to have permitted the groups against whom both Hartmann and Linville directed their charges an opportunity to be heard in their own defense with the same amount of latitude as was allowed these gentlemen.

At the end of the testimony given by Dr. Linville, Congressman Starnes remarked, somewhat encouragingly, "It is probably a matter of interest to you to know that the committee which is conducting these hearings—all three of us [Starnes, Mason, and Voorhis]—are former teachers ourselves, and we have listened with a great deal of interest to the testimony today." [55]

8 THE COMMITTEE REPORTS

IT IS NECESSARY to distinguish between the hearings and the reports of the Dies committee. The so-called *hearings* are the published proceedings of the committee and run into thousands of pages. They include the questions addressed to witnesses, the statements and answers made by witnesses, statements made by members of the committee in the course of the proceedings, and letters, affidavits, and other communications addressed to the committee. The *reports* of the committee were prepared by the committee for submission to the House of Representatives. They indicate the committee's findings and recommendations, and are much briefer than the hearings.

It is the writer's opinion, after carefully reading both the hearings and the reports, that the latter are not dependent on the former. The reports simply amplify points of view which Martin Dies expressed to Congress even before President Roosevelt's first inauguration. The reports refer to the testimony of the hearings to prove certain things; the determination of what things were to be proved, however, was not a product of the testimony itself. Given a desire to reach other conclusions, Dies could easily have found an equal amount of testimony in support of them. As it was, although the hearings contained little testimony from witnesses who did not share Dies' own views on what is "un-American," the hearings nevertheless contain much evidence contrary to the "findings" of the committee as set forth in its reports. The committee refers to its hearings in the case of testimony supporting its own hunches, but does not refer to the hearings in those cases in which testimony ran counter to the committee's own presuppositions.

It is evident that the important thing was not the testimony itself but the ideas of the committeemen, the ideas which they had at the outset of the investigation. The investigation found what it set out to find. Despite the fact that witnesses were carefully selected and hostile witnesses were compelled to confine their testimony within narrow limits, the most fundamental declarations set forth in the committee's reports were not dependent on the testimony. On the contrary, one finds stated there basic assumptions which the committee set forth in its first report and seems to have taken for granted throughout the entire investigation without feeling any need for testimonial or documentary support.

The writer has read every speech made by Dies in Congress, as reported in the *Congressional Record*, every word spoken by him and recorded in the hearings and in all reports of his committee. This reading makes it clear that Dies had very definite ideas on subversive and un-American activities and propaganda long before his committee came into existence. The Dies committee later investigated and found out what Dies knew even before the investigation began. The hearings were organized as an agency to prove certain things that Dies wanted to prove; consequently he often rejected witnesses whose testimony might have led to other conclusions than the ones which he had in mind at the outset.

The views of the committee, allegedly based on the hearings, were first set forth in reports submitted to the House on January 3, 1939, and on January 3, 1940. These first two reports were signed by all members of the committee. Dies has stated that the second report—a twenty-five-page report submitted on January 3, 1940—was not "entirely in harmony" with his own views,[1] although his signature was attached. Our preoccupation will be with the first report. We shall consider as an expression of Dies' own views only those parts of the second report which are an extension of views he expressed as his own in the course of the hearings themselves. In general it will be noted that the second report, with which Dies was not in complete agreement, is a much more liberal document than the report to which he took no exception.

The third report, twenty-five pages in length, was submitted on January 3, 1941; it, too, was signed by all members of the committee. The next was a "special" report and consisted of two parts, a majority report of twenty-two pages submitted on June 25, 1942, unsigned by members of the committee, and a minority report of seven pages submitted on July 7, 1942, signed by Jerry Voorhis. The fourth annual report was submitted on January 2, 1943; it was sixteen pages in length and included a majority report of thirteen pages signed by Dies, Starnes, Thomas, and Mason, and a minority report of three pages signed by Jerry Voorhis.

THE FIRST REPORT

The first report of the Dies committee starts with a criticism of the Administration for its failure to co-operate with the committee. Not only had the heads of certain departments failed to co-operate, "but some of them deliberately sought to discredit the investigation by ridicule and misrepresentation." It was claimed that the witnesses who had appeared before the committee were a representative group of American citizens from nearly all sections of the country and from nearly all walks of life. It was emphasized that the committee had been "non-partisan" and "fearless"; it had felt obliged "to focus the spotlight of publicity upon every individual and organization engaged in subversive activities regardless of politics or partisanship." [2]

The second section of the report defines "Americanism":

Americanism recognizes the existence of a God and the all-important fact that the fundamental rights of man are derived from God and not from any other source. Among these inalienable rights which are the gifts of man from his Creator are: (1) Freedom of worship; (2) freedom of speech; (3) freedom of press; (4) freedom of assemblage; (5) freedom to work in such occupation as the experience, training, and qualifications of a man may enable him to secure and hold; (6) freedom to enjoy the fruits of his work, which means the protection of property rights; (7) the right to pursue his happiness with the necessary implication that he does not harm or injure others in the pursuit of this happiness.[3]

Further, "Americanism" is "class, religious, and racial toler-ance." It would thus appear that no matter how great the injustice suffered by a particular class or religious group or race, there must be no hatred on the part of the underprivileged, for that is "un-American." "Americanism" includes the protection of "the God-given rights of man" by means of "an independent Congress, an untrammelled judiciary, and a fair and impartial Executive operating under the American system of checks and balances." It would appear, then, that an individual who sought to use the method of Constitutional amendment to eliminate checks and balances from the American system of government would be running counter to the basic principles of Ameri-canism.

"Americanism" involves not only majority rule but the "recognition of certain rights of minorities which majorities cannot alienate." Thus the property rights of a minority are entitled to protection against a covetous majority, although it is not equally clear that the rights of a Communist minority are entitled to an equal measure of protection. Dies seems less concerned over the violation of the "God-given rights" of Jehovah's Witnesses than over the threatened violation of prop-erty rights.

All of these definitions of "Americanism" are attributed to the Declaration of Independence and the Constitution of the United States. Yet no mention is made of that section of the Declaration of Independence which refers to "the right of the people to alter or abolish ... any Form of Government ... and to institute new Government, laying its foundation on such principles and organizing its powers in such form, as to them shall seem most likely to effect their Safety and Happiness" or to the clauses of the Constitution which provide for the amend-ment of that document. In other words, Dies and his committee feel that "Americanism" requires the preservation of the status quo, and label as "un-American" whatever seems to threaten the status quo no matter how constitutional be the means whereby it is proposed.

As a matter of fact, the only reference to anything like "God-given rights" in either the Declaration or the Constitution is the statement in the Declaration of Independence "that all men are created equal, that they are endowed by their Creator with certain unalienable Rights, that among these are Life, Liberty and the pursuit of Happiness." The Constitution makes no mention of God and provides that "Congress shall make no law respecting an establishment of religion, or prohibiting the free exercise thereof." In other words, the Constitution makes definite provision for the separation of church and state. When Dies attempts to drag in theological sanctions in support of his own pet notions he is reverting to a presecular theory of government of which the Constitution of the United States marked an end in American government.

Seeking to contrast communism, fascism, and nazism with Americanism, the committee found them all "forms of dictatorship which deny the divine origin of the fundamental rights of man." In Russia, Italy, and Germany the citizens had no right which government was required to respect; the state was everything and the individual was nothing. Contrasted with communism, founded on class hatred, and nazism and fascism, founded on racial and religious hatred, "Americanism is a philosophy of government based upon the belief in God as the Supreme Ruler of the Universe." Communism denied, and nazism and fascism ignored "the existence and divine authority of God."

Communism was defined in the report:

Communism is a world-wide political organization advocating: (1) the abolition of all forms of religion; (2) the destruction of private property and the abolition of inheritance; (3) absolute social and racial equality; (4) revolution under the leadership of the Communist International; (5) engaging in activities in foreign countries in order to cause strikes, riots, sabotage, bloodshed, and civil war; (6) destruction of all forms of representative or democratic government, including civil liberties such as freedom of speech, of the press, and of assemblage; (7) the ultimate objective of world revolution to establish the dictatorship of the so-called proletariat into a universal union of Soviet socialist republics with its capital at Moscow; (8) the achievement of these ends through extreme appeals to hatred.[4]

This definition, the committee acknowledged, was a paraphrase and elaboration of a definition provided by Representative Hamilton Fish in 1930.[5] It should be noted that when foreign isms, such as communism, are defined by the committee, these definitions are derived from sources opposed to the isms defined; but that when Americanism is defined, that definition is formulated by its friends. Such discrimination in the matter of definitions hardly conforms to the canons of fairness or objectivity. Certainly no political scientist, aside from Hamilton Fish, would accept these definitions.

According to Dies, communism, fascism, and nazism "advocate that it is the duty of government to support the people and the right of government to exact blind obedience on all matters from the people." They "seek to regiment the people under bureaucratic and paternalistic governments through a system of planned economy"; they seek to transform individuals into slaves of the state through substituting collectivism for individual initiative, but "the economic security of collectivism is the security of a prison."

Having defined Americanism and its enemies, Dies proceeds to catalogue the qualities which therefore constitute un-Americanism. Thus:

(1) Any organization or individual who believes in or teaches the destruction of our sevenfold freedom is un-American; (2) Any organization or individual who preaches or promotes class, religious, or racial hatred is un-American; (3) Any organization or individual who believes in or advocates the destruction of the God-given rights of man is un-American; (4) Any organization or individual who believes in or advocates disrespect for or the violent overthrow of our constituted authorities is un-American; (5) Any organization or individual who believes in or advocates a system of political, economic, or social regimentation based upon a planned economy is un-American; (6) Any organization or individual who believes in or advocates the destruction of the American system of checks and balances with its three independent co-ordinate branches of government is un-American.[6]

Dies' reasoning here is astonishing. He starts out by reading his own articles of faith into the Declaration of Independence and the Constitution, omitting any references to those sections which run counter to his articles of faith. Then, without documentation, he attributes to communism, and to a lesser degree to nazism and fascism, those social and economic doctrines which he himself heartily dislikes. Finally, contrasting his articles of faith, described as "Americanism," with those things which he dislikes, he labels "un-American" those who disagree with him.

However, the report does say that "Americanism permits American citizens to believe in, advocate, and teach doctrines which are contrary to it. In America, citizens have a right to believe in and advocate communism, fascism, nazism or any other system of government that they approve, subject to certain restrictions and regulations which in nowise destroy the principles of freedom.... While Congress does not have the power to deny to citizens the right to believe in, teach or advocate communism, fascism, and nazism, it does have the right to focus the spotlight of publicity upon their activities and to outlaw any organization which is found to be under the control of, or subject to the dictation of a foreign government." [7] In other words, while Congress has no legal right to interfere with the free speech of minority groups, it is possible to destroy by official censor at public expense minor political parties and other minority groups by representing them as under the domination of foreign nations. If evidence to prove foreign domination were available, all that would be necessary would be a law passed by Congress and signed by the President of the United States to the effect that foreign-dominated political parties and groups were illegal. On the basis of such legislation, the courts of the United States could weigh the evidence and determine questions of guilt and punishment in accordance with the law.

The report includes what is alleged to be a history of communism; and documents are cited which lead the committee to declare that American Communists are "merely carrying out the instructions of the Communist International." [8] The Communists are said to be highly organized, and successful because of their "Trojan Horse tactics" by means of which they insinuate themselves into positions of leadership and control in numerous "front" organizations, which have laudable public objectives but which are used by the Communists to serve the purposes of Moscow. It is this "subtle and indirect influence" of the Communists which is dangerous. Moreover, "the minds of most Communists are diseased and . . . their thinking and process of reasoning are fantastic and often border on insanity. Indeed the very philosophy of communism is fantastic and unreal. There is nothing in the experience or reason of man to justify it; it is the product of mental warping." This analysis is apparently assumed to be self-evident, inasmuch as the committee gives no evidence whatever in its support.[9]

Communists "make a great deal of noise" about civil liberties, said the committee, but they are interested in such liberties only "as a tool with which to destroy all civil liberties." Communists hate publicity; they silence critics by accusing them of red-baiting. They bore from within. The Communist party has gained many "controlling positions" in the C.I.O. The sit-down strike was "largely imported from abroad" and was used "for the purpose of paralyzing industry and producing a revolution."[10]

"Fellow travelers," or those "middle-class intellectuals—professors, writers, clergymen and government officials" who serve the purpose of the Communist party, were said to be particularly active in "front" organizations.[11]

There was "no excuse for the failure of the Labor Department to deport . . . aliens [like] Harry Bridges."[12] The danger of Nazi and Fascist activities in the United States was very briefly discussed in the report.[13] However it is evident from an examination of the report that the committee was much more fearful of communism than of either nazism or fascism.

While admitting that the committee had "only scratched the surface of the un-American and subversive activities of those who are invading America with their alien ideologies," the report declared that there was "ample evidence" to prove that the Communist party was "under direct control of the Third International" at Moscow and was trying to overthrow the American system of government through Trojan Horse tactics and through associating itself "with every crack-pot scheme to undermine our system of free enterprise and private initiative." The Communist party feared publicity and would "stop at nothing to discredit" those who "fearlessly exposed its activities." Communists were "actively boring from within, churches, schools, youth organizations, and every other organization and institution into which they can find entrance." Nazi activities in the United States were linked with Nazi Germany and should be immediately checked if the United States was not to suffer serious consequences.[14]

The report emphasized that the great majority of American citizens of all races, creeds, and classes were loyal and patriotic American citizens and opposed to communism. The committee recommended that its investigation be extended for a two-year period and that it be allowed a minimum of $150,000 to carry on its work "along nonpartisan and courageous lines." No group or individual "engaged in un-American activity should be shielded because of political expediency." The future success of the investigation would depend entirely on "the courage, fearlessness, and the thoroughness with which it is conducted, and upon the assumption and maintenance throughout the investigation of a strictly nonpartisan attitude and policy."[15]

The first report is the *magnum opus* of Dies committee reports. Not only is it longer than all the others put together, but it laid down the philosophical principles and conclusions which subsequent reports have merely fortified and ramified. It throws no light on the problems which it assays to clarify, but it does indicate the prevalence of hysteria in America in 1938.

THE SECOND REPORT

The second report has little of the dogmatism which characterized the first. "Un-American activities" are defined as those "which are directed, controlled or subsidized by foreign governments or agencies and seek to change the policies and form of government of the United States in accordance with the wishes of such foreign governments." Both Stalin and Hitler are declared to be engaged in building up groups and organizations

146

in the United States devoted to serving their purposes. And "the difference between various kinds of totalitarian governments is much more apparent than real." However, each extreme has tried to convince well-meaning people in the United States that the only defense against violence from the other extreme is the use of violence in its own behalf. The report warned against the tendency of rightists to classify as "Communist" all those who were to the left of center, and of leftists to classify as "tools of Hitler" all those who were to the right of center. Moreover, the report insisted that the way to deal with "un-American activities" is "by duly constituted law-enforcing bodies of America operating under our Constitution and with the support of an informed public opinion." [16]

The report then summarized the evidence which led the committee to the conclusion that the Communist party was a branch of the Soviet Union and operated in the United States as "a foreign conspiracy masked as a political party." The present writer is in no position either to affirm or deny this assertion. Neither is the Dies committee. This is a problem in evidence and should be referred to "the duly constituted law-enforcing bodies," which under our Constitution are not the Dies committee but the courts. It is a judicial and not a legislative problem. The committee, having described as "un-American" any effort to undermine our system of "three independent co-ordinate branches of government," might do well to set a good example by confining its own efforts to the legislative area, and not getting over into the judicial area.

"The committee finds," read the report, that certain organizations are "front" organizations, controlled by the Communist party. The committee advised "earnest" Americans either to stay out of such organizations or to make sure that the organizations were not foreign-controlled. The committee also found Communists in control of certain C.I.O. unions and wanted the American labor movement to "free itself." At the other extreme from the Communist party was the German-American Bund. It, too, was found to have "front" organizations and to be engaged in "united front" tactics.

The committee declared that its purpose was to protect "our

147

constitutional democracy by turning the light of pitiless publicity" on organizational activities "seeking to work the will of foreign dictators in the United States or to destroy our constitutional democracy and set up a totalitarian regime of some sort in its place." This is clearly a noble purpose. It should be remembered, however, that even dictators claim to be working for noble purposes. The trouble with the Dies committee is that it has assumed legislative, executive, and judicial powers in dealing with minority groups in the United States. In doing so, it has followed the totalitarian pattern which it so vigorously condemns across the water. The Dies committee is virtually an executive committee of the two old-line parties, which through Congressional immunity exercises totalitarian and dictatorial powers in fighting minority groups.

In concluding its second report the committee acknowledged that not over one million people in the United States had been "seriously affected by these essentially foreign or un-American activities" against which the committee inveighs. Said the committee:

That leaves about 131,000,000 Americans who in spite of the efforts of Nazis, Fascists, Communists, self-styled saviors of America, and in spite of the suffering and distress of 10 years of unemployment and depression, are still as sound and loyal to American institutions and the democratic way of life as they ever were. We owe something to these 131,000,000 people—especially to the poor, the unemployed, the distressed among them. We owe something to our farmers, our workers, our business and professional people who have so nobly stood by America, her institutions and ideals through these difficult years. We owe them a solution of the economic and social problems and unnecessary poverty in the midst of possible plenty.[17]

One other remark made by the committee in the second report is interesting in the light of subsequent events. "The question of the form of government of the German or any other nation," said the committee, echoing the view expressed by Dies in Congress, "is not one that concerns either this committee or the American people." But the committee was concerned with "attempts by any foreign agency to influence American citizens in favor of a foreign form of government and against American democracy." Apparently the committee's interpretation of history is not infallible. Since 1940 the American people have decided that the German form of government *is* a matter of very definite concern to them. However, there has been no evidence from Dies since 1940 that he has repudiated his earlier stand in this matter. Also of interest is the opposition of the committee to any effort by a "foreign" agency to influence public opinion in the United States against American democracy or in favor of any "foreign" form of government. There is a great deal of evidence to indicate that by "foreign" the committee means having ideas which are fundamentally different from those of Martin Dies, and that its concern with "foreign" agencies advocating "foreign" forms of government is actually a concern with any agency, no matter how indigenous to America it may be, advocating anything different than the two-party system in which all members of the committee firmly believe.

THE THIRD REPORT

In the third report,[18] issued January 3, 1941, the committee started out by drawing a very clear distinction between "foreign-controlled" groups attached to some foreign power, and "those who simply hold unorthodox economic views and hence advocate changes in the status quo which they sincerely believe would benefit the majority of the American people." The implication here is clear that "loyal Americans, exercising their own constitutional freedom of thought and speech, [have a right] to advocate changes which the majority may consider radical." However, it is one thing to draw a distinction between groups, and it is another thing to treat them differently. Dies may verbally distinguish between the two groups, but he has treated them much alike. In the second sentence the word "sincerely" and in the third sentence the word "loyal" are what Theodore Roosevelt called weasel words, because they suck the blood out of otherwise meaningful sentences. Who is to decide sincerity and loyalty? Dies thinks he has an infallible insight into people's intentions and purposes, an insight which is denied the courts, the attorney general, the executive department of

149

the government, the people themselves, and even the other members of his own committee. Consequently, the above assurances, in effect, conceal rather than reveal what Dies has been doing to the American Bill of Rights. What Dies says, should never be mistaken for what Dies does; his actions speak much louder than his words.

Dies urges "all genuinely progressive and prolabor groups" to "dissociate themselves with all possible emphasis from those who follow Moscow's leadership and principles," and "all genuinely patriotic and conservative groups" to "dissociate themselves with all possible emphasis from those who follow Axis leadership and principles." Note clearly the effect of the words "genuinely" and "principles" in the above quotations. These words leave the door wide open for Mr. Dies to reach the final decision as to what is genuine and what is not, and which "principles" are foreign and which are not. It is not necessary for Dies to prove that an organization is foreign-controlled; all he has to do is to assert that an organization follows foreign "principles." He reverts to a pressure device which he has used very effectively to destroy organizations whose principles are at variance with his own. This pressure device has been his insistence that those who belong to such an organization are somehow responsible for, contaminated by, and to be blamed for, the aims and purposes of the least popular sector of its membership. Instead of judging an organization by its own stated purposes or by its actions, Dies singles out the most socially offensive individuals in the group and holds the organization responsible for the purposes which he alleges that this minority group seeks to promote.

We are told in the report that "the illusion that Stalin's regime was a progressive one and that his leadership was the world's best protection against the spread of nazism has now been exploded by Stalin himself. His government today stands forth as one of naked opportunism, conquest, and power politics." In the same way, we are told that Hitler's protection of the world against communism has shown itself to be an illusion. Then, we learn from Dies that both "totalitarian" regimes have designs against the United States. But a major part of the report is devoted to showing the designs of Moscow to worm its way into the American labor movement and, ultimately, to take over our country by violent revolution.

The committee somewhat modestly acknowledges its achievements as an educator of American public opinion. It says:

> One accomplishment will, by universal consent, be credited to the committee: We have educated and awakened the American people to a far better understanding of the sinister character and wide extent of subversive activities. We may justly claim to have been the decisive force in shaping the present attitudes of the American people toward the activities of the "fifth columns" which aim at our destruction. Our work has been a type of public education whose importance cannot be exaggerated.

The committee goes on to explain how it destroyed or weakened the organizations which it did not approve. It "kept the spotlight of publicity" turned on them until they finally "gave up in despair" or "went out of existence." Organizations were "killed by exposure." (When the committee had evidence, it turned it over to the "law-enforcement authorities" and these authorities secured convictions. In those cases the committee did not find it necessary to use what it refers to as "relentless exposure.")

The committee reported that it had built up a very complete file on "fifth columnists." Listed in these files were the "names and records of several hundred thousand individuals." These were not the names of individuals who had violated the law; they were the names of individuals who were suspected of having "subversive" ideas. Here were listed the names of individuals who at one time or another had belonged to "fifth column" organizations. A list of this kind is actually a black list in the hands of American reaction, prepared at federal expense to be used by those now in power against any group or individual who seriously challenges the status quo. This is typical pressure-group technique: to destroy the reputations of potential leaders of the opposition, picking them off, one individual at a time. It is utterly undemocratic, but altogether in harmony with totalitarian practice. It is an American equivalent of certain European secret police practices. The power of the system lies in the fact that it permits those in possession of black lists to inflict, on groups and individuals who are guilty of no violation of law whatever, punishments as severe as if the law itself had been violated. If you destroy a man's reputation by false accusation, against which he has no legal recourse, and thus deprive him of means of making a livelihood, you actually impose upon him a penalty just as if he had committed a legal crime. And after a few outstanding individuals have been destroyed in this manner, for thinking differently, or for participating in organizations which think differently, a state of fear can be created in the minds of less resolute individuals which, in time, permeates the rank and file of the American people and effectively discourages and stops all effort to bring about social change by the constitutional means of freedom of speech, freedom of assembly, and freedom of press.

The Dies committee declares that it has found "a way to combat the 'fifth column' without creating a Gestapo. It is a way of exposure which conforms to the letter and the spirit of democracy, and is at the same time more effective than a Gestapo." In both Russia and Germany, say the committee, "half the population spies on the other half. That is the logical end of a system which depends exclusively on methods of counter-espionage." Now, let us interpret this statement. Dies has found a way to fight those whose ideas of social and economic constitution are fundamentally different than those of the reactionary group which he represents. There has been no need to create a "Gestapo"; the creation and functioning of the Dies committee has served the same purpose. The method of making charges against individuals and groups, destroying them without evidence and without trial by jury, assuming that individuals are guilty until they are able to prove themselves innocent, does not conform to either the letter or the spirit of American democracy. But it is no doubt more effective in America than a "Gestapo," because a Gestapo in America. if it were called that, would arouse vigorous and effective opposition from the American people. Public allegations, backed by the prestige of a "Congressional investigating committee," and widely publicized by certain newspapers in such a way as to make allegations look like "findings," can, even when the individual has not been proved guilty, do him as much damage and injury as if he had fallen into the hands of a Gestapo. The Dies committee, and especially Dies himself, have been so free with ruinous unsupported charges against organizations and individuals that there has been no need for public spying.

In its third report the committee recommended legislation to crack down on aliens, totalitarian propaganda from abroad, passport violations, employment by the federal government of noncitizens, and political organizations in the United States which are "shown to be under the control of a foreign government." The committee wanted these latter organizations to be outlawed. The writer of this book thinks that that would be an excellent idea, but he would want the decision as to which organizations were foreign-controlled to be rendered by the courts, and not by the Dies committee.

Another legislative recommendation of the committee was:

Withhold all Federal financial support from any educational institution which permits members of its faculty to advocate communism, fascism, or nazi-ism as a substitute for our form of government to the student body of these educational institutions. (This particular recommendation is not concurred in by Mr. Voorhis, not because of disagreement with the principle involved but on the ground that the administration of such an act is impossible without risking grave injustice being done to people seeking merely to explain the principles involved in totalitarian philosophy.) [Parentheses in report. W. G.]

This recommendation is interesting because it seems to indicate a lack of faith in the ability of our form of government to withstand an intellectual attack by proponents of rival theories. The writer is of the opinion, on the contrary, that the American form of government has so much to recommend it that it can easily hold its own in intellectual discourse against any of the rival doctrines and practices in the world today. In times of peace, most universities proceed on the assumption that a major function of institutions of higher learning is to further the quest for truth, and not to propagandize for any one set of principles or beliefs, no matter how widely these are accepted in a particular time and place. Belief in our democratic form of government is very nearly all-pervasive in America, but it is generally recognized that a clash of doctrine is highly desirable from an educational standpoint.

Independent judgment comes to a student through encouraging him to select from among the various facts and interpretations which he observes to be in basic conflict. Facts and interpretations are best presented by those who believe in them. The bias of one teacher tends to be counterbalanced by the biases of other teachers with opposing viewpoints. Educators have generally had sufficient confidence in human intelligence to believe that a student, exposed to conflicting points of view expressed without equivocation by those who have sincerely accepted them, would be better educated than if exposed to only one point of view.

The American scholar has so much confidence in the American form of government that he has no fear of rival doctrines, no matter how radical they may be. The case for our American form of government is so strong that it need not fear any other theory or form of government. Introducing students to rival doctrines has the advantage of showing American students, by the test of intellectual battle, just how strong our form of government really is. Their understanding and appreciation of democracy increases as they come better to understand its meaning and advantages.

Dies considers himself competent to determine the one true faith; and he would have scholars teach it to students as he has proclaimed it. But scholars believe in academic freedom, which includes the right of a teacher to declare his own findings, whatever they may be. Academic freedom ends when teachers are told that they must teach "accepted maxims," and must avoid certain forbidden subjects for fear that they will be accused of advocacy and will be subjected to persecution. Scholarship would not be scholarship if inquiry were compelled to end where Dies' ignorance begins.

The third report urged a two-year extension of the committee, and pointed to things which it had been able to accomplish because its "power" was so much greater than that of other agencies of government. It frankly admitted that there are "many phases of un-American activities that cannot be reached by legislation or administrative action." In other words, the committee admitted, in effect, that it was essentially nihilistic insofar as American law and the American system of government are concerned. It is believed that "fearless exposure, coupled with effective enforcement of the laws that are on the statute books, is the democratic answer to the 'fifth colmn.'" The word "fearless" in the above quotation should not be permitted to hide the tacit admission by the committee that the kind of persecution which it exercised under the name of "exposure" was not authorized by any law on the statute books. In other words, the Dies committee is an extralegal agency created and sustained by Republicans and anti-New Deal Democrats in the House of Representatives, and is invested with sufficient power to rise above the laws on the statute books and, in so doing, to rise above the Constitution.

THE SPECIAL MAJORITY REPORT

Anyone who reads the first three reports of the Dies committee must be impressed with the moderation of the second and third as compared to the first report. In the second and third reports Voorhis seems to have cramped Dies' style. There is a reasonable quality about Voorhis that has no place in a Dies report. Dies sees things in terms of black and white, whereas Voorhis insists that there are intermediate shades. You either agree with Dies and are a good American, or you are a Red Russian Communist; but Voorhis permits people to disagree with him, without doubting either their sincerity, their patriotism, or their intelligence. A special report to Congress was issued on June 25, 1942, six months after Pearl Harbor. It was divided into two parts, an unsigned majority report,[19] and a minority report [20] which was signed by Jerry Voorhis.

This special report was on "Subversive Activities Aimed at Destroying Our Representative Form of Government." The majority declared that "the essence of totalitarianism is the destruction of the parliamentary or legislative branch of govern-

ment" and went on to "take cognizance of a wide-spread movement to discredit the legislative branch of our Government."

Dies found that there was an effort to purge certain members
of Congress. "Many of the efforts to purge individual Members
of Congress are based upon an assumption which reflects discredit upon the entire legislative branch of Government." This
assumption was that "the sole remaining function of Congress
is to ratify by unanimous vote whatever wish is born anywhere
at any time in the whole vast structure of the executive branch
of Government down to the last whim of any and every administrative official." Dies is back at his old tricks, assuming that
an effort to purge Dies and others like him is an attack on "the
entire legislative branch of the Government," and also using
the fallacy of extension, pretending that those who think that
Congress should co-operate with the President to win the war
seek to reduce Congress to a state of subservience, which they
do not. Dies' statement of what his opponents intend to do to
Congress is typical of Dies' tendency to see things in terms of
black or white. If you do not agree with Dies that his committee
should carry on against Russia as it did before the war, but
think that this is a good time to promote better relations between America and Russia, it does not follow, as Dies implies,
that you favor a Congress which yields "to the last whim of
any and every administrative official." There is a lot of ground
between these two extremes. Dies would exclude the middle
ground, with all of the angels in his camp and only devils in
the other.

Dies says that it is one thing to criticize an individual member
of Congress and a very different matter to "scoff" at Congress as
an institution. The Union for Democratic Action, in collaboration with the *New Republic,* had published a document entitled
"A Congress to Win the War" in which it was shown how the
members of Congress had voted on foreign and domestic policy.
This booklet urged the re-election of certain congressmen and
the defeat of others, to facilitate the winning of the war. According to Dies, "this vituperative and scurrilous document"
showed its "viciousness" by including "a cowardly lie" about
some congressmen (including Martin Dies). Its line of argu-

ment showed that the Union for Democratic Action belonged to "that relatively small group of radicals who are trying to use the war emergency to advance their own revolutionary programs within the United States." Instead of attempting to answer the argument contained in the thirty-two-page document, Dies and associates reverted to *argumentum ad hominem* and attacked the men who advanced it.

Incorporated in the majority report is a chart listing fifty leaders of the Union of Democratic Action and indicating, after the names of each of these fifty leaders, to which of twenty-five organizations described by the Dies committee as "agencies and fronts of the Communist Party" each of these fifty leaders belonged. This chart is reproduced on pages 158-161. It made "clear" to Martin Dies that "the Union for Democratic Action is composed chiefly of individuals who have been a significant part of the interlocking directorate of the Communist movement in the United States." (As we shall see later, the chart's meaning was not equally "clear" to Jerry Voorhis.) Individual members of the Union for Democratic Action were singled out for special defamation. Each of the twenty-five organizations was classified (for example, the American League for Peace and Democracy was "nothing more or less than a bold advocate of treason"), and the relationship of each of the fifty leaders to each of these twenty-five organizations was indicated. (Actually the majority report was nothing but a campaign document, issued at government expense, in answer to the *New Republic*'s supplement.)

THE SPECIAL MINORITY REPORT

We come now to Jerry Voorhis' minority report, which was dated approximately two weeks later than the majority report. Voorhis declared that the majority report was considered at only one committee meeting, when only four members of the committee were present. Voorhis had not heard of the report before this meeting and was struck by the "vigorous attempt ... to secure immediate adoption of the report" before he had even had a chance to read it. His failure to sign the majority report about which he had heard nothing before the meeting,

	American Committee for Democracy and Intellectual Freedom	American Committee for Protection of Foreign Born	American League for Peace and Democracy	American Student Union	American Youth Congress	Champion	Communist Party	Communist Publications	Conference on Pan-American Democracy	Descendants of the American Revolution
1. Amlie, Thomas R., director, Washington Bureau, U. D. A.		X			X	X				
2. Axtelle, George, sponsor, U. D. A.										
3. Bates, Ralph, sponsor, U. D. A.								X		
4. Bowman, Leroy, sponsor, U. D. A.			X		X					
5. Bradley, Dwight, research council, U. D. A.		X								
6. Brennan, Eleaor, sponsor, U. D. A.			X							X
7. Cochran, William F., board of directors, U. D. A.			X							
8. Corey, Lewis, research director, U. D. A.							X			
9. Counts, George S., board of directors, U. D. A.	X	X	X	X					X	
10. Crawford, Kenneth, executive committee, U. D. A.										X
11. Crosswaith, Frank, vice-chairman, U. D. A.										
12. David, Henry, sponsor, U. D. A.			X					X		
13. Dennen, Leon, sponsor, U. D. A.							X			
14. Douglas, Melvyn, board of directors, U. D. A.			X							
15. Edelman, John W., board of directors, U. D. A.										
16. Fischer, Louis, board of directors, U. D. A.			X							
17. Forsyth, Margaret, sponsor, U. D. A.			X						X	
18. Frank, Waldo, sponsor, U. D. A.		X		X			X	X		
19. Gannet, Lewis, sponsor, U. D. A.								X		
20. Graham, Frank P., sponsor, U. D. A.	X	X	X							
21. Granger, Lester B., board of directors, U. D. A.			X							
22. Harrison, Charles Yale, sponsor, U. D. A.							X			
23. Hardman, J. B. S., sponsor, U. D. A.			X		X	X	X			
24. Henson, Francis, board of directors, U. D. A.; research council, U. D. A.		X								
25. Herberg, Will, sponsor, U. D. A.							X			

Friends of the Soviet Union	International Labor Defense	International Workers Order	League of American Writers	National Committee for Defense of Political Prisoners	National Committee for Peoples Rights	National Federation for Constitutional Liberties	National Negro Congress	New Masses	Open Letter to American Liberals	Open Letter for Closer Cooperation with U. S. S. R.	Soviet Russia Today	Spanish Aid Organizations of the Communist Party	Washington Committee for Democratic Action	Workers Alliance
X												X		
	X					X						X		
			X					X				X		
												X		
						X						X		
		X						X				X		
						X								
X											X			
				X	X							X		
						X							X	
							X							
X								X			X			
												X		
		X					X					X		
	X								X		X	X		
X														
X	X		X	X	X	X		X		X	X	X		
X												X		
	X											X		
		X					X							
								X						
								X						

	American Committee for Democracy and Intellectual Freedom	American Committee for Protection of Foreign Born	American League for Peace and Democracy	American Student Union	American Youth Congress	Champion	Communist Party	Communist Publications	Conference on Pan-American Democracy	Descendants of the American Revolution
26. Hicks, Granville, sponsor, U. D. A.		X	X			X	X	X		
27. Himwich, Harold E., sponsor, U. D. A.										
28. Isaacs, Stanley, board of directors, U. D. A.	X	X							X	
29. Jackson, Gardner, board of directors, U. D. A.			X		X				X	
30. Kenyon, Dorothy, sponsor, U. D. A.	X	X			X				X	X
31. Kingdon, Frank, president, U. D. A.	X									
32. Kirchwey, Freda, board of directors, U. D. A.	X		X	X						X
33. Lane, Robert E., sponsor, U. D. A.				X						
34. Lewis, Alfred Baker, board of directors, U. D. A.										
35. Lore, Ludwig, sponsor, U. D. A.		X	X				X	X		
36. Neilson, William A., board of directors, U. D. A.	X	X								
37. Niebuhr, Reinhold, chairman, U. D. A.		X	X	X						
38. Randolph, A Philip, board of directors, U D. A.			X		X				X	X
39. Redefer, Frederick L., sponsor, U. D. A.	X				X					
40. Reissig, Herman F., sponsor, U. D. A.		X	X	X				X		
41. Rome, Harold, sponsor, U. D. A.										
42. Schnapper, M. B., sponsor, U. D. A.			X				X	X		
43. Sibley, Norman, sponsor, U. D. A.	X		X							
44. Spivack, Robert, sponsor, U. D. A.			X	X		X				
45. Stewart, Maxwell, sponsor, U. D. A.	X	X	X		X				X	
46. Totten, Ashley P., sponsor, U. D. A.			X							
47. Weinstein, Jacob, sponsor, U. D. A.		X	X							
48. Welsh, Edward, sponsor, U. D. A.								X		
49. Wiggins, Lee Manning, sponsor, U. D. A.				X						
50. Williams, Howard Y., organizer, U. D. A.			X							

Friends of the Soviet Union	International Labor Defense	International Workers Order	League of American Writers	National Committee for Defense of Political Prisoners	National Committee for Peoples Rights	National Federation for Constitutional Liberties	National Negro Congress	New Masses	Open Letter to American Liberals	Open Letter for Closer Cooperation with U. S. S. R.	Soviet Russia Today	Spanish Aid Organizations of the Communist Party	Washington Committee for Democratic Action	Workers Alliance
X	X		X	X	X			X	X	X	X			
	X													
					X						X	X		
	X					X							X	X
	X											X		
				X				X				X		
							X							
					X							X		
												X		
	X							X				X		
X	X	X	X					X	X			X		
	X		X			X			X		X	X		
								X						
						X								
X				X	X			X	X	X	X	X		

161

and which he had had no opportunity to read, was "interpreted in the press as an attempt to protect Communists." No hearings were held by the committee concerning the matters considered in the report. It was issued without any further consideration, subsequent to the meeting which Voorhis attended. Voorhis had no opportunity to vote for or against the majority report or to suggest any changes in it. "The majority report was just issued all of a sudden without any action at all in which the minority had any opportunity to participate."

While Voorhis held no brief for the Union for Democratic Action and disagreed with its analysis of Congress, he did not consider it desirable for the committee to "descend to the undignified position of engaging in a name-calling contest with an organization whose ideas the committee just doesn't like." It is evident that Voorhis did not consider it the "proper business of the Committee on Un-American Activities" to challenge the right of the Union for Democratic Action to engage in criticism of congressmen, or to take part in political action, and that he did not consider the Union for Democratic Action "primarily responsible for the attack on Congress as an institution." Voorhis was himself concerned over the attacks on Congress and over the concentration of power in the executive agencies, but considered the latter an inevitable product of the war. He recognized that under our system of representative government congressmen must expect to be subjected to criticism and attack. Congressmen thus attacked should not confuse an effort to defeat them in an election with an attack on Congress as an institution.

Voorhis was convinced that the attacks on Congress could be remedied if Congress improved its own conduct. Voorhis explained his position, as follows:

A courageous, effective, and constructive job of doing all things to push forward the war effort, of stopping waste in war expenditures, of protecting small business and combating monopoly controls so far as possible, of equalizing the burdens of war, of sincerely abandoning the advocacy of special interests, of keeping the people so far as possible informed as to the real facts connected with shortages, rationing, price control, contracts and the like and of

162

preparing now to meet effectively the after-war domestic economic problems—these are the things Congress could and should do to combat these attacks.

It is ineffectual and undignified for Congress or any committee of Congress to attempt to answer attacks by mere assertion that the attackers are not good Americans. That is the main thing the majority report does.

There was no substantiation of the charge that any member of the Union for Democratic Action was now a Communist. The majority report went ahead on the assumption that once a person was a Communist he was always a Communist, although the Communist party had actually attacked the Union for Democratic Action. The "test," from Voorhis' standpoint, was "not one of past opinions but of absolute and unquestioned loyalty to our country for her own sake as she fights this war." Voorhis saw no evidence that these people did not possess such loyalty or that their loyalty was a consequence of the fact that the Soviet Union was an ally of America in the war.

"It is nothing short of inexcusable in a report which attempts to imply Communist charges against this organization without actually being able to make such charges, to include in the chart incorporated in the majority report the names of many people whose sound Americanism no sane or fair person would question." In the future many people would say of these Americans that the Dies committee had found them to be Communists. The majority report had taken no precaution whatever to prevent any such accusation from being made against these people.

Then Voorhis included in his own report these highly significant lines, setting forth his own position:

The Dies committee is supposed to investigate subversive activities—which to the minority at least means activities seeking the overthrow by force of our Government and especially those activities which are directed from abroad. Once, however, the committee undertakes to accuse people of un-American activities because they criticize certain features of our economy or say unkind things about finance capitalism, or because they come out for a greater degree of cooperation in our economic life, it is in danger of becoming an

163

agency which arrogates to itself the right to censor people's ideas. That in itself is un-American.

For any man has a right in America to believe in, advocate, and work for economic change and reform so long only as he never seeks to gain his ends except by the Constitutional method of attempting to persuade a majority of the people by American political methods that he is right. The majority report is shot through with statements accusing people of being un-American not because they are Nazis, Fascists, or Communists, but because their political or economic beliefs or opinions are not orthodox as judged by the committee majority.

Voorhis said that Westbrook Pegler and the late Raymond Clapper, neither of whom could be charged with Communism, had delivered through their columns much more devastating attacks against Congress as a whole than anything in the Union for Democratic Action's attack on specific congressmen. The latter's attack was not, in fact, an attack on Congress as a body but an attack on individual congressmen. If the majority of the committee was going to prepare a report on attacks on Congress it should have included all such attacks, instead of singling out one group for special attention and neglecting attacks which emanated from conservatives. But not even a report of that kind would do any good. Voorhis declared that Congress could "completely justify itself and meet every attack simply by going ahead with its work in a courageous, effective, and high-minded way." And that was what Voorhis wanted Congress to do. He said that the record did not support the charge that the Union for Democratic Action was either communistic or Communist-dominated; to say that it was "un-American" anyhow "because some of its members [were] radicals . . . put the Committee on Un-American Activities in the position of judging people not on the basis of their fundamental loyalty to the United States and its constitutional form of government but on the basis of the particular economic beliefs which they may hold and which are not in accord with those of the committee."

"This Nation is at war," said Voorhis, and at such a time, "one thing above all else is important—that is loyalty to America and her cause." "It makes comparatively little difference in these critical hours what happened in 1936. The fact regarding an organization or a person that is all important is: Does that organization or that person, entirely regardless of its opinion of our Committee on Un-American Activities or its members, support with all its strength the war in which the United States is now engaged?"

Voorhis continued:

The position of the minority [of the Dies committee, namely, of Jerry Voorhis] is ... that when the majority accuses people of being un-American because their political or economic views are at variance with those of the majority it is committing an error that is not only contrary to every tradition of democratic government but is of a sort that no committee of this character can commit and continue to do effective work against subversive elements. To include the long list of people in the chart presented by the committee and put into it the names of people who by no stretch of anyone's imagination can be considered Communists is to strike a blow at liberty of the most serious kind.

The minority believes that a man has a right to be either an extreme reactionary or a radical in his economic views and still be regarded as a good American so long as his whole-hearted loyalty is to the United States and its constitutional form of government. Much as the minority disagrees with the analysis of Congress put out by the Union for Democratic Action it believes that either this organization or Raymond Clapper or Westbrook Pegler, or Time, or Life, or the Washington Times-Herald has a basic American right to criticize people in official positions in the American Government, including the minority as well as the majority of this committee, without being accused of being tools of communism, nazi-ism, or fascism.

All the minority is contending for is the right of loyal American citizens to disagree politically with a majority of the Dies committee without being branded subversive and un-American.

THE FOURTH REPORT

The fourth annual report [21] of the Dies committee was issued on January 2, 1943, two years after the third annual report, more than a year after Pearl Harbor, and six months after the special report attacking the Union for Democratic Action. Jerry Voorhis had signed the first three reports; he issued his minority report as Part 2 of the special report. In the case of the fourth annual report he prepared a minority statement which followed that of the majority but was incorporated in the same pamphlet. The fourth report was entitled "Special Report on Subversive Activities Aimed at Destroying Our Representative Form of Government." After a brief initial statement indicating that the committee was aware of the fact that there was a war going on "against the existence and spread of totalitarianism," the majority defined its own function as discovering and exposing "enemy groups which fight with nonphysical weapons as a fifth column on our home front." The report announced the committee's decision, reached many months before, not to hold public hearings dealing with Axis sabotage in this country during the war because of the danger of premature disclosure.

After explaining that when the committee started its work in 1938 its efforts had not received the attention they "deserved" in "certain official quarters," the majority report went on to acknowledge its own efforts. While in 1938 the committee's records required only 2 filing cabinets they now required 135 filing cabinets. The committee had built up an index indicating "subversive" records of organizations and individuals on more than 1,000,000 cards. This material had been gathered largely in consequence of the committee's possession of the right to use Congressional subpena, a power denied other governmental agencies. Because of the exhaustive materials in its files the committee had been able, it said, to render invaluable assistance to other government agencies. During the preceding fourteen months it had received 1,600 calls from other agencies. The committee had given the President a list of 17,000 individuals connected with Nazi activities in the United States. Furthermore, the committee's 11,725 pages of testimony and 3,000 pages of reports on "subversive" activities had been of assistance in enlightening the American people as well as in providing federal agencies with information "of immeasurable value." The committee had called to the attention of the President the names of many high-ranking government officials who were connected with "Communist-front" organizations. Nevertheless, many of these officials were still employed in the government. When Congress provided the funds necessary to investigate these federal employees, the Attorney General had "utterly failed to carry out the mandate of Congress," according to Chairman Dies.

The majority declared that the American Peace Mobilization, successor of the American League for Peace and Democracy, and later succeeded by the American People's Mobilization, was "completely under the control of the Communist Party." The committee had investigated sabotage strikes in defense industries and found them not only Communist-led and -inspired but "in every instance, the union involved in these interruptions of production was affiliated with the Congress of Industrial Organizations." The committee had investigated the Japanese living on the Pacific Coast, and "a direct result of the committee's report on Japanese subversive activities in this country was the removal of the Japanese population from vital west-coast areas." In January, 1942, in executive session, the Dies committee had investigated "alleged anti-Semitic activities," but the testimony was "of such extreme and fanatical tenor" that it was the committee's opinion that "no good purpose could have been served by taking it to the public." The Union for Democratic Action was referred to as "one of a considerable number of agencies" in the country which sought to discredit the legislative branch of the government; it was claimed that since the publication of its "special report the committee had gained further evidence concerning this organization which, if it were published, would demonstrate that the organization was 'an un-American sham.'" It was charged that the National Federation for Constitutional Liberties was controlled by the same group as the American Peace Mobilization. Credit was claimed for much assistance rendered to other departments in securing the conviction of persons who had been connected with the Axis front movement in the United States.

Voorhis wrote that whereas previously he had signed the annual report of the committee, it was necessary in this instance to dissent from the majority report. First, because the report, after being prepared without committee members being given a chance to discuss or amend it, was submitted to committee members "on a 'take it or leave it' basis." Second, he thought the report should have been devoted primarily to helping the American people "identify, avoid, and combat the propaganda and activities of agents and friends of enemy nations of the United States in the current war." A report showing activities in the United States favorable to the Axis had been prepared, but it had not been approved by the committee and it seemed highly problematical, said Voorhis, whether it ever would be approved. This was the major reason for Voorhis' dissent. Third, the majority report contained materials on alleged communistic affiliation which represented action by the chairman, not by the committee.

Voorhis agreed that neither communists nor fascists should be employed by the government. But his fourth objection to the majority report turned on the question of whether the individuals against whom charges of subversion had been made were really "subversive" or were "simply people whose views don't agree with the majority." It did America no good to use the words "Fascist" and "Communist" indiscriminately as epithets applied to political opponents; certainly such words should not be applied to "persons whose patriotic devotion to America and her basic institutions cannot be questioned." The fact that a person's name was on the mailing list of one of the organizations which Dies called "subversive" seemed to Voorhis "to constitute no substantial evidence" of "subversive" activity. In many instances the person's name was included without any action on his part or even without his knowledge. Therefore Voorhis was not surprised that the Department of Justice had discovered no substantial evidence of subversion on the part of many individuals included on Dies' lists. Voorhis explained:

To attempt to indicate that everyone whose name was carried on the list of the Washington Committee for Democratic Action, the Washington Cooperative Bookshop, or the Washington Committee to Aid China, is thereby to be regarded as per se subversive is, in my opinion, as false an implication as it would be to attempt to say that every member of the America First Committee was sympa-

168

thetic with fascism or the Nazi cause. The latter statement no thoughtful American would make, even though we know that attempts were made in certain sections of the country to use the America First Committee as a vehicle for pro-Axis propaganda and activities.

The above quotation provides a very interesting analogy. The America First Committee included a number of distinguished Americans, and no doubt also included a considerable number of Bundists. The American League Against War and Fascism included a number of distinguished Americans, and no doubt also included a considerable number of Communists. Why did Dies, long after Russia had become an ally of ours in the war against the Axis, persist in the persecution of those suspected of belonging to left of center groups without attempting to "expose" those who, by the same kind of reasoning, could be accused of belonging to fascist-front organizations?

The fifth reason for Voorhis' dissent was his opinion that while the committee's investigation of the Japanese on the Pacific Coast had been one of the factors bringing about Japanese relocation, such relocation had not been "a direct result of the committee's report" as the majority claimed.

Sixth, he had wanted the report to acknowledge, in discussing the sabotage strike of 1941, "the unquestioned loyalty and record of outstanding production of the great rank and file of American workers." Voorhis made it very clear that he did not agree with the charge that the Dies committee had not investigated Nazi and fascist groups in the United States. In fact, the committee had done "a very good job" in this respect. But the majority report had not placed sufficient emphasis on the importance of exposing Axis activities and propaganda. Voorhis felt that the "main excuse for the committee's existence" was to facilitate the winning of the war against the Axis, that in its annual report the committee had "neglected" an exceptional "opportunity to strike a blow in that direction."

169

PART III
THREAT TO AMERICA

9 DIES UNDER FIRE

ALL HAS NOT BEEN plain sailing for Dies. From the beginning his committee has been severely criticized, and the volume of protests, particularly as reflected in the successive debates on the question of renewal, has increased.

When he submitted the first report on January 3, 1939, Dies was referred to by the *Washington Post* as the outstanding winner of the "Americanism award for 1938" in consequence of his "outstanding patriotic service." [1] He submitted a resolution to authorize the continuance of the committee, and another providing $150,000 for its expenses.[2] (In its initial request for funds the Dies committee had asked for $100,000 but got only $25,-000.) [3]

On February 3, 1939, the Rules Committee submitted Dies' resolution with an amendment that his committee report not later than January 3, 1940, instead of January 3, 1941, as provided in his original resolution.[4] The resolution was not subject to further amendment except upon the motion of the Rules Committee, of which Martin Dies was a member. It is worthy of note that the time allowed for debate was divided equally between the leaders of the majority and minority sides of the House, and was not divided equally between those who were for and against the resolution, and that only one hour was allowed for this discussion.

In the discussion it was brought out that when the Rules Committee had considered continuing the Dies committee, not "more than one or two" witnesses had voiced opposition. Representative Cox was sure that if the committee were continued, it would "avoid repetition of any mistakes and . . . escape the criticism . . . heretofore . . . directed against it." Representative Taylor of Tennessee considered "the type and character of the opposition to the Dies committee . . . perhaps the strongest argument and recommendation for its continuation." He said that "the bulk of the opposition" came from "well-known and well-recognized un-American activities," and that "the only difference between ultra-liberalism and communism was one of degree." He had observed that "it is always the 'hit dog that howls,'" and so would not "crucify" a committee which had shown such "courage and determination in its efforts to expose radicalism in our midst." Congresswoman Norton, while favoring the investigation, considered $100,000 "a large sum of money to be spent on an investigation unless the investigation is conducted according to the rules of evidence as they would be in any court of justice."

Representative Keller said there was consensus among both elected and defeated congressional candidates in 1938 that the Dies committee had "contributed largely to the result" of the election. He asserted that Dies' report to Congress was "not an honest report" because it was not based on the hearings before the committee. Complaining that the investigation had been "a one man investigation and carried on apparently with one principal objective—that of getting publicity for the chairman"—Keller said Dies had used his position as chairman "to attack and injure those Departments of Government with which his own ideas were not in sympathy," and to attack organized labor. Dies' labor record was "more spotted than the leopard's skin." He called attention to the fact that Shepard Knowles, erstwhile secretary of the Associated Farmers, had provided much testimony before the Dies committee, and that Knowles had claimed he represented the American Legion, a statement which the Legion subsequently denied, without any recognition of this disclaimer getting into the record.

Keller included in the *Congressional Record* telegrams exchanged between committee members during the election campaign of 1938. In the first of these telegrams, dated October 26, 1938, Healey and Dempsey expressed to Chairman Dies their concern over charges that the committee was being "improperly

174

used for election purposes." They considered it unfair to continue hearings when they could not be present "to participate in the determination of proper procedure and take responsibility for its proceedings." Dies replied that a majority of the committee had authorized him to continue the hearings in spite of the campaign. He added that there were certain questions "much bigger than mere partisanship" and that "preserving the fundamental principles of Americanism transcends in importance political expediency"; that it would be "cowardly" to postpone the hearings until after the election, since "to do so would imply that the Democratic Party is unwilling for the people to have the facts when they go to the polls." Dempsey replied that he considered "nothing more cowardly than to permit wild and irrational statements which have no basis in fact and have only for their end the assassination of characters of men who are outstanding . . . American citizens of the highest type."

Keller said the Dies committee would be continued because the Republican party which had profited so much from the activities of the committee had pledged itself to vote for its continuance—in a sense the money so voted was "a Republican campaign fund." In his opinion the United States did not need "the suspicion, fear, resentment, distrust, dissension, jealousy, prejudice, and disorganization of American public opinion which the Dies procedure has stirred up." Keller added:

What we do need . . . is the broadest possible tolerance along all lines. Tolerance of religion; tolerance of race; tolerance of national origin; tolerance of ideals; tolerance of opinions; and, most of all, at the present time we need an all-embracing tolerance of economic proposals. . . . Only through the greatest consideration for one another—the broadest tolerance for the expression of ideas—can we hope to receive and consider the best ideas looking to the solution of this the greatest of all problems—that of assuring through government an opportunity for a job for every man and woman who wants to work.

Representative Fish was of the opinion that the "Communists" and "radicals" were "up to their old tricks" of "trying to smear" the investigation by "ridicule, distortion, and falsehood." Said

Fish, "I love the Dies committee for the enemies it has made."

Representative Hook objected to the failure of the committee to confine itself to an investigation of un-American activities, and declared that in Michigan the committee had made "political capital for the Republicans out of a prejudiced hearing of prejudiced witnesses" while neglecting to investigate activities in the state which were actually un-American, such as the connections of the Black Legion with corporate wealth. Hook presented a resolution passed by the convention of the Upper Peninsula Association of American Legion Posts condemning "the practice of the Dies committee in permitting [the] publicizing as facts [of] matters which were only hearsay and caused unjust reflections on good Americans." He insisted the American people wanted "action and legislation, not dreamy investigations" which created "unrest and bewilderment" throughout the nation. He asked:

Is this Congress going definitely to act to curb un-American activities by legislation, or is it going to allow this investigation to carry on to such a point that any political philosophy that does not meet with the personal approval of the committee will be assassinated as un-American?

Marcantonio of New York objected to the "undemocratic," "unjust," and "un-American" way in which the resolution was being "railroaded through." Denied time to speak against the resolution for more than a half minute, he took advantage of the opportunity to extend his remarks in the *Congressional Record*. He had no objection, he said, to "an investigation of subversive and un-American activities" but thought any such investigation "should be carried on by a committee of fact-finding, fair-minded, and impartial Members of the House." He considered the existing Dies committee unqualified to carry on that kind of investigation, because it had been used by "native Nazi representatives" and other "un-American" and subversive groups as a sounding board to smear and besmirch the reputations of progressive Democrats as well. The committee had heard witnesses who were themselves "un-American" and "did one of the foulest political jobs in the history of this country." Marcantonio pointed out that Edward F. Sullivan, the committee's chief investigator, had sponsored witnesses with criminal records, and had himself been associated with activities against Catholics and Jews in co-operation with men like James True and Gerald Winrod. Marcantonio said Sullivan had made "one of the filthiest racial hatred speeches on record." When these facts about Sullivan were called to the committee's attention, he was "dropped, due to lack of funds"; but no condemnation of him found its way into the report of the committee. The "Sullivan incident" was not an isolated one. Another representative of the "native Nazi" group was Walter S. Steele, editor of the *National Republic* magazine, and "A No. 1 witness of the Dies Committee." Declaring Dies and the committee had failed to investigate "native Nazi, anti-Semitic, and anti-Catholic organizations," Marcantonio said the committee had not investigated the Silver Shirts, Pelley, Mrs. Dilling, the Ku Klux Klan, Gerald B. Winrod, and other spokesmen of the "native Nazi" of America, in spite of their attacks on the President, the Catholic Church, the Jews, "and against everything that is decent."

Representative Dingell stated that the Dies committee had been in serious error in giving the country "the impression that Frank Murphy is a Communist, that our Detroit schools are shot through with communism, and that our school teachers are injecting the virus of un-Americanism into the tender beings of our school children." Dingell said "nothing could be further from the truth" but "nothing in the world could be more helpful to communism than to link it with the respected names of some of our best citizens, holding office or in private life." While he favored continuing the investigation, Dingell wanted a new committee appointed to carry the investigation forward.

Representative Voorhis, who was not yet a member of the Dies committee, expressed fear of "a concerted attempt to identify every clean, decent American progressive movement in defense of the rights of the common people of this country with communism," and said in America "we have got to have room for honest divergences of opinion on the problems we face without trying to link our opponents with some un-American movement. Unless we keep alive the spirit of tolerance and fair play we are in danger of losing our liberties. It will loose a vindictive spirit of hate and prejudice and it will be hard to control." His vote against the resolution was a protest against the committee's methods, he explained, not against setting up another committee to carry on the investigation. He opposed "what has happened to the reputations of a great many sincere, patriotic people in this country," and giving publicity to "unsubstantiated charges" and condemning people "before they have fair opportunity for defense."

Representative Coffee of Washington objected to having "reputable citizens ... indicted before a congressional agency in their absence by innuendo, gossip, guesses, hearsay, and wishful thinking." He cited a statement by Arthur Garfield Hays to the effect that men like Congressman Dies think "the only permissible views are those which they approve.... These men start with a will to believe—a will to believe those witnesses who, because of ignorance, prejudice, malice, personal aggrandisements, desire for publicity ... come before a committee and are permitted to express opinions which, since they are the opinions of the committee, are accepted by the committee as facts." Coffee indicated that the Dies committee had not given the American Civil Liberties Union an opportunity to be heard in its own defense although numerous charges had been made against it. "It seems perfectly obvious from the record," said Coffee, "that any committee under Congressman Dies is wholly incapable of giving the American public a fair inquiry or honest conclusions." He wondered if the effort to extend the life of the committee was not based on a desire to influence the outcome of the 1940 election. What other functions, he asked, could this committee perform which could not be handled by the Department of Justice, a joint committee of the House of Representatives, "which would rise above the suspicion of reactionary partisan ends," or the enactment of appropriate legislation? Coffee cited a report of 150 "lawyers of national repute" which revealed numerous instances of bias on the part of the Dies committee. Coffee pointed out that "approximately 90 per cent of the hearings reveal the chairman's cross-questioning and exclusive handling of the hearings." He continued:

The question is, Has the committee sought and obtained facts rather than opinions and conclusions? Has it ever defined the amazing word "un-American"? Has it not, rather, pictured any citizen of liberal or progressive leanings as being tinctured by the virus of communism? Could any lawyer of experience enthuse over the admission of inadmissible evidence? Are we justified by the past conduct of the committee in continuing its operation?

Is a Congress which reduced the appropriation to provide work for the unemployed in the amount of $150,000,000 in a position logically to authorize the expenditure of a large sum of money to ascertain whether discontent exists in the United States?

Coffee expressed wonder that fascists and communists in America numbered no more than they did, since so many Americans were "ill-housed and under-nourished and lacked a job." He pointed out that the Dies committee had not heard both sides and had allowed "witnesses of dubious antecedents to give publicity to slanderous utterances before a tribunal which the law has surrounded with legal immunity. If these witnessses had made the same statement elsewhere, they could have been held to strict account by the reputable citizens impugned." He attributed to the committee considerable responsibility for the defeat of Governor Benson of Minnesota and Governor Murphy of Michigan. Calling attention to the fact that opponents of continuing the Dies committee had been allowed only thirteen minutes to present their side of the case, Coffee declared the resolution was "being railroaded through . . . without careful consideration," and predicted it would receive unanimous Republican support because it was so clearly designed "to wreck the New Deal."

Representative Coffee quoted President Roosevelt's reference to the Dies Committee, as follows:

Most fair-minded Americans hope that the committee will abandon the practice of merely providing a forum to those who for political purposes or otherwise seek headlines which they could not otherwise obtain. Mere opinion evidence has been barred in court since the American system of legislative and judicial procedure was started . . . I was disturbed . . . because a congressional committee, charged with the responsibility of investigating un-American activities, should have permitted itself to be used in a flagrantly unfair and un-American attempt to influence an election.

Coffee included in the *Congressional Record* excerpts from twenty-odd newspapers and magazines, both liberal and conservative, which expressed opposition to the investigation as conducted under the leadership of Martin Dies.

Speaking in reply to his critics, Dies declared "this campaign of abuse and misrepresentation was no new thing," and pointed out that many of his present critics had opposed the investigation even before it began. From the very outset there had been an organized effort to discredit the investigation by misrepresentation and ridicule. He said that although repeated invitations had been issued to those against whom charges had been made to appear and answer the charges, these invitations had not been accepted. He denied that the committee had attempted to "smear" the Administration or the New Deal and said his committee had been subjected to "personal abuse and vilification."

In spite of inadequate funds and other handicaps the committee had done "everything in its power to render a patriotic service to this country" and to give "to the Nation a unanimous report . . . based upon facts and not upon opinions or hearsay." Declaring "the Democratic Party not in sympathy with communism," he expressed his resentment at the charge that it was and, particularly, the fact that certain Cabinet officers had gone "out of their way" to attack an independent agency of this Congress, and shouted:

I love this Congress. My father served in this House for 10 years. [Applause] And during all the time he was here he defended the integrity, the dignity, and the prerogatives of this House. When, therefore, Cabinet officers—appointive officials of the Government— went out of their way not merely to attack me, for I am merely an humble and insignificant member of a great body—when they attacked this committee they attacked the greatest deliberative body on earth, and I resent such action. [Applause]

Dies expressed gratitude to the members of his committee for their "loyalty" and "courage" at a time when "radical writers" had attempted to "smear" the committee "with deliberate lies and misrepresentation" while it was "honestly and sincerely undertaking to do a patriotic service to the people of this country." Liberals, he said, had nothing to fear from the investigation because "true liberals are as much opposed to communism as are the conservatives."

The "intolerant ideologies of Europe," he said, had been "transplanted to our shores" and sought to "change the structure of this Government by intrigue and by violence." He was pained at the charge that he had tried to hurt the Democratic party and administration, and added:

I am thinking of one whose memory will ever dwell in my heart and for whom I entertained profound love and devotion. He left me as a priceless heritage a record in this House which was distinguished by courage and patriotism. No man loved the Democratic Party more than he did. And yet at a moment of crisis he did not hesitate to place this country above partisanship. I would be unworthy of him and the heritage of unselfish service which he left me if I did not place the interest of our beloved country above what some misguided partisans conceive to be the interests of the party.

As a matter of fact, this is not a partisan question. Here we are dealing with the life of America, with the fundamentals, with that concerning which all men of all parties, of all creeds can unite in a common defense.

Dies was convinced that his committee had not erred or shown partisanship "in exposing men prominent in this Government who by their own admission subscribe to communism," or in showing "by uncontradicted evidence" that communism had infiltrated into the labor movement. "America comes before all questions of partisanship [Applause]."

Representative Shannon of Missouri said Dies was "very closely related by blood ties to Mr. Hitler's country" and therefore "unsuited for the chairmanship of the committee." He thought the Dies committee sought to "camouflage its racial prejudices and antilabor feelings by going 'hog wild' on the subject of communism." He did not believe there was any kangaroo court in the large city jails that would be "as unfair and as high-handed in its methods as was this committee in conducting its investigation." He declared Dies' "antilabor record

181

[was] unexcelled by any Member of [the] House" and called it "effrontery [for] a man with such a record [to ask] respectable labor leaders to appear before him for quizzing." He showed how Dies had fought the wage-hour bill in Congress. He declared the Dies committe in 1938 became "a first aid agency in the movement to elect Republicans" and had thereafter the full support of the press. He warned the Republicans, "Beware lest the Dies torpedo which proved so useful to you in the 1938 campaign turn out to be a boomerang and hoist you by your own petard in 1940." [5]

In an extension of his remarks Representative Voorhis explained (February 1, 1939) why he opposed continuing the Dies committee. Considering knowledge the best defense against those "boring from within," he wanted the facts. In his opinion there should be no secret political organizations in America. If every political organization were required to be "an open book for all to read," there would be need for fewer investigations. Although the hearings of the Dies committee contained much "so-called evidence," there was also much "pure hearsay," he felt, and some material which was "absolutely false." Saying the Dies committee had not always been "careful" and "fair" and had "certainly disregarded completely certain fundamental rules of evidence," Voorhis claimed the major result of its work had been to confuse the public mind by lumping progressives, liberals, and communists all together. In his opinion every effort should be made to protect innocent persons from character assassination. "Either there will be fairness and justice for all, either everyone will be considered innocent until proven guilty, or else," he said, "in the course of time no one will enjoy such rights and our liberty and democracy will be no more."

Voorhis pointed out that democracy can be destroyed much more rapidly than it has developed. He feared its destruction through the activities of subversive groups, the continuance of unnecessary poverty and economic stagnation, and the destruction of the democratic spirit of tolerance and justice. An effort to destroy subversive groups might destroy the spirit of tolerance and justice which is "the very spirit and substance of democracy." Voorhis recalled how the Dies committee had called in question the patriotism of such men as Bishop Francis J. Mc-Connell of the Methodist Church, Professor Paul H. Douglas, and Stuart Chase. Of Dies' efforts to compel the registry and licensing of all civilian military organizations and to deport all aliens who owed loyalty to any other government, Voorhis said:

In the declining years of every civilization there have been scape-goats—groups of people upon whom all the ills of the time were blamed. I need only mention the Christians in imperial Rome, the outcasts of India, the Jews in Germany, "political enemies" in Russia. Are we looking for scapegoats in America today? Will we find them in the migratory laborers of our farms, the unemployed, the members of a particular religion ... Or will we find our scapegoats by branding as Communists all who question the eternal rightness of anything in the economic status quo and calling down upon their heads the blind wrath of the very people they have sought to help?

Voorhis considered it important to "draw a clear distinction between real disloyalty to the United States on the one hand, and divergent views on economic policy upon the other." It was disloyal to the United States to feel first allegiance to another country or to seek to overthrow our form of government by force or violence; but it was certainly not disloyal to strive to see the country improved or the lot of the underprivileged bettered.

The cure for the extreme movements in the United States was a "release of the productive energies of our businessmen, our farmers, our workers"; through governmental help abundance might take the place of artificial scarcity; freedom for the maximum number of people could only be gained through restricting the freedom of the few. President Roosevelt had followed these principles in his administration of the government; and the Dies committee had been "in very important respects, the willing or unwilling tool" of a movement to discredit the Roosevelt administration.[6]

When the vote on continuing the Dies committee was taken, there were 344 yeas, 35 nays, 2 "present," and 51 not voting.[7] On February 6, 1939, Dies introduced a resolution authorizing the payment of the expenses of the committee.[8] On February 8, 1939, the Chair appointed Jerry Voorhis of California to fill a vacancy on the committee.[9] On August 5, 1939, Representative Healey resigned from the committee. Casey of Massachusetts was appointed to take his place.[10]

On October 25, 1939, Representative Coffee of Washington protested against the threat of the Dies committee to publicize the names of government employees who were members of the American League for Peace and Democracy. He maintained that government employees had "the indubitable and inalienable right to join organizations of their own choosing," and added, "If the aim of the Dies committee is to preserve this Nation from the curse of dictatorship, that aim cannot be achieved by introducing the methods and standards of dictators here [Applause]."

Coffee commended Voorhis, Casey, and Dempsey, Dies committee members, for their objection to such publication, and pointed out that were it not for his "Congressional immunity," Dies "might be liable for plenty of libel suits in the courts of the land" from people whom the press said Dies had called "reds." [11]

Starnes of Alabama inserted in the *Congressional Record* (October 31, 1939) a radio address delivered shortly before by Martin Dies. In this speech Dies explained that in undertaking the investigation of un-American activities he had "made a covenant with the American people that [he] would keep faith with them, and with them alone, on a matter which rises above all party interests and considerations." He said he expected to be a Democrat as long as he lived, although, like his father, he would break with the leaders of his party "when his conscience persuaded him that the interests of his country transcended those of his party." He continued: "I would be faithless to my father's memory and to my public trust if I failed to put America first. I cannot and will not bow to the leadership of my own political party when my conscience tells me that the vital interests of America and the views of my party's leadership are in conflict." Dies expressed himself as "deeply grieved" that the President had described the procedures of his committee as "sordid." He did not propose to "enter into controversy with" the President. He knew, nevertheless, that there were Communists in key positions of the government and "hundreds, yes, thousands, of members of Communist-controlled organizations scattered throughout the departments and agencies of [the] Federal Government." And nothing would deter him from "apprising the American people of this fact." Dies expressed profound regret that the President and his Cabinet had not supported the committee with the same unanimity as "the people of this country." He said the President had not complained of sordid procedures when the committee was investigating fascists, and added, "If we are not free to reveal the identity of the parlor pets of Moscow who plot the overthrow of our Government over their teacups, then we can have no investigation worthy of the name." Pointing out that the nine members of the House of Representatives who had served on the committee, including the two appointed to fill vacancies, were agreed that the American League for Peace and Democracy was a "front" of the Communist party, Dies declared the American League was "simply the Communist Party travelling on one of its many false passports under the aliases of peace and democracy," and continued:

It is high time that innocent and gullible people begin to learn to discriminate between organizations that are controlled by the Communist Party for its own purposes—the purposes of Stalin—and organizations that truly represent legitimate American interest. It is high time that leaders in government and trade-unions cease lending their names as propaganda assets to the Communist Party and its front organizations. Otherwise they must be prepared to take full responsibility for their connections with these un-American and subversive groups. . . .

I believe that more consideration is due the person who openly and above board accepts a Communist Party membership card than is due the fellow traveller who conceals his real political alinement from the public by professing to be interested only in the advancement of worthy causes, such as peace and democracy . . .

. . . The Nation must be informed by fearless investigation of every menace of those who would steal from us . . . our priceless heritage of freedom and democracy . . . the menace of those who hate the Bill of Rights even while they are clamouring for its protection from the exposure of their own misdeeds.

While Dies wanted "more effective legislation against sub-versive elements," he opposed "repressive measures that would detract from the dignified strength of free men." He continued:

Liberty is born of the confidence of strong men. Our American democracy must continue to demonstrate the capacity of man for self-government—with tolerance for all that is nationally tolerable, and without fear in exposing and punishing that which is nationally intolerable.

There must be a new insight into the true meaning of liberalism. Whether men call themselves conservatives or progressives, all those who love America and its free institutions can unite on a platform of liberty. Of one thing we must be certain, conservatives and pro-gressives alike, and that is that economic security and economic progress depends upon the preservation of liberty, upon maintain-ing inviolate the Bill of Rights. Many people in the modern world have sacrificed their hard-won liberty in the pursuit of economic security. They have been rudely awakened to find that both their liberty and their economic security are gone. They have followed demagogues who promised them economic security in exchange for their liberty. They have found, at the end of the road, that their economic insecurity is multiplied a hundred times in the loss of their liberty. All those who believe that liberty is the keystone in the arch of our social structure are true liberals. They may call them-selves conservatives or they may call themselves progressives, but together they can unite in rejecting all forms of totalitarianism.

To the people of America I refer my case. After all, this is your investigation, and if you want it continued along honest, coura-geous, and nonpartisan lines; if you want those in high positions as well as those in low positions exposed when they are guilty; if you agree with me that this is no time for concealment or soft-pedaling on account of partisan interests, you have but to make known your views and wishes to your servants in Washington. As for me, I shall not swerve from the path of duty as God gives me the light to see it.

May the God of our fathers vouchsafe to us the light and the strength to keep America the land of the free.[12]

On November 1, 1939, Dies introduced a resolution for the continuation of his committee.[13] The next day Representative Coffee inserted in the record an editorial from the *Boston Eve-ning Transcript,* and an article by Jay Franklin published in the

Washington Evening Star. Both accounts discussed the Dies committee. Coffee pointed out the injustice of concluding, as Dies had, that one's name on a mailing list meant one's membership in the organization doing the mailing. The receipt of Pelley and Coughlin publications by all congressmen he cited as in no way indicative of their membership in fascistic organizations or agreement with such views.

The *Boston Transcript* cited Dies' statement that "There isn't a leader of any of these organizations (Fascist or Communist) who hasn't violated some penal law" and that there was plenty of evidence to prove this statement. That being the case, asked the *Transcript*, what need is there for the Dies committee? Fear was expressed that the committee, thriving on war hysteria, might undertake a "red" hunt such as that of A. Mitchell Palmer and further uproot the Bill of Rights.

Franklin in the *Washington Post* had said that "If [the fact that] there are Communists in the League for Peace and Democracy ... makes the League a communist 'front,' and if members of that 'front' are also members of Phi Beta Kappa, that makes Phi Beta Kappa another communist 'front.' And that makes me a Communist. Q.E.D." He was greatly "worried," he said, that by standing near a Communist in a subway he might have "accidentally become un-American" by contagion.[14]

DEBATE ON COMMITTEE EXTENSION

Shortly after the session of Congress got under way in January, 1940, the House debated whether to continue the Dies committee investigation for another year.[15] The debate was limited to two hours, with the time equally divided between the two sides of the House. The resolution was passed by a vote of 344 to 21, with 1 absent and 57 not voting.[16] The committee had asked that its life be extended two full years, but the House voted an extension of one year only.[17]

Although the vote was overwhelmingly in favor of prolongation, the debate showed much more resistance to the committee than in the two earlier debates. One feature of the debate was the absence of Martin Dies himself. He was confined to his home in Texas by illness.[18]

Letters, telegrams, and editorials were read into the record both for and against continuance of the committee. In favor of continuance were petitions signed by approximately 400,000 persons who had responded to an appeal by Gerald L. K. Smith of Michigan, national chairman of the Committee of 1,000,000, an organization claiming to represent the leadership of 141 patriotic and civic groups.[19] There was also a letter from William Green, president of the American Federation of Labor, indicating that that organization had officially approved the "excellent, splendid work" done by the Dies committee, and desired that its work be continued.[20] Various units of the American Legion wired their support of the committee and urged continuance.[21] All World War Veterans' organizations, including the Veterans of Foreign Wars, and the Spanish-American War Veterans were declared to have gone on record in favor of continuing the committee.[22] The Gallup Poll was cited to show that 75 per cent of the American people favored a prolongation of the Dies committee.[23]

Nevertheless, there was formidable opposition. Among those opposed to the committee were the American Civil Liberties Union, the Civil Rights Federation, the Consumers' Union, the Committee for People's Rights, the Public Affairs Committee, the National Association for the Advancement of Colored People, the American Federation of Teachers, the American Committee for Democracy and Intellectual Freedom, the League of Women Shoppers, the National Board of the Young Women's Christian Association, the Democratic Club of Glendale, California, the National Board of the National Negro Congress. Opposition was also expressed by over one hundred outstanding American intellectuals, scientists, and writers.[24]

Representative Sabath of Illinois, who in 1938 had favored the formation of the Dies committee and in 1939 had voted for an additional appropriation of $100,000 to continue the investigation, now opposed it because it had "unfairly" attacked and stigmatized many outstanding persons and organizations. He charged that the Republicans favored the resolution because the Dies committee had served Republican political interests by attacking Democratic leaders as well as "progressive labor organizations throughout the United States." [25]

A communication from the American Federation of Teachers, while not objecting to the "stated purposes" of the Dies committee, said:

The Dies Committee has itself clearly violated democratic procedures and therefore been truly un-American (1) by calling witnesses without due regard to their credibility; (2) by accepting testimony unsupported by trustworthy evidence; (3) by releasing to the public press testimony which attacks the reputations of these individuals and organizations without affording them the semblance of a fair chance to refute irresponsible charges; (4) by condemning individual people, through association; and (5) by summoning witnesses without due notice, thus preventing adequate opportunity to secure data either for complete clarification or defense.

The methods of the Dies Committee violate the civil liberties guaranteed in our Constitution by un-American treatment of dissident minority groups.

The action of the Dies Committee has brought attacks upon organized labor, threatened its security, and thus endangered the most important movement in advancing and protecting our American democracy.

The Dies Committee has failed to define Americanism and thus confuses the entire country, embarrasses all liberals, including teachers, students, and others who sincerely believe in democracy, and generally discredits free thought and expression.

The Dies Committee has not been impartial and comprehensive in its choice of organizations to be investigated and thereby testifies to its own confusion or prejudices.

The methods of the Dies Committee discredit all Government agencies with investigatory powers by reason of its obviously political motives in contradistinction to its stated purposes.

The Bill of Rights should remain inviolate especially in view of the present international crisis.[26]

A similar communication came from the American Committee for Democracy and Intellectual Freedom urging that Congress grant no further appropriations to the Dies committee because of the treatment which it had accorded the educational world.

Its objections to the Dies committee are partially set forth in the following paragraphs:

1. The use of the phrase "un-American propaganda," which is vague, undefined, and undefinable, left the committee free to follow its own bias and prejudice. The result has been something approaching the character of a witch hunt, reminiscent of the activities of Attorney General H. Mitchell Palmer and the Lusk committee in the heat of the period of the first World War. Political phrases have been manipulated as epithets in order to discredit individuals and organizations. Public attitudes of intolerance and hatred have been created which discredit minorities—political, cultural, religious, labor—and greatly lessen their effective appeal. "The fundamental right of free men," said Mr. Justice Brandeis (Justice Holmes concurring), "to strive for better conditions through new legislation and new institutions will not be preserved, if efforts to secure it by argument to fellow citizens may be construed as criminal incitement to disobey the existing law—merely because the argument presented seems to those exercising judicial power to be unfair in its portrayal of existing evils, mistaken in its assumptions, unsound in reasoning or intemperate in language."

2. The Dies committee has attacked freedom of teaching and investigation in leading institutions of learning (Harvard, Vassar, Stanford, California, Columbia, among others), by recognized scholars (Albert Einstein, Dean Grayson N. Kefauver of Stanford, Prof. Kirtley F. Mather, of Harvard; Prof. Max Radin of California; Prof. Paul Douglas, of Chicago; Dr. Eduard C. Lindeman of the New York School of Social Work; Prof. Wyllistine Goodsell, of Teachers College, Columbia, among others), and by professional associations of educators (American Association of University Professors, American Federation of Teachers, Progressive Education Association, Commission of Social Studies of the American Historical Association, among others).

Reduced to its essential implication, these attacks mean that our universities, educators, and learned societies must give up their intellectual freedom and conform to the views held by a congressional committee or else be pilloried by the publicity it can command and be threatened with legislative interference. We cannot accept such an unwarranted assumption of authority and retain our integrity.

3. The Dies committee has attacked freedom of association and

debate among students. We believe that our students think their own way through the political, economic, and social philosophies of our time. Any attempt to exercise tyranny over the minds of youth not only exceeds the authority vested in Congress, but is bad pedagogy and likely to produce results contrary to those desired. The safeguard of the United States tomorrow is the free minds of its youth today.

The Dies committee has sat in judgment upon current books, periodicals, plays, and works of art. We assert that the very foundations of intellectual liberty are shaken when any congressional committee can hold even the shadow of a threat over the books we read or the plays we see.[27]

Representative Keller of Illinois objected to the sensationalism which characterized the publicity of the Dies committee and expressed the opinion that the true purpose for which Congress had instituted the committee had been subverted by its publicity-loving chairman. He charged that Dies "from the beginning . . . made himself the whole committee" and ignored the other members "completely and entirely." This "one-man" Dies committee had "gone forward with insistent deliberation not to get information which would help the House in any way to pass necessary remedial legislation but to destroy the New Deal, which he has hated from the start; to destroy organized labor and to embarrass the Roosevelt administration, and where possible, to aid the Republican at the expense of the Democratic Party." It was not hard to understand, he said, why the Republicans had voted for a continuance of the committee.[28] Jerry Voorhis of California, now a member of the Dies committee, wanted the resolution to be amended to prevent certain abuses. He favored regular executive meetings of the committee at least once each week, authorization of public statements and press releases by a majority of the committee before they were issued, giving accused persons an opportunity to be heard in their own defense, and no public speeches, charges, or predictions by committee members concerning matters which were under investigation by the committee until they were "substantiated by evidence." Such a modification in procedure would have seriously interfered with Dies' freedom of action and would have re-

191

duced the volume of publicity which Dies enjoyed. The Voorhis amendments did not get to first base in Congress.[29]

Congressman Celler of New York said the committee on "un-American activities" had itself employed "un-American procedure." He declared a committee report alleging communistic activities in consumer organizations had been published without any witnesses being heard by the committee, without any hearings on the subject before the committee, and without the knowledge of any committee member except the chairman. He suggested that the committee investigate the so-called Christian Front conspiracy to overthrow the government, which had been "aided and abetted by the writings and mouthings of Father Coughlin." [30]

Geyer of California charged that the Dies committee had "timed its appearance in certain cities to coincide with the holding of National Labor Relations Board elections, or the settlement of serious labor disputes," and had in this way "used its unquestioned influence to affect the outcome of... elections and... settlements... in a manner inimical to the interests of the workers involved." President Roosevelt, said Geyer, had characterized the committee's influence on national elections in at least three states as "unfair and un-American." [31] The effect of the Dies committee had been "to undermine American democracy by terrorizing the American people into the surrender of their traditional rights." The objectives of the committee, he said, were the same as those of the Chamber of Commerce, the National Association of Manufacturers, the Associated Farmers, the Christian Front, the reactionary press, Wall Street financiers, munition makers, and "all the most powerful and richest enemies of democracy." Consequently the committee had no difficulty whatever "in making itself heard." In fact, the ineffective opposition to the Dies committee by labor unions and other progressive groups was "itself a measure of the extent to which the Dies committee has already succeeded in weakening and intimidating the progressive forces in this country." He charged that the Dies committee was engaged in attacks not only on freedom of teaching, and freedom of speech, press, and assembly, but had endangered "that inalienable right of freedom to think for ourselves." [32]

That the investigation should be intrusted to the Justice Department rather than the Dies committee was the contention of Representative Hook of Michigan. He questioned the committee's impartiality and wondered why no list of fascists had been published by the committee, but only "a list of names published smearing innocent people with a 'red tinge.'" The committee had been much too selective in its investigation. For example, there were members of Congress who had received the votes of less than 5 per cent of the people in their own districts. Was it not "un-American" asked Hook, to exclude 95 per cent of the people from the right to vote because of race, color, or creed, intelligence tests, or the poll tax? [33]

Shannon of Missouri noted with suspicion "the admiration shown the gentleman from Texas, Chairman Dies, by his new-found Republican friends...and his labor-hating [Democratic] friends." Shannon preferred that the committee be discontinued, but urged that if it were continued a provision be enacted to prevent any committee member from receiving "one dollar of revenue" for newspaper articles or speeches. This suggestion was applauded by Congress but no action was taken to carry it into effect.

Most devastating of the criticisms directed against the Dies committee was that by Congressman Coffee of Washington. In the Dies committee he saw an effort to deal with the symptoms. rather than with the causes, of "un-American activities." There were in America 9,000,000 heads of families who were out of work. It did no good to "inveigh at groups with whose philosophy we are in diametrical disagreement." What we must do is to enact legislation which will take away the dreadful insecurity which hangs over these people. "Remove the curse of unemployment, of hunger, of want, of lack of opportunity, of sickness, of malnutrition, and our problem is settled," said Coffee. How absurd, he argued, to say that no money could be found to support those on W.P.A. at the same time that another $100,000 was voted by Congress "to engage on a witch-hunting, bogey chasing expedition, in which rules of evidence will be flouted and in which hearsay testimony will be allowed to be introduced in that record which would not be admissible in any court of record in the United States; in which unsupported and readily refutable assertions made by unqualified witnesses will be allowed to be spread on the record; in which reputable citizens will be assailed and accused of being Communists and will be charged with engaging in un-American activities, but not in the presence of the accusers; and in which, when persons and groups so slandered have asked to appear before the committee and deny the charges, frequently they have not been accorded that opportunity."

Coffee indicated numerous fascist organizations which the committee had had neither the time nor the inclination to investigate. He listed outstanding people charged with communism by the committee, and indicated scores of prominent American citizens who were opposed to continuance of the committee. He cited numerous editorials from leading American newspapers; for example, an editorial from the *New York Times* concluding that "from some of the testimony given before the House Committee on Un-American Activities it is now possible to be a Communist without knowing it. One may think he is merely working for peace and democracy, or against war and fascism, but in the background, if one takes this testimony at its face value, is the sinister figure of Stalin and the Ogpu." And the *St. Louis Post-Dispatch* saw evidence of the "unjudicial" character of the Dies committee "in its chairman's boast that it has paralyzed the left wing of the Democratic Party, discredited John L. Lewis and the C.I.O., and driven Elmer F. Andrews from his post as Wage and Hour Administrator."

The lawless character of the Dies committee was recognized by Walter Lippmann in a column published in the January 11, 1940, issue of the *Washington Post,* which read in part as follows:

The Dies committee are not really a legislative committee. They are a kind of committee of public safety set up by Congress to suppress activities which, though detested by the great majority of the people, are in themselves either not unlawful, or, even if they were outlawed, could not be dealt with by the ordinary procedure of the law. The Dies committee are official vigilantes operating in an area, that of the political underworld, where there is as yet no effective law and there is, therefore, no order. The committeemen, like their vigilantes predecessors, on the American frontier, are therefore themselves often lawless in spirit and disorderly in their methods.

This accounts for the somewhat shamefaced approval which thoughtful men have given to the work of the committee. The public is confronted with the ancient moral question of whether the end justifies the means, thus, only the very innocent and self deluding have any doubt that the Dies committee have been attacking a formidable evil in modern society. The menace is real. It is not imaginary. And it must be met. Yet there is no doubt also that the procedure of the Dies committee is itself a violation of American morality; it is a pillory in which reputations are ruined, often without proof and always without the legal safeguards that protect the ordinary criminal; it is a tribunal before which men are arraigned and charged with acts that are, as a matter of fact, lawful.[34]

Representative Casey of Massachusetts, a member of the Dies committee, expressed himself in favor of a discriminating attitude toward the Dies committee, rather than one of complete approval or disapproval. He considered that the committee had done a "great" and "commendable" job in "exposing" Earl Browder and Fritz Kuhn, but did not approve of the "infamous report of Communist activities in consumer organizations" which Voorhis described as "purely and simply the opinion of one man," viz., J. B. Matthews, "a renegade Communist," and now chief investigator of the Dies committee. Casey decried the theory that if a man spoke to a group in which there were Communists he himself became a Communist, by association. A man might speak to a group which included Republicans, without himself either being or becoming a Republican, said Casey, and he might speak to the American Association of University Women without either being or becoming a woman in the process.[35]

Those who favored a prolongation of the investigation capitalized on the enemies which the commitee had gained; that

Earl Browder, Secretary Ickes, and Secretary Perkins were "unfriendly" to the committee was considered an argument in its favor.[36] "I like the committee," said Congressman Robison of Kentucky, "for some of the enemies it has made. It put the 'reds' on the run. [Laughter and applause]"[37] He declared that the committee had "rendered a great service" to the country by "exposing these termites and vipers here in the United States who have been and are injecting their poisonous venom into the very heart of this great Republic."[38] The achievements of the committee were also indicated; the country had been saved from totalitarianism; Kuhn and Browder had been sent to jail; people had been taught "the important lesson of caution before joining organizations with high-sounding names and sinister purposes." Representative Thomas, a member of the committee, declared that the committee's work "rises far above all partisan questions and commands the whole-hearted support of all Americans. [Applause]" Thomas listed ten points made clear by the investigation:

First. It has exposed the fact of widespread passport frauds by Communists.

Second. It has established the connection between Stalin and a gigantic counterfeiting plot in this country.

Third. It has shown by hundreds of pages of testimony, that the Communist Party in this country is a branch of Stalin's government and, as such, is guilty of violation of the act requiring the registration of foreign agents with the State Department.

Fourth. It has proven that numerous auxiliaries of the Communist Party, such as the American League for Peace and Democracy, have violated the same act by failing to register.

Fifth. It has adduced substantial evidence that the Communist Party has been engaged on a wide scale in espionage and sabotage in this country through the instrumentality of Stalin's Ogpu.

Sixth. It has revealed an alarming penetration by the Communist Party into the ranks of labor and the penetration of communism in our schools, colleges, and governmental agencies.

Seventh. It has shown the direct link between Hitler and the German-American bund.

Eighth. It nipped in the bud a crude move of the Mosely-Deatherage-Gilbert-Campbell group to launch a race-hating violent American fascism.

Ninth. It has exposed from top to bottom the un-American character of Pelley's Silver Shirts, and a score of kindred Fascist outfits including the Christian Front.

Tenth. It demonstrated again and again, long before the Stalin-Hitler alliance, the essential identity of all the totalitarians—the Communists, the Nazis, and the Fascists.[39]

Cox of Georgia took Hook of Michigan to task for having attempted to attack Chairman Dies because one of Dies' sponsors, when he spoke to a New York audience, was alleged to have been a Mr. James Wheeler-Hill, secretary of the German-American bund. Hook had also charged Dies with "guilty association" with Pelley. Cox pointed out the defect in logic which held Dies responsible for guests at a luncheon at which he merely spoke and for private correspondence between men over whom Dies had no control whatever.[40]

Representative Case of South Dakota asked the Dies committee to investigate a National Labor Relations Board order to the effect that Henry Ford must desist from distributing pamphlets indicating his attitude toward labor. Such an order, said Case, was contrary to the First Amendment to the Constitution.[41]

Smith of Ohio, defining communism as "the abolition of property" and declaring that that was how it had been defined by Karl Marx, expressed wonder that the Dies committee had not yet investigated "communistic programs" such as the Tennessee Valley Authority, the use of "irredeemable paper money" in the United States, the United States Housing Authority, and the Export-Import Bank of Washington, D. C. These were but a few of the "great many" communistic programs adopted by the federal government in recent years. If the Dies committee investigates these matters, "they will see," said Smith, "that the real promoters of communism in this country do not live in dark, subterranean haunts of illicit intrigue but that they live in marble palaces and other respectable places." [42]

Congressman Brooks of Louisiana emphasized the importance of publicity in attaining the results achieved by the Dies committee. By means of publicity and exposure it had been possible for the Dies committee to deal with problems "difficult to handle under our system of government and under the terms of our Bill of Rights." The focusing of "public indignation" had turned the trick. [43]

Congressman Ham Fish of New York wished the Dies committee to investigate immediately "the insidious, dangerous, and un-American activities of foreign war mongers who [were] spreading poisonous war propaganda in our midst." He urged exposure of "all foreign agents and propagandists ... trying to inflame our passions and hatreds and to drag us into foreign entanglements and wars." [44] Starnes of Alabama, a member of the Dies committee, warned that the Communists, not the Fascists or the Nazis, were "the most dangerous dissident minority" in the United States. [45]

There is, however, a topic which should not be overlooked in connection with the debate. On the day before the House discussed the question of continuing the Dies investigation, Representative Hook of Michigan introduced in the House certain letters purporting to show a connection between Dies, Pelley, and the Christian Front. Subsequently, it became clear that Representative Hook had been the victim of a hoax and that the letters were actually forged and completely unauthentic; although Representative Hook had not recognized their unauthenticity at the time he presented them to Congress. [46]

Subsequent to this debate there were minor references in Congress to Dies and his committee, but little was heard from Dies himself. On February 1, Representative Voorhis expressed a desire that the Dies committee clarify "the very essential difference" between progressives and Communists, and make a similar distinction between conservatives and Fascists. He opposed "unsubstantiated accusations or name calling," and while reserving the right to call anyone a reactionary who called him a radical, he agreed to call anyone a conservative who called him a progressive. Voorhis was opposed, however, to calling people "un-American" merely because they were "concerned with the plight of the people" and wanted economic problems solved.[47] A week later Voorhis complained in Congress that Dies' articles in *Liberty Magazine* had complicated the work of the committee by expressing the chairman's views prior to any investigation by the committee itself.[48] The following week Representative Bradley of Pennsylvania referred to Martin Dies as one who had been "the self-constituted president of the cloak-room Demagog Club" for an eight-year period. Bradley proclaimed Dies "a pretty smart fellow," who was not willing to share "publicity" with anyone else.[49] On February 26, 1940, Representative Smith of Ohio objected to secret hearings but was assured by Representative Thomas of the committee that secret hearings had not been voted by the committee.[50]

Dies himself took action in Congress when James H. Dolsen refused to answer certain questions asked him by the Dies committee. Thereupon, Chairman Dies came to the House on March 29, 1940, with a resolution to authorize the committee to proceed against Dolsen.[51] On April 2, 1940, similar authorization was asked to proceed against George Powers, another who had refused to answer questions.[52] Phillip Frankfield, Dr. Albert Blumberg, and Thomas F. P. O'Dea also refused to answer questions, and proceedings were instituted against them.[53]

DIES WARNS AMERICA

Dies made a one-hour address on May 17, 1940, in which he summarized the findings of his investigation and indicated certain conclusions and recommendations.

Speaking on "The Fifth Column, or Trojan Horse, in America," Dies declared that democracy was challenged throughout the world. We in America are in no danger of foreign invasion, said Dies. "No power or combination of powers could ever successfully invade our country even if they dare to try, so long as we are adequately prepared and stand united in allegiance to the God of our fathers and the Constitution upon which our economic and political institutions are founded."

The fifth column, however, seeks to destroy our unity. It is this enemy within, which is most to be feared. Both Hitler and Stalin are undermining our strength by creating internal divisions within the United States. Dissident minorities were responsible for the downfall of Austria, Czechoslovakia, Poland, Finland and Norway, Holland and France. Treason from within is a greater danger than invasion from without. Nazism, fascism, and communism are world theories, "not to be confined to any one country, but to embrace the proletariat of every country." Therefore Italy, Germany, and Russia have set up organizations throughout the world which pretend to be fraternal, patriotic, or social groups, and often masquerade as political parties, but these organizations are actually "foreign conspiracies under the control of foreign dictators." "For two years," said Dies, "I have been stressing the fact that communism, nazi-ism, and fascism are fundamentally alike." In each instance, he said, the state is everything, and the individual is merely a cog in the wheel.

The American Communist party operates under the Communist International. It is a conspiratorial party and uses illegal as well as legal methods "in obedience to orders from Moscow." The party has 5,000 branches in the United States and claimed a membership of 100,000 members in 1939. It is the policy of the Communists to underestimate their strength. For example, the Communists claimed only 60,000 paid-up members in Russia at the time of the Russian Revolution, but were able nonetheless to seize the government of Russia. Communists in America are more loyal to the Soviet Union than they are to the United States. They have worked their way into the American labor movement on orders from Moscow and have "wanted to establish industrial unions in the United States under a central control." They have tried to seize control of strategic positions in the labor movement. They do everything in their power to facilitate the industrial type of organization represented by the C.I.O. True, most of the people in both the A.F. of L. and the C.I.O. labor unions were "loyal, patriotic American citizens," but there were at least ten national C.I.O. unions in which Communist leadership was intrenched and there were, likewise, certain "front organizations," such as the American League for Peace and Democracy, which were Communist-controlled and whose policies were determined by Moscow in spite of the fact that only a small proportion of the membership might be Communist. The Communists claimed a unit in every naval yard in the United States, and directed their members to form units in every vital industry, such as aircraft.

The Fascist and Nazi organizations had also seized key positions in basic industries. These people are "fanatical followers of their pagan religion." Their loyalty is not to the United States. "You are dealing with people who are willing to follow the dictates of foreign governments even if this involves betrayal of their own country." The Communists have receipts in the United States of $10,000,000 per year and distribute 600 publications. Their income is derived in part from contributions made by people who are able to give from $10 to $3,000 per year. The Communist party has 50,000 members in labor organizations, one-third in the A.F. of L. and two-thirds in the C.I.O. The Communists are actually under the control of Joseph Stalin, said Dies, and are in effect "an espionage system in the United States which Russia does not have to pay for." The fifth columns which Hitler and Stalin in this way had at their disposal in the United States included "many sincere and fanatical followers who can be depended upon to be loyal, faithful, and zealous." Furthermore, they consist largely, not of noncitizens residing in the United States, but of naturalized citizens. For example, Dies estimated that 95 per cent of the 100,000 members of the German-American Bund had come to the United States after 1918 and were now naturalized. The Bund had 100 units in 47 districts in the United States, and cooperated with the Christian Front, Christian Mobilizers, and the Christian Crusaders.

While not all members of the Communist party or the German-American Bund were "traitors" to the United States, it was "fifth column ... technique to use innocent and sympathetic people for the purpose of obtaining valuable military and industrial information, and to support the foreign policies of the dictatorships, and to undermine national unity." Communist leadership was "entrenched" in "vital and basic industries in America that affect our national defense." To handle these "undemocratic minorities in our midst," Dies recommended strict enforcement of laws on immigration, deportation, income tax evasion, foreign agent registration, and passports. American citizens should discontinue their affiliation with front organizations. More stringent deportation and immigration requirements; and registration of, and full publicity given to, foreign organizations in the United States would also help. Dies exonerated John L. Lewis of the "Communist" charge, but wanted the C.I.O. to expel all "Communist" leaders, such as Harry Bridges. If the C.I.O. would "clean house," the Dies committee would give it "a clean bill of health." Since Dies' committee had never had more than seven or eight investigators, and was dealing with a problem of such crucial importance, Dies asked that the government "here and now co-operate with this committee to the fullest extent possible." The committee, he said, had been "handicapped in every conceivable manner." Dies concluded:

I appreciate very much the opportunity I have had to bring some of these facts to the attention of the House. I want to make myself perfectly clear, that there is no indictment or intended indictment of a great majority of the American people. But minority movements, highly organized, constitute the greatest threat to modern democratic governments. We have seen the ability of a small group, tightly organized as a kernel, holding strategic and vital jobs in utilities, in shipping, in transportation, and in communications, to deliver a whole country over to an invading host.

We have seen their ability to promote strife and hatred in a country in order to divide it into hostile camps either along racial, religious, or class lines. We have seen the disastrous results that have come to other republics and other democracies by such a course.

If we are to be preserved as a democracy we must match the brains, the ingenuity, the patriotism of men who believe in democracy against this new and sinister influence. We must revitalize democracy and offer it as a challenge to the fanatical followers of Hitler, Stalin and Mussolini. I believe that democracy can develop a tremendous enthusiasm for the principles of freedom and constitutional government. I believe that through voluntary and cooperative union on the part of all classes in America, labor and capital, all races and all creeds, that we can meet the challenge that has been flung at every democracy on the face of the earth; and, as one people under one God, regardless of our differences of race, religion, or class, we can unite in the defense of the greatest democracy the world has ever seen. [Applause, and Members rising] [54]

Maintenance of the Monroe Doctrine was Dies' topic when he again delivered a major address to the House of Representatives, on June 18, 1940. Moved by the tragic fate of France, he attributed her downfall to the propaganda with which "Hitler, Stalin, and Mussolini" had "flooded France," and to the organizations which they had built up in France to sow disunity and divide the country into hostile groups. The Communist, Fascist and Nazi organizations which had undermined the national unity of France and England had also been at work in the United States, but "on a larger and more active scale." Dies proclaimed a new Monroe Doctrine to prevent an ideological and propaganda invasion from Europe which had not been contemplated at the time the Monroe Doctrine was originally formulated. "Traitorous" organizations, like the German-American Bund and the Communist party, which were "linked to foreign governments," should be declared illegal. Foreign agents should not be admitted to America under the guise of refugees. If anybody likes any other country more than the United States, said Dies, "accommodate him by putting him on a boat and sending him to the country of his affection [Applause]." Propaganda, Dies added, was "the strongest arm of despotism and tyranny"; it could result in "a weakened and disunited nation." [55]

A month later Dies was back on the floor of the House with more on the same subject. He could solve the problem of the Trojan Horse in America if only the administration would co-operate with his committee.[56] (The President of the United States had not accepted the leadership which Martin Dies had volunteered in both foreign and domestic policy. The administration had not co-operated with the gentleman from Texas, in the sense in which the word "co-operation" is understood by Mr. Dies.)

In November, 1940, Representative Dickstein described an

attack by Dies on the Department of Justice as "shameful and disgraceful." Dickstein declared one G-man or one Department of Justice man worth more than all the Dies committee investigators put together. The Dies committee, he said, had gone out for "ballyhoo" instead of making an investigation or suggesting remedial legislation. Dickstein further chided Mr. Dies on the publication of a book, *The Trojan Horse in America,* which sold at $2.50 per copy and was in no sense a report to the Congress which had put up the $220,000 to carry on the Dies investigation. Dies' book was a report to "so-called public suckers." Dickstein urged that book writing by congressmen be stopped; he said Dies seemed "much more interested in making reports to the public than ... in making his report to the Congress [Applause]." [57]

Not all members agreed with Dickstein. Mundt of South Dakota described Dies' article in *Liberty Magazine,* "More Snakes Than I Can Kill," as "a clear-cut revelation by one of the most clean-cut Members of [the] House." [58] Representative Rankin referred to the Dies committee as "putting on a real investigation, measured by old-line American standards." [59] Representative Hall of New York expressed deep regret over "an apparent coldness" toward the Dies committee in the executive department. [60]

It is interesting to note that in 1940 Representative Voorhis of California agreed with Dies in thinking that the problem faced by the committee was not "the old problem of free speech that liberals used to talk about when it was a case of dissident minorities that have a different idea from what the majority of the people hold about current questions." He made this statement on December 12, 1940, and said also that the totalitarian groups, which were opposed by the Dies committee, had no independent ideas of their own but pursued "ideas ready made and patterned for them from across the sea." And, he added, it was no easy matter for democracy to combat these organizations and their propaganda because "many, many of the activities that are carried on by such people are not technically violations of law." [61]

When Congress got under way in January, 1941, the Dies committee was not long out of the limelight. Dickstein of New York, increasingly critical of the Dies committee, called the committee's current report to the attention of the House, and taking up its nine recommendations one by one, subjected them to critical analysis. He was of the opinion that the committee had "let the cat leap out of the bag" when, after having had two and one half years for "sleuthing and talking," it now asked for at least two more years "to formulate and put into effect a long-range program." Asserting that the committee had not presented a single bill to eradicate the evils it charged, Dickstein declared that Congress had authorized no committee "to formulate long-range policies by sleuthing and talking." If it were necessary to continue the committee for such a long time "to expose conditions" rather than to recommend remedial legislation, it would be desirable to convert it into a standing committee of the House, provided with a permanent staff. As a standing committee, it would "not be necessary for it to seek continuous publicity."

Dickstein charged that the entire subversive element in the United States could have been cleaned up within a year's time; there had been no occasion for the investigation to take two years and an appropriation of $235,000 in addition to a huge printing bill of "several hundred thousand dollars more." Dickstein thought it "very strange" indeed that Dies was "a close friend" of Merwin K. Hart, president of the New York State Economic Council, who had been a supporter of Franco in Spain. He indicated well-known subversive groups against which the Dies committee had failed to act. Moreover, the so-called "un-American activities" against which Dies inveighed appeared to be much worse, said Dickstein, when seen through press releases than when appraised on the basis of such evidence as had been actually gathered by the Dies committee. If these press releases were correct, Dickstein wanted a standing committee to assist the Department of Justice in finding out who in the United States actually advocated the overthrow of our government. Dies wanted $1,000,000 for his investigation; Dickstein favored giving that amount to the Department of Justice because it would do a much better job. What Dickstein desired was "laws in place of talk, talk, and more talk by a one-man committee." [62]

On February 5, 1941, Thomas of New Jersey, a member of the Dies committee, complained that the House had not yet taken action to continue the committee. "The minions of Stalin and Hitler want the Dies committee killed," said Thomas, adding that the only ones who benefited "by the inexcusable delay in this matter" were the members of the fifth column.[63] In extension of his remarks Thomas said that the Dies committee had "established the fact that there are no important differences between the brutalitarian regimes of Stalin and Hitler." The Administration could not abolish the Dies committee, but it had done the next best thing: it had delayed the committee's continuance. The country "needs the Dies committee to protect it against the Administration's indifference toward the menace of communism." Since there were persons in the Administration who were "still toying with the idea that Communist Russia is some kind of a utopia," the Dies committee was, in fact, "the only agency in government" which could keep before the American people "the basic identity of the Stalin and Hitler regimes." [64]

Finally, on February 11, 1941, the House considered a resolution to continue the Dies committee until April 1, 1942. There was only an hour's debate, with the time evenly divided between the two sides of the House.

Representative Sabath urged the Dies committee to devote more time to Nazi and Fascist activities because Nazi and Fascist propagandists and agents were "far more active in this country, and far more dangerous, than the Communists." He thought that Fascist agents had cleverly misled Dies to concern himself primarily with Communist activities, and public attention had been diverted from the more dangerous activities of these Axis agents.[65] Michener of Michigan declared the Dies committee had "rendered a splendid service to the country" and indicated that the committee and the F.B.I. had recently worked in close co-operation.[66]

Representative Fish praised the committee's accomplishments, insisted that the opposition to its work had receded, and attributed the defeat of certain members of the House in the last Congressional election to the fact that they had opposed continuation of the Dies investigation. Nevertheless, Fish himself had a few criticisms. He thought the committee should bring to the House legislative measures providing for "drastic deportation, ... outlawing ... the Communist Party, taking the Communists off the ballot, and not permitting Communists or Bundists to hold office in the Federal Government." In fact, Fish wanted the committee to produce legislation to send all alien Communists and Nazis back to their native lands. This suggestion was applauded by the House.[67]

Thomas of New Jersey, Republican member of the Dies committee, listed twenty-six accomplishments of the Dies committee, claiming, among other things, that it had revealed to the American people that "the sit-down strikes were instigated by the Communist Party," that certain federal agencies were being used to disseminate Communist doctrines, that the Communist party controlled labor unions in the United States and hoped "to capture the trade union movement ... by infiltrating in the C.I.O.," that Moscow controlled the Communist party in the United States, and how that party had used front organizations to serve its purposes. Of the twenty-six accomplishments of the Dies committee listed by Thomas, sixteen were concerned exclusively with communism, five with fascism, and five with both. This would tend to substantiate Representative Sabath's charge that the committee had been primarily preoccupied with communistic rather than with fascist activities.[68]

Representative Bradley of Michigan complained that the Dies committee had not investigated "groups that are trying to stick America's nose into a foreign war and send our boys overseas when the American people do not want it." This "highly organized un-American group, ... since the start of the European war, [had] been trying to get this country into it 100 per cent and [to] shed American blood on foreign soil. [Applause]" Declaring that the American people were overwhelmingly opposed to our participation in "this unfortunate European war" and that they considered our participation in World War I a mistake, Bradley wanted Dies to investigate "insidious propaganda" from a "vicious group" which was seeking to involve America in World War II on the side of Great Britain.[69]

Representative Dickstein created a storm in the House by charging that "110 Fascist organizations in this country had the back key, and have now the back key to the back door of the Dies committee." Dies denied this. Representative Rankin of Mississippi then asked for the floor and moved that Mr. Dickstein's entire speech be expunged from the record. In the discussion that followed, Dies spoke in his own defense, insisting that no matter how bitter a member of the House became, there should be no impugning the motives or the integrity of any other member of that body. He asserted that his committee had "exposed numerous Fascist and Nazi organizations" and had shown no partiality whatever in the investigation of "un-American" groups. His committee had not hesitated to expose organizations which disseminated "hatred against the Jewish race." No distinction had been made between different kinds of "foreign ideology"; the committee sought to expose them all. Nevertheless, in spite of his efforts, certain congressmen "who professed to be [his] friends" had met, when he was at home in Texas, "sick in bed for six weeks, under the care of a doctor," and had sought to destroy him, "at a time when [he] was unable to defend [himself]." At that time forged letters, purporting to show a tie-up between Dies and Pelley, had been read on the floor of the House; these letters were widely publicized throughout the country; Dies was "bitterly attacked by some people as a pro-Nazi."

There had been a constant effort to malign him and the other members of the committee, said Dies. For example, one congressman had made the "ridiculous" charge that he [Dies] had made $100,000 out of lectures and writings since the investigation began. It was true, said Dies, that he had written magazine articles, and a book called *The Trojan Horse in America*. He had also made 160 speeches since the outset of the investigation. He had been compelled to speak and write because of the concerted effort made by Secretary Ickes, Secretary Perkins and others, to discredit his investigation. Another reason for writing and speaking, however, had been the need to acquaint the American people with their peril from abroad. Dies' speaking tours also put him in contact with sources of information about subversion which would otherwise not have been available to his committee. For 105 of the 160 speeches which he had made, Dies received no honorarium, and for 35 per cent of these he was not even reimbursed for his expenses.

On speaking tours it was often necessary to take his family with him because they "could not be separated day in and day out"; moreover, his wife "was constantly frightened by threatening notes and the fear of having [their] children kidnapped." Since the expenses of his family's traveling could not be paid for by the committee, these expenses were often paid for out of the fees received for speaking and writing. Nevertheless, on these trips he frequently "conducted executive hearings for the committee." He had spent more money for the investigation, he said, than he received in Congressional salary, and "not once but many times took money out of his own pocket and spent it on the investigation." In fact, his expenses because of the investigation had been so heavy that he had been compelled to borrow on his salary by making assignments to banks. His telephone and telegraph bills, paid out of his own pocket, often amounted to $150 or $200.

Moreover, there was considerable precedent for accepting fees and honorariums, as Dies pointed out. President Roosevelt had received $35,000 for three articles written for a magazine. The President, members of the Cabinet, high government officials—and even Mrs. Roosevelt—had received fees for writing and lecturing. Mrs. Roosevelt had been "paid as much as $1,500 for one lecture." Members of Congress had long "supplemented their salaries in this manner," and Dies said he had never "condemned" them for it because on his travels he had "seen the derelicts of public service, men . . . who for many years devoted their energy and ability to the service of our country . . . retired to private life without any business or income, and in great poverty." But in order that there could be no question concerning the use he made of the net proceeds derived from writing and speaking in connection with the investigation, he had published a statement promising that none of these proceeds would be used by him for his own personal benefit. "While there would be nothing illegal" about using such funds for his own "personal use and benefit," it would, he feared, "tend to cheapen the great cause and cast a cloud upon the motives" which prompted his utterances and activities. Therefore, he had decided that he would consult with leaders of patriotic groups to determine how most effectively to use this money "in order to promote Americanism in this country." He would "carry out this promise to the letter," after, of course, deducting "all legitimate expenses" incurred in connection with his activities.

Dies said that he had received 2,800 invitations to speak and that these invitations had come from every section of the country. These numerous requests showed that the people wanted to learn the truth. It would bring him "a deep sense of personal relief" if the investigation were terminated by the Congress, owing to the great stress and tension resulting from the efforts of some people to "trap" and "discredit" the investigation. The committee had said to the country that it would not "become partisan" or " 'crook the pregnant hinges of the knee where thrift may follow fawning.' " The committee, getting off to an early start, had got a supply of information about "enemies within" such as no country had ever possessed. Despite having said earlier in his speech that termination of the investigation would bring him "a deep sense of personal relief," Dies at this point thanked Congress for having had the "courage and patriotism" to continue the investigation, in spite of the fact that it had been "denounced, misrepresented, and maligned by 'fifth columnists' and their dupes, and by those who have misunderstood this question and the seriousness of it." And, said Dies, speaking with a sense of assurance and finality as to both facts and interpretation which has usually been denied historical scholars even a century after such events:

I plead with this Congress and with the President, let us not make the mistake that was made in France when the People's Front, initiated by and controlled from Moscow, undermined the national unity of France, drained her resources, and left the country relatively defenceless before the blitzkrieg of Hitler's invading horde. It was the People's Front, composed of radicals of every shade and description, and led by militant and aggressive Communists, which promoted continual strikes, sit-downs, and slow-downs and prevented the French industries from competing with the Nazi industrial system. It was the People's Front, which included professional reformers and misguided idealists and aided by Nazis and Fascists which was in large measure contributory to the undoing of France.

Explaining that since Hitler and Stalin had entered into their "unholy alliance" the Nazis and Communists in the United States had been "in active collaboration and co-operation," Dies went on:

I can see no distinction between brands of totalitarianism. To my mind all of them are based upon the materialistic concept of life and upon an ideology that preaches exaltation of the state at the expense of the individual. Any ideology that would deprive you and me of the right to live free, to worship our God in accordance with the dictates of our consciences, any ideology that is predicated upon the atheistic philosophy that the state must be everything and the individual nothing, whether it masquerades under the name of communism, nazi-ism, or fascism, is un-American and is diametrically opposed to all our country stands for. [Applause]

Dies insisted that his committee had "done more to resist, to oppose, and to abate racial and religious prejudice and hatred" than any committee ever established by Congress. He and the President had not "always seen things eye to eye," and, said Dies, "I do not say that I am always right." Dies felt, however, that recently the President had somewhat changed his attitude and "realized some things" which he had not realized before. Dies wanted to drive foreign agents out of defense industries; if he had his way, he would not "sit idly by" hoping that he might "detect some of them in the commission of an offense" before any action was taken against them. Ninety per cent of the members of both the German-American Bund and the Communist party were born in foreign lands, said Dies, and he suggested that Mr. Dickstein would do well to quit criticizing the Dies committee and begin strengthening the immigration and deportation laws. There was no foundation to Dickstein's charge that 110 organizations had the key to the back door of the Dies committee; this was shown by the bitterness with which these organizations attacked the committee in their publications.[70]

After Dies concluded his speech, Dickstein's speech was expunged from the record, and the resolution extending the life of the Dies committee was adopted by a vote of 354 to 6, with 71 not voting, and 34 pairs announced. Immediately thereafter a resolution was introduced providing $150,000 for the investigation, bringing the total sum available for the investigation before April, 1942, up to $409,302.42, or "more money than ever heretofore appropriated by the House for the use of a special committee."[71] Later that same day Representative Hook, warning that it was "not yet treason to reason," reverted to the forged documents which he had attempted to put into the *Congressional Record*. Hook emphasized that Mayne, who prepared these forged documents, had been on the payroll of the Dies committee at the time and was kept on the payroll after he had forged them. Representative Voorhis denied the latter part of this assertion.[72]

The next day Representative Eliot of Massachusetts warned that while the Dies committee dealt with foreign agents in an effort to combat disunity in the United States, it had itself become a source of disunity by casting "scorn and obloquy" upon those "patriotic Americans whose political opinions" differed from its own. Dies had failed to hold regular committee meetings and had often acted without any meeting, discussion, or vote on the part of his committee. Consequently, the good the committee might do was "more than outweighed by the damage, both to genuine law enforcement and to American unity, that can result from an unconsidered course of action. [Applause]"[73] On February 25, 1941, Representative Dickstein, returning to battle, asserted that he was the father of the fight on un-American activities and declared that on April 8, 1937, he had introduced a resolution to implement that purpose. The Dies resolution, when later introduced in Congress, was "in the identical language in which the Dickstein resolution was phrased." Mr. Dies was made chairman of a committee brought into being by a resolution which Mr. Dickstein had first introduced in the House of Representatives. Dickstein reiterated that his criticism of the Dies committee was based solely on the ground that its investigations had not been sufficiently comprehensive.[74]

DIES WARNS THE PRESIDENT

A month later Dies told the House his committee had "indisputable proof that the agents of the totalitarian powers [were] busily engaged in a vast conspiracy against the security of the American people." The Communist party was "diametrically opposed" to our policy of national defense and aid to Britain. The most important issue before the American people was whether we were going to "flounder in the incredible folly which destroyed France" by permitting the agents of Stalin and Hitler to occupy important positions in our defense industries and thus to cripple our national defense efforts. These enemies within the gates could and should be convicted under existing laws.[75] In this speech, and in several thereafter, Dies listed individuals and organizations which he charged were active in Communist sabotage against America's war effort.[76] Dies noted the extent to which Communists had infiltrated the steel industry "for the sole purpose of obstructing" our national defense efforts. He said it was a reflection on the Steel Workers Organizing Committee that it allowed so many known Communists to get on its payroll as organizers.[77] Dies declared that the National Maritime Union was "a completely dominated Communist organization,"[78] and indicated a similar situation in other unions.[79]

In August, 1941, Mr. Dies, speaking to the House on selective service extension, predicted great sacrifices ahead for America. At the ballot box the American people had decided to enter world affairs; they had committed this country to aid the democracies "in every possible way short of war." Such a program would involve tremendous sacrifice by every group in America; the defense program was "no glorified W.P.A. project." It would involve taxes up to 50 per cent of our incomes. It was "cowardly" to preach all-out defense and at the same time encourage labor to believe that it could have high wages, low prices, and low taxes. This was the disastrous error which, under the Popular Front in France, had led to the collapse of the republic. "Cowardice" and "cheap demagoguery" had "betrayed" France during a period when she should have been preparing for battle, said Dies. He continued: "The popular front, initiated by and controlled from Moscow, composed of radicals and professional reformers of every shade and description, and led by Moscow, the country that we now propose to make our partner in the great task of defending democracy, undermined the national unity of France." Dies declared that he did not want the American people to "make the great mistake of opposing totalitarianism in Europe and embracing it in America." [80]

Extended military service for draftees, like higher taxes for civilians, will be hard on those immediately affected, said Dies, but "all of us will be compelled to sacrifice to preserve our democracy." In such a period Congress should prevent inflation by increasing taxes and reducing non-defense expenditures. And, said Dies, "if we believe in defense, and are going to prepare this country for defense, then the first step is for the President to stop dodging [the issue of men in high office "whose allegiance is to a foreign power"], and get rid of the Communists and Fascists and Nazis." When President Roosevelt did this, Dies said, he would "have more confidence in the safety of the country." [81] On September 25, 1941, Congressman Leland M. Ford of California suggested that Congress not pay the salaries of federal employees whom the Dies committee considered subversive.[82] The same day Representative Mason of Illinois, a member of the Dies committee, gave instances in which "the Dies committee told you so." He pointed out that in spite of the fact that the Dies committee had clearly shown the Amtorg Trading Corporation was "Communist controlled," the President of the United States had recently ordered that $50,000,000 of credit be advanced to it to purchase supplies for Russia. Mason warned "that one of these days the policy of collaboration with the totalitarian tyrant of Moscow is going to be revealed as one of the tragic mistakes of this era." [83]

If the President of the United States has not seen the light, it has been through no unwillingness on the part of Martin Dies to provide him with unsolicited counsel and advice. For example, on October 1, 1941, Dies wrote President Franklin D. Roosevelt a letter setting him right on the subject of freedom of religious worship in Russia. Dies did not want the truth about communism in any way obscured; he was determined "at whatever cost...to let the American people know that the similarities between Stalin and Hitler are far more striking than their differences." President Roosevelt in a press conference called attention to Article 124 of the Soviet Constitution, which guaranteed freedom of religious worship to the people of Russia. "In the name of tens of thousands of voiceless Christian martyrs who have been murdered by the Soviets," Martin Dies wrote to President Roosevelt, "I rise to protest against any effort in any quarter to dress the Soviet wolf in the sheep's clothing of the four freedoms." Dies explained to President Roosevelt that "the very essence of Communist strategy is double-dealing," and he pleaded, "Believe me, Mr. President, we have not seen the end of Soviet and Communist double-dealing. The ever zig-zagging line of the party will zig-zag again."

Dies explained that the Soviet constitution was a "device for hood-winking foreign liberals into Stalin's camp." Religious freedom was "nonexistent" in Soviet Russia. Stalin himself had said, "The party cannot be neutral toward religion, because all religion is something opposite to science." Religion could not survive the triumph of either communism or nazism. "The truths which Americans hold most dear," wrote Dies, "are in as much danger from Communism as they are from nazi-ism." Dies asked Mr. Roosevelt to "clarify the situation with respect to Stalin and the four freedoms by making it unmistakably clear that the Soviet regime is utterly repugnant to the American people." [84]

On November 19, 1941, Dies read into the record a letter which he had written to James Lawrence Fly, chairman of the

Federal Communications Commission, protesting the appointment of Goodwin Watson as chief broadcast analyst at a salary of $5,600. He declared that Watson was "a propagandist for communism and the Soviet Union." With his "frequent eulogies on the Soviet way of life," Watson had customarily coupled "emphatic disparagement of the American way of life." Moreover, he had been active in many "Communist-front" organizations which Dies listed.[85] On November 25, Dies objected to the employment of Robert A. Brady and others in the Office of Price Administration because of their "long records of affiliation with Communist organizations" and because their writings showed that they "were opposed to the American system of democratic free enterprise." Dies said that he had called this information to the President's attention three months before.

Dies was concerned because he realized that price control involved "a temporary suspension of at least a part of our system of free enterprise." Whether, when the war was over, we would "return to the system of free enterprise with which our system of democratic government is inseparably linked depends in large part upon the character of the persons who administer ... such measures" as price control. Such measures should not be administered by "declared enemies of the system of free enterprise" like Robert A. Brady, head consultant of O.P.A. at a salary of $7,500, who as late as 1937, "and not in the period of the collapse of 1929," had expressed "simon-pure Communist doctrine with respect to our system of free enterprise." An "unwise bill" might be successfully administered, said Dies, by "wise and patriotic men," but a wise bill, put in the hands of "crackpots" or "men who do not believe in our system of free enterprise and are seeking to use their opportunities to revolutionize that system, will result in failure," he added.[86]

When Leon Henderson failed to fire Brady and others designated by Dies, Dies asserted that he was "sick and tired of the arrogance of the bureaucrats that have infested this Government," and would vote to recommit the price control bill because he refused "to put into the hands of the enemies of this country vast powers to strangle our whole economic and political system." So much impressed were certain congressmen with Mr. Dies' position in this matter that they rose to "Thank God for the gentleman from Texas [Mr. Dies]." "God bless him," cried Representative Rich of Pennsylvania.[87]

Dies made an omnibus speech in Congress shortly thereafter, discussing a number of topics more or less at random. He opposed passing any price-fixing bill until Congress received "definite assurances" that those who would be "charged with the administration of the act shall be loyal, patriotic Americans who believe in our system of free enterprise and who will seek to preserve it." Our enemy Germany is "a planned or regimented economy"; "American democracy is based on free enterprise." His vote to recommit the bill was, he said, "a protest against the coddling of totalitarians in the United States." He complained that his pleas to the executive department of the government had been "spurned and ignored." He had decided to plead no longer. Consequently he listed, for Congress, information with which he had provided the executive department of the Government indicating the subversive character of certain federal employees.

Particularly annoying to Dies were the circumstances under which he had been called to Washington from his home in Orange, Texas, by the President. After leaving for Washington with his family and completing "a long and tedious trip," Dies came to the White House to keep an appointment with the Chief Executive at twelve o'clock, only to be kept there for forty-five minutes "cooling [my] heels" while Gardner Jackson, a man "who has one of the longest records of activity in Communist-front organizations of any man in the country; the man who admitted he had put up the money to buy the letters that attempted to link [Dies] with William Dudley Pelley," was in conference with the President. Then, when Gardner Jackson had left, and Dies, "after I had sat there for 45 minutes," entered the Chief Executive's private office, "there, sitting across the table was a court reporter to take down the conversation of the President of my country and myself, after I had worked for three years—hard, difficult, and discouraging work—in the interest of the American Government."

217

In spite of all the evidence which Dies had presented against Gardner Jackson, in spite of "what Gardner Jackson had attempted to do to me," that man Jackson was still employed as principal economist in the Department of Agriculture at a salary of $5,600 per year. In thousands of other cases no action had been taken against men who had been designated as subversive by Dies and his committee. Dies could not see how we could hope to "defeat the enemies abroad" until we were "prepared to defeat the enemy within our own country."

Dies read a letter from Goodwin Watson and others relative to Earl Browder's prison sentence. In this letter Goodwin Watson and others expressed agreement with a statement by Wendell Willkie that "if you truly believe in the protection of civil liberties, you will wonder whether Mr. Browder was sentenced to four years in jail and a $2,000 fine because he made a false statement on a passport application, or because he was a Communist Party member." [88] (Dies did not say whether he considered Willkie an "enemy within," but it was clear that he classified Goodwin Watson under that heading.)

DIES AND LABOR

Discussing labor legislation on December 2, 1941, five days before Pearl Harbor, Dies said "the beginning of the C.I.O. was marked by a coalition of communism and criminality." Dies did not assign crime or communism to "the millions of men and women who work and who alone are entitled to be dignified by the term 'labor,' whether they belong to one union or another or to none." And he did not want labor "curbed in the interests of national defense." Quite the contrary! He wanted labor emancipated from the "shackles" imposed upon it by "Communists and criminals." John L. Lewis was "in part at least, the creature of the very Government which he had recently defied"; he "and his mobs" had grown "powerful and defiant" because the government had "let [them] alone in their lawlessness and violence" during the period of the sit-down strikes. The silence of officials and their tolerance of the sit-down strikes had actually encouraged the "arrogance" of John L. Lewis. Dies prayed that the day might soon come when a clear distinction would be drawn "between labor's gains on the one hand and the irresponsible power of labor bosses on the other hand."

Communists in the C.I.O. "were in the forefront of the sit-down-strike movement and they... remained in positions of leadership in many of the C.I.O. unions." This leadership "victimized" American working men and women. Not only were there thousands of C.I.O. leaders who were Communists, but "time and time again [the Dies committee] discovered that C.I.O. leaders had both Communist and criminal records." Dies listed the crimes of which some twenty of these C.I.O. leaders had been convicted.

Dies saw "an inexorable logic" in the "coalition between communism and criminality." Criminals "saw Government yield disgracefully before the revolutionary lawlessness of the sit-down strike. They figured that there was at least one racket beyond the law and that they had only to masquerade as labor leaders in order to ply their old trades. The result has been that hundreds of men have stepped out of prisons into union jobs. The records speak the ugly, naked truth of the matter." When the Communists were driven from cover they cried "red baiter"; when the labor "criminals and racketeers" were exposed, they cried "labor baiter." But Martin Dies would "refuse to be intimidated either by the Communists or the criminals, either by the radicals or the racketeers." He was voting, he repeated, "not to curb labor but to aid in its emancipation, not to force labor into any form of totalitarian slavery—whether it be Hitler's brand or that of John L. Lewis—but to aid in driving both the Communist and the criminal from the labor scene." [89]

The following day Representative Bradley of Pennsylvania pointed out that it was no fairer to convict the entire labor movement because twenty of its leaders had been convicted of crime "at some time in their careers" than "to tear down our governmental institutions because many men in public life have been guilty of far greater offenses than these individuals to whom he refers." To this, Dies replied that he was prepared to give the House the records of 1,000 labor leaders. [90] Dies

219

proposed legislation to take away labor organization status from any labor union which "knowingly or negligently" permitted members of certain subversive groups, or ex-criminals, to hold appointive or elective offices in them. Dies said that, four years before, he had urged John L. Lewis "to get rid of the Communist element in his unions." Not only had no action been taken by Lewis in response to Dies' counsel, but "from that moment" C.I.O. leaders had "consistently condemned me [Dies] throughout the United States."

Marcantonio of New York fought the Dies proposal on the ground that it was not only an attack on "the fundamental rights of labor" but was "aimed at the constitutional rights of American citizens." Dies' proposal followed the pattern of fascism and nazism. "Anti-labor laws have always been imposed on people behind an anti-Communist smoke screen," said Marcantonio, asserting that he could mention criminals on the payroll of the Dies committee.[91]

On December 19, 1941, Dies argued in Congress for specific mention of such organizations as the Communist party and the German-American Bund in a bill requiring members of foreign-controlled groups to register, on the ground that unless they were specifically mentioned the Department of Justice would not compel them to register. Dies also wanted these groups compelled to file information concerning their membership, officers, and directors. He declared that the specific mention of such groups in legislation requiring alien registration was in no sense a bill of attainder, but merely an effort to protect this country from the "fifth column." [92]

10 DIES IN RETREAT

IT is not to embarrass but to aid the administration that I
speak," said Dies, somewhat reassuringly, when, on January 15, 1942, he embarked on his first major address to the
House in the second session of the 77th Congress. This was the
first address in which he took cognizance of the Japanese attack
at Pearl Harbor. This attack, said Dies, showed that he had
said too little, rather than too much, and that the American
people had heard too little, rather than too much, about the
menace of the "fifth column" as an instrument of conquest employed by totalitarian dictators. A great deal still remained to
be done "in defense against our internal enemies." Not only
had the Nazi fifth column been well organized and financed in
the United States. Not only had it disseminated much propaganda. But, we should be on our guard against another enemy!

"The very fact that we are at war with the Axis Powers probably means that our alertness is better organized against the
Nazi fifth column than it is against the Communist fifth column." The fact that the Russians were making a "heroic" fight
against the Nazi hordes should not cause us to close our eyes
"to the nature and ultimate aims of the Communist Party in
the United States." On the contrary, "closing our eyes" would
be "wholly devoid of logic." Even if Russia completely anni-
hilated the German armies, that "would not make communism
one iota more compatible with the American way of life."

Although we had undertaken to work with other nations to
destroy Hitlerism, it was "no part of that enterprise that we
embrace communism. Neither is it any part of that enterprise
that we permit Communists to entrench themselves more

221

deeply in our life and institutions." We could "welcome unreservedly" the "assistance" of the Russian armies in beating the Germans, but that had "nothing whatever to do with our firm conviction that the spread of communism to new territories would be in the nature of unmitigated tragedy." We "condemn" communism just "as much in 1942 as we did in 1938." Stalin was fighting Hitler, said Dies, not because Stalin believed in democracy but because Hitler had invaded Russia. We, too, want to destroy Hitler, but "for reasons which are strictly our own, and not Stalin's." Hitler's destruction is "the one and only point on which the interests of the Soviet Union and the interests of the United States converge." We must be on our guard lest the communists in America try to use the present international situation to lay the foundations for a future Soviet America.

The Civil Service Commission, in recommending the dismissal of Mr. and Mrs. Robert A. Brady from their positions in governmental service, had acted "courageously," said Dies, and had "given the American people new grounds for confidence in our Government." Many other persons, however, "of provable connections with un-American activities" still held their positions on the federal payroll. Among these was Harold Loeb, who, with Leon Henderson, had at one time been connected with the technocracy movement. Dies found that Loeb, although holding a job as senior business specialist in the O.P.A., had gained no distinction in the field of business, but had written books—novels which were somewhat "pornographic"— books on technocracy which were "emphatically to the crackpot side." Dies referred to Howard Scott, head of the technocracy movement, as "a charlatan and a crackpot."[1] A week later Leon Henderson denied that he had been connected with Howard Scott in the technocracy movement, whereupon, Dies virtually called Henderson a liar by reaffirming his charges.[2]

Dies' legislative amendment "requiring the Communist Party to register and give the names of officers and members" was taken out of the registration bill by House and Senate conferees. Inasmuch as his committee had "conclusively shown" that the Communist party in the United States was controlled by the Communist International, Dies insisted that the Communist party should be compelled to disclose the names of its members. There were some who thought that such a requirement might "antagonize the Soviet Union and, to some extent, embarrass our war efforts." Dies wanted to know if the time had come when we no longer dared to legislate in domestic matters "because someone fears that our action may displease a foreign dictator." [3]

Out of the four-year investigation by the Dies committee, said its chairman, "there ... emerged one fact the importance of which probably exceeds that of all others—the Communist Party is an agency for the planning and perpetuation of misdemeanors and high crimes." Lenin had said, "Revolutionaries who are unable to combine illegal forms of struggle with every form of legal struggle are very poor revolutionaries." Consequently, the Communist party in the United States is "a foreign conspiracy masked as a political party," its members are "foreign conspirators who cannot honorably or safely serve the American Government." Stalin certainly would not permit an American organization to promote Americanism on Russian soil, nor would he permit Russians who believed in Americanism to occupy important positions in Russian government, labor, or defense industry.

"A fear of displeasing foreign powers and a maudlin attitude toward fifth columnists was largely responsible for the unparalleled tragedy of Pearl Harbor," Dies asserted. If his committee had been "permitted to reveal the facts ... on Japanese espionage and sabotage" in September, 1941, "the tragedy of Pearl Harbor might have been averted." Although the information had been turned over to high officials in Washington their attitude had been one of such indifference that appropriate action had not been taken.

Dies was convinced that if his committee had proceeded with its hearings on the Japanese situation in September, 1941, undeterred by a letter from the State Department advising him that the President, the State Department, and the Department of Justice were opposed to such hearings, "the Pearl Harbor tragedy never would have occurred." (This is an important statement. Reference was frequently made to it in House discussion thereafter.) But Dies, in his "anxiety to cooperate with the administration and not to do anything to embarrass it, . . . yielded." Events had shown that the Administration was "wrong" and Dies would have been "right" if he had gone ahead with the exposure. That was why Dies was now so determined not to "weaken" in the exposé of fifth columnists who occupied "key positions" in government, defense industries, and labor organizations. If he weakened, and another tragedy occurred, "I would blame myself," said Dies. He hoped that the indifference of the executive department to the fifth column in America might change to one of aggressive action "while there is still time."

In his struggle to recommit the bill, in which the Senate and House conferees had failed to specifically mention certain groups as foreign-controlled and, therefore, required to register, Dies was unsuccessful. The vote against him was 228 to 40. This vote came only after Dies had been denied time for further debate to which he deemed himself entitled. No doubt a contributing factor in the defeat of Dies' proposal was a speech by Sumners of Texas emphasizing that this was "no time for child's play . . . [and] no time to play to the galleries." If we were "seeking to kick Russia," which happens to be "doing the best fighting of anybody in our crowd just now," it would be "good sense" to sustain the Dies proposal; but this was not the time to bring up that issue.[4] Within six weeks thereafter Dies admitted that although he still held the same opinions as before, he believed that "under all the circumstances . . . the House and Mr. Hatton W. Sumners were wiser than I was to this extent: that I believe that while it is absolutely essential for this committee to investigate and expose communism, I agree with the great majority of this House that there is no occasion, regardless of the facts, to risk antagonizing any other foreign country that happens to be allied with us at the present time."[5]

On January 26, 1942, Dies introduced a resolution for the continuation of his committee.[6] Discussing the committee on February 18, 1942, Eliot of Massachusetts objected to the "irresponsible" manner in which the committee had acted. Eliot said that he had objected to this a year before; but now that "the national danger [was] far greater," it was doubly desirable for Congress "to repudiate [the] committee's way of doing things." It was "heedless folly" to permit the Dies committee to divide the Nation and play into the hands of the enemy any longer. President Roosevelt at a recent press conference had referred to a "Cliveden set" in Washington which Congressman Eliot said was seemingly "more interested in creating conflict between us and Russia than in beating the Axis." And that was precisely what Martin Dies was doing, in "raking up old hatreds and implying that our most dangerous enemy today, our most sinister fifth column, is Russian and not German or Japanese." Eliot called the attention of Congress to a letter from the Chairman of the Federal Communications Commission, indicating that Dies had been "frequently and favorably quoted" by Axis propagandists broadcasting to the Western Hemisphere.[7]

Eliot alleged that the word "subversive," as defined by Dies, was "so fantastic as to defy belief." The Dies committee, he said, had, for example, named a man "subversive" because he favored legislation endorsed by Warden Lawes, by several members of the House of Representatives, and even by a member of the Dies committee itself. Another man had been called "subversive" because his father had been a member of a Council Against Intolerance, which included such "sinister, dangerous revolutionaries" as Thomas E. Dewey, Alfred E. Smith, Senator Carter Glass, and the Reverend Maurice E. Sheehy, head of the Department of Religious Education at the Catholic University of America. While we were "in a deadly war with dangerous enemies," the Dies committee was sending Federal investigators on "fools' errands." Representative Eliot continued:

George Saunders, of the Office of Civilian Defense, ... is on the [Dies] blacklist. The committee's file says that he is a Communist living in Pittsburgh. Actually the George Saunders in the Office of Civilian Defense lives in San Francisco where he was active in the Junior Chamber of Commerce. His former professor, Senator Elbert Thomas of Utah, tells me he is a Roman Catholic. But our eagle-eyed committee tells the F.B.I. to track him down just the same.

And while they demand the scalp of this Catholic layman and call him Red, do you know what is happening only a hundred miles away? George Deatherage, the frank American Fascist who used to head up the Knights of the White Camelia and who planned a Fascist coup to seize the Government, is executive engineer at an immense naval construction project right down here at Norfolk. But our alert Dies committee did not know about that; they were too busy worrying about [a certain] Mary Johnson, [whom the Dies committee alleges once drew a cartoon for the *Daily Worker,* and whom they now claim is a Federal employee; but who turns out actually not to be the same Mary Johnson at all], and that revolutionary organization headed by Al Smith and Governor Saltonstall and Father Sheehy.

As a matter of fact, the Dies committee has never done much about the Fascist front organizations. The chairman has said a lot about them, but the record is largely one of words, not action.... The committee's record on Fascist organizations is a sorry one of big promises and little or no performance.

Representative Eliot, then, listed a score of absurd charges which the Dies committee had made against individuals, charges which, if they were universalized, would prove "Mr. Wendell Willkie is some kind of a 'pink,' " and make it "un-American" to oppose the Dies committee. Eliot pointed to the "amazing and smug self-righteousness" of the committee, and declared that the committee had become "a dangerous and expensive luxury." The Dies committee had a record, said Eliot, of "high-handed hearings, high-sounding promises, very little accomplishment, and endless, ridiculous, unforgiveable smearing of decent and loyal Americans." Dies had cried "Wolf!" too heedlessly to be longer "trusted to guard Americanism." In a period when there was great need for national solidarity Dies had attacked President Roosevelt's policies and had made "false charges" against men who were trusted by the President and by the country as well. Although it might seem "politically safe" to continue the Dies committee, it would not be actually safe for the United States to perpetuate "a committee which is only a source of futile confusion, suspicion, absurdity, doubt, and hatred." The committee should be disbanded.[8]

In reply Congressman Hoffman of Michigan asserted that while the New Deal administration has been "trying to destroy our constitutional form of government," the Dies committee has been "trying to get rid of the Reds and the Communists." Meanwhile, "the President's wife has been taking them in; taking them to lunch, feeding them, and sleeping them." We should watch Russia, to see that Russia does not "stick a knife in our backs" or trip us. It does not matter much to "the common people" of America, said Hoffman, "whether Hitler gets us and skins us from the top down, or whether our ally, Joe Stalin, gets us and skins us from the heels up. We do not want to be taken over by either." There were "too many . . . folks down . . . in the executive department" who did "not even have good intentions. Some of them apparently wish to follow the party line," said Hoffman.[9]

On March 4, 1942, Martin Dies rose in the House to a question of "personal privilege." The Washington *Star* and other newspapers had reported, he said, that Representative Eliot of Massachusetts had hurled a direct "lie" charge at Dies over his assertion that the Administration had prevented him from exposing Japanese fifth column activities prior to Pearl Harbor. Representative Eliot thereupon said that he had not used the word "lie" but had simply said that he had received a letter from the Attorney General saying that no effort had been made to prevent the Dies committee from revealing facts about the Japanese in September, 1941. In response Dies said he rose less in his "own personal defense" than "in defense of the dignity of the House of Representatives," and it would be "a great blow to the cause of democracy" if "the confidence of the American people in the legislative body is undermined by slander and misrepresentation." In consequence of his eleven years as a member of the House, he knew that there was "no more patriotic" group of men and women in America. Although he might "differ with gentlemen in this House on political matters," no difference could "justify me in impugning their motives, or warrant me to give expression to thoughts or views that would bring in question their honesty and their patriotism."

Then Dies read a letter supporting his earlier assertion that the Attorney General had advised him, in September, 1941, that the President and the Secretary of State both felt "quite strongly" that hearings on Japanese activities in the United States would be "inadvisable," and that he, the Attorney General, was of the same opinion. Dies also read correspondence with Secretary of the Navy Frank Knox concerning the employment of George E. Deatherage at the naval operating base at Norfolk, Virginia, indicating that this correspondence had led to Deatherage's discharge from such employment one week after Eliot had mentioned the matter in Congress. Dies recognized that his committee had made mistakes. His objection to Eliot's criticism was that it was "not constructive."

McGranery of Pennsylvania interrupted to bring out that Dies had been in error when he had declared that the evidence on Japanese fifth column activities had "been turned over to the Justice Department" by the Dies committee prior to Pearl Harbor. Dies now admitted that he had been in error in that particular, and that this had not been done. Consequently, McGranery declared, Dies in his appeal to personal privilege was only "shadow boxing," because there was actually no point at issue between him and Eliot.

Representative Colmer wanted to know why Eliot had permitted a week to go by without explaining, retracting, or apologizing for the statement in the press that he had called Dies "a liar." Eliot asserted that a week had not elapsed; moreover, he declared he "did not know such thin skins were possessed." Dies insisted that calling a member of the House "a liar" was "no small matter." Dies continued as follows, addressing Representative Eliot:

If the gentleman serves in this body long enough—I have known the Members of this House many years. My father had his office in that corner over there for a decade during one of the most difficult periods in the history of this Republic, and I have seen press reporters, not a majority, but some of them, deliberately distort the facts and do all in their power to undermine the confidence of the American people in this body. Let me say to the gentleman that whether he serves here a long time or a short time, the first thing is to learn to love and respect the Members of this House.

After giving this fatherly advice to Eliot, Dies declared that those who were opposed to his committee were "for the most part" representatives of organizations which his committee had exposed. Then, considering the charge that the Dies committee had devoted itself primarily to exposing communism, not nazism and fascism, he undertook to answer "here and now, and for all time" this "cleverly disseminated" propaganda against his committee. He recalled how "the wife of the Chief Executive appeared with the witnesses, sincerely and honestly believing in her idealism that [the American Youth Congress] was a bona fide organization, and she believed that the Dies committee was the instrumentality of the reactionary forces of this country; and she permitted those witnesses to be her guests at the White House during the time the investigation took place." But "finally" Mrs. Roosevelt "discovered the truth" and "publicly admitted that she had been deceived."

Yes, there were people who had had "the audacity to stand before the American people and say that Martin Dies is a Fascist sympathizer," said Dies, but what were the facts? His committee had heard 129 witnesses on fascism and nazism and had approximately 3,000 printed pages of testimony on the subject. The reports issued by the committee on Nazi activities were as large as the reports on Communist activities. No honest member of the House of Representatives, said Dies, would say that his committee had been derelict in its investigation of fascism, if he would only study the hearings and reports of the committee. If Eliot had in mind any organization which he thought the Dies committee should investigate, "I would be glad for him to tell this House. I pause for him to tell this House," said Dies.

At this point Coffee of Washington asked Dies to yield him the floor. Dies thereupon acknowledged Coffee to be "an honest critic, but a gentleman with it all." To this Coffee remarked, "The gentleman takes all the steam out of a man." To this, Dies said he did "not mean to do that," and told Coffee to "Go right ahead." Coffee then remarked that he was "so fond of the gentleman from Texas" that he hesitated to ask him a simple question, but he knew that Dies would have "a very logical answer" and that all would be enlightened by Dies' reply. Coffee wanted to know why Father Coughlin's organization had not been investigated. "The answer to that," said Dies, "is that Father Coughlin's organization has been investigated." Dies wanted to give the House "the facts"; he was "ready to answer any questions at any time." Why had Father Coughlin not been brought to Washington? Why had he and Gerald Winrod not been subjected to questioning? The committee had gathered "all of the evidence that we could possibly secure" but had not brought priests or preachers to Washington for fear that they might refuse to testify, in which case, if they were "held in contempt, ... from all over the country there would have arisen an outcry denouncing us as being against certain religions." The committee had been "wise" not to call these people to Washington but, instead, to gather evidence on them in other ways. This the committee had done.

Dies said there had been an effort by the Axis to "smear" the President "personally," not just to "attack his policies, for that is the right of every citizen." Of course, there was nothing wrong with criticizing the President's policies. "In fact," said Mr. Dies, "I am one of those who believes that the greatest service that can be rendered to the President is to give him the benefit of honest, constructive criticism." When the time came that members of the House were "not permitted, in a spirit of honesty and fair dealing and common love of our country, to stand on the floor and, with respect and dignity, urge that certain things are wrong in the executive department," the House of Representatives would have "lost its dignity and its great independence" and might as well "quit and go home." But it was not this kind of criticism which Dies had in mind—it was

Axis propaganda "designed to undermine the confidence of the people in the integrity of the Chief Executive."

Dispassionately viewing the work of his committee, Dies found that it had "performed a wonderful service" because it had "been able to seize records and to compel people to testify, while other agencies of the Government have been unable to do that." It would certainly be "no personal favor" to any member of the Dies committee if the House continued the committee. It was most difficult to deal with an "explosive subject" of this type. Obviously, it was much easier to criticize the committee than to do the things which were recommended to it by its critics. Never in the history of the country had there been greater need for "sincerity, honesty, and zeal in the discharge of public duty" than at this time of "great crisis." Dies concluded with an appeal that "whatever may come, whatever the provocation may be, let each of us have a spirit of tolerance and good will toward the rest of us." And as if overwhelmed with emotion, he added, "Even though—even though—we disagree with one another let us be patient and tolerant and let us continue to be friends fighting in a common cause for the greatest Republic that ever existed in all the annals of history." Here the gavel fell! [10]

Two days later Representative Eliot was back on the floor stating reasons why, in his judgment, the Dies committee should be discontinued. He insisted that Dies' exposé of Japanese plans against the United States consisted of quotations "taken in toto from publications ... months and years old [and] lifted without benefit of quotation marks"; that the "secret Japanese naval map" published by the committee had appeared in a Japanese magazine of wide circulation in January, 1935. While Eliot wished to continue, his remarks were terminated at this point by adjournment of the House.[11] Although Eliot had had little success in gaining the floor of the House, he inserted, from time to time, certain documents in the Appendix to the *Congressional Record*. On February 12, 1942, he inserted a letter from James Lawrence Fly, chairman of the Federal Communications Commission, showing that Dies had been "quoted with approval many times by the Axis." [12] Again, Eliot produced a chart modeled on one published earlier by the Dies committee, in which he showed that if a person became "subversive" merely by belonging to organizations which were dubbed "Communist-front organizations" by the Dies committee, it was possible to prove that Chief Justice Charles Evans Hughes, Justices Jackson and Black, Secretaries Knox, Stimson and Ickes, Vice President Wallace, Senator Carter Glass, Governor Thomas E. Dewey, President William Green of the American Federation of Labor, Mayor La Guardia of New York City, Walter Dill Scott of Northwestern University, and dozens of others, were "subversive." [13]

On March 7, 1942, the day after his speech was discontinued by adjournment, Eliot extended his remarks in the record. He said that the committee's report on the Japanese fifth column in America contained nothing new and nothing important. He cited chapter and verse, showing the ancient and irrelevant quality of the materials in the report. Eliot said that, with the same "great difficulty" as Dies committee agents, he had himself gone to the Library of Congress and found there the "sinister" materials which were published in the Dies report as something new, but which had actually been available in the Library of Congress for several years. The administration had not been given Dies' secret information before Pearl Harbor, as Dies had stated at first, but later denied. The administration had not prevented Dies from publishing his report whenever he wished; it had only "discouraged the holding of public hearings." Eliot declared the "headline-hunting [Dies] committee ...a dangerous bull in a china shop." Its report could have been written without cost by consulting the Library of Congress and a few newspaper files, and getting together a few lists which were in no way secret. The Dies committee was indeed a costly "fifth wheel" in fighting the fifth column.

Eliot referred to Dies' "remarkable" speech of two days before in which "the gentleman from Texas announced the forthcoming publication of still another report...designed to show that the Nazis are organizing a smear campaign against President Roosevelt." Obviously, this report would include "a tremendous amount of documentary evidence of...filthy, rotten smear literature" seized by the Dies committee. Its publication would be "the answer to a Nazi prayer," and such would be the case "however patriotic the motives of Mr. Dies may be." Somewhat sarcastically, Eliot exclaimed:

O, Mr. Speaker, I hope and pray that in his enthusiasm, his zeal to defend the President, whom he loves so well, the gentleman from Texas will burn this rotten stuff instead of publishing it. But I have little hope. The gentleman shows his love for the President in such curious ways. Am I wrong in assuming that it is his love for the President that leads him to criticize so freely the President's policies, the President's appointees, and even the President's wife?

Eliot pleaded for discontinuance of the Dies committee because it served Nazi purposes. This was shown by the fact that Dies was so frequently and favorably quoted in Axis broadcasts.[14]

Two days later Eliot inserted in the record editorials from newspapers sharply criticizing the Dies committee. The *St. Louis Post Dispatch* pointed out that Dies had been "operating for a long time . . . by virtue of a statute which authorizes Congress to conduct investigations with a view to the enactment of legislation" without producing any "meritorious suggestion of that nature." The Dies "show" was "little better than a personal racket," and it was time to call a halt. The *York* (Pa.) *Gazette and Daily* took Dies to task for his attack upon the President "in his usual veiled and insinuating manner." Referring to Dies as "vicious," "outrageous," and lacking in decency, it said, "He is either too ignorant to realize the effect of his actions or he is the most insidious influence in this Nation." Martin Dies, continued the editorial, "wittingly or unwittingly . . . has served the cause of the Fascists well" in following "Hitler's anti-Communist line" and in "hitting below the belt" at the President.[15] On March 10, Eliot added six additional editorials criticizing the Dies committee, most of them arguing that the Dies committee imperiled national unity and should be discontinued, at least for the duration of the war.[16]

The discussion of the Dies committee by members of the House of Representatives was more extensive in 1942 than in any previous year. No longer was the limitation of debate on the extension of the committee an effective factor in restricting discussion. Often materials were inserted in the Appendix to the *Congressional Record,* and congressmen often discussed the committee on the floor at times other than that apportioned for debate on that topic. Congressman Sheppard of California introduced a letter from the American Civil Liberties Union criticizing the "unsavory" record of the Dies committee, as well as his reply thereto, indicating the letter contained language which was "personally offensive" to him.[17] Thomas of New Jersey called attention to a letter sent out by the National Federation of Constitutional Liberties urging its members to send telegrams to congressmen and use other pressure tactics in an effort to prevent continuance of the Dies committee. Thomas charged that the officers and sponsors of the National Federation of Constitutional Liberties were Communist-affiliated. He also inserted in the record a press clipping in which Lynn U. Stambaugh, national commander of the American Legion, declared the Dies committee "must" be continued.[18]

Representative Marcantonio of New York joined Representative Eliot in attacking the committee. He inserted in the record a radio speech in which he charged that Dies' statement that the President and State Department had prevented Dies from publishing information which would have prevented Pearl Harbor was untrue. They had "merely [advised] Dies not to hold public hearings." There was a difference between holding "public hearings" and revealing information which would have prevented Pearl Harbor. The Dies committee had not only "failed in its duty" but had become an instrument used by the enemy in its propaganda attacks on the American people.[19] Marcantonio also recorded a letter from Philip Murray, president of the Congress of Industrial Organizations, indicating that the executive board of the C.I.O. opposed continuation of the Dies committee because the committee had created disunity, undermined national morale, and "harassed" labor unions "with the sole known purpose of aiding the enemies of labor." The resolution of the executive board of the Congress of Industrial Organizations read as follows:

RESOLUTION ON CONDEMNATION OF UN-AMERICAN ACTIVITIES OF THE DIES COMMITTEE

Whereas (1) The record of Chairman Dies of the House Committee to Investigate un-American Activities has been one of the [most] sordid and reprehensible in the annals of the American Congress in that the name and the status of a House committee have been used:

(a) To attack and weaken bona fide labor unions when engaged in the life and death struggle with employers and at the very moment when such attack was intended to lend aid and comfort to the employers;

(b) To attack the liberal and progressive policies and administrators of the Federal and State Governments under the guise of red-smearing tactics but with the intent of undermining and destroying such policies for the sake of enhancing the interests of reactionary groups;

(c) To interfere and harass The President of the United States in his conduct of foreign affairs and the establishment of co-operative relations with the Allies of this Nation;

(d) To sow the seeds of disunity and discord among the people of this Nation by creating evil hatred against labor unions, aliens, and other minority groups. Thereby weakening the national unity so earnestly desired by most Americans, which policy, if continued, merely offers aid and comfort to the axis powers; and

(2) Chairman Dies has most carefully refrained from having the House committee really investigate the un-American activities and Axis influences within this country at any time during the history of the committee, except to the extent of announcing such investigations immediately prior to a request for more funds, which, upon the appropriation of the same, the announced investigations are discontinued; now, therefore, be it

Resolved, That the Executive Board of the Congress of Industrial Organizations recommends to the House of Representatives, in the interests of our Nation and in order to achieve the national unity so necessary to the successful prosecution of the war, that if Congress believes it to be necessary to have a continuation of any investigation of un-American activities in this country, or of any activities intended to disrupt or weaken the united war effort, a new committee with responsible and fair-minded leadership be established in lieu of the un-American Dies committee.[20]

Representative Voorhis thought that henceforth the attention of the committee should be focused on groups "working for or friendly to" the Axis. One reason, he said, why the committee had done so little in this field was that it had on its staff no expert who knew fascism and nazism from the inside. Voorhis disliked "a growing tendency to say, in effect, 'So-and-so may not be a Nazi or a Communist, but I do not like his ideas or his point of view: Therefore some punishment should be inflicted upon him.'" It was "not un-American for a man to pioneer new paths for the solution of the problems of his country." Voorhis referred again to the rules of correct procedure which he had long advocated that the Dies committee follow, but which the committee had never adopted. The committee should be aware of the fact that there was a war going on. "The only proper course of action for a committee of this kind now is to throw its effort into the work of assisting in every way it can to help frustrate the designs of the Axis Powers," said Voorhis.[21]

Representative Marcantonio on March 7, 1942, compared many sentences and paragraphs of the Dies report on Japanese activities with a newsletter put out earlier (July 9, 1941) by News Research Service, Inc., and found them identical; the committee had published these statements without acknowledgment. When an effort was made to interrupt this comparison of the texts of the two documents, Marcantonio declared it a "sad reflection" on the House that a member could speak "only ... with permission of members of the Dies committee." Marcantonio declared that this "report of a committee which has cost $385,000 to date" had been "copied" from a newsletter which could have been purchased for a dime. When interrupted by Hoffman of Michigan, Marcantonio said: "The gentleman reminds me of an old steamboat up on the East River that had a 2-inch boiler and a 6-inch whistle. Every time the whistle blew the boat stopped. Every time we mention the Dies committee the gentleman just stops."

Marcantonio's exposé was referred to as a "farce," a "spectacle," and "facetious" by Representative Mason of Illinois; but Marcantonio demanded an investigation of the report and inserted in the record several pages of material indicating the resemblance of the Dies committee report to the newsletter published by News Research Service.[22]

Representative Voorhis defended the right of a member of the House to oppose the Dies committee. It was his opinion that the Dies committee had no information "which could have prevented the Pearl Harbor disaster." He acknowledged that the report to which Marcantonio had taken exception, although prepared by persons in the employ of the committee, had been submitted to the members of the committee and approved by them. He did not know "exactly" who wrote the report, but frankly admitted that the committee's report had been taken in part from the newsletter. Permission had been obtained from the writer of the newsletter to use the material, but the writer preferred not to have his contribution acknowledged; as a result, the committee had made no acknowledgment. Voorhis did not criticize the State Department for having requested the committee not to hold public hearings on the Japanese question at a time when the government was making an effort to avert war with Japan. Moreover, although he felt that some of the material in the hands of the Dies committee before Pearl Harbor was "important," he did "not think any of it was of such a nature as to determine definitely what the Japanese were going to do and when they were going to do it." [23]

Congressman Eliot called attention to a statement by Dies that before we entered the war, Germany had requested that the committee be discontinued. Eliot indicated that the United States Department of State had no evidence of any such protest. Eliot reminded the House again that Dies was "the man ... so frequently and so favorably quoted on the propaganda broadcasts of our deadly enemies." [24]

DEBATE ON COMMITTEE EXTENSION

On March 10, 1942, the Rules Committee of the House presented a resolution to continue the Dies Committee, with the stipulation that the committee report not later than January 3, 1943.[25] The resolution came up in the House on the following day. Originally provision was made for three hours' general debate, but the time was finally cut to one hour, and as usual it was equally divided between the majority and minority. Sabath began the debate by declaring that the country was faced with more important matters than the life of an investigating committee which had been in existence for three years and ten months and had spent $385,000 plus an additional $90,000 for printing. Sabath opposed continuance of the committee on the ground that it had not investigated "the real Fascists and Nazis of this country that are really the greatest danger to our country." He called attention to a suit instituted by Henry Ford against the Ku Klux Klan because it had used Ford's name in anti-Semitic publications. Sabath indicated that the Ku Klux Klan not only favored continuance of the Dies committee but urged that the committee be provided with ample funds.[26]

Representative Sabath said he had "originally helped to create the Dies committee, and in great measure was responsible for the gentleman from Texas being made chairman of that committee." He had done this because Dies had "assured" him that he would investigate "all" subversive activities. Within a short time after the committee got under way, Sabath had urged Dies to investigate Nazi activities "as he [Dies] had promised." Sabath called Dies "capable," "resourceful," and "a splendid publicist," but declared him "misled by shrewd and vicious Nazi-Fascist propagandists." Sabath named numerous organizations and individuals who had not been investigated by Dies but "should have been." He said some members of the House supported Dies "because of his activities against organized labor." Sabath thought "we should desist from attack on" Russia while that country was fighting valiantly to defeat Hitler. He introduced more than forty letters urging discontinuance of the Dies committee.[27]

Representative Mason, a member of the Dies committee, asserted that 129,000,000 out of the 130,000,000 Americans were "friends" of the Dies committee, and that 95 per cent of the membership of the House of Representatives believed the committee's record justified its continuance. Representative Coffee of Washington thought otherwise. He declared that Fritz Kuhn

238

of the German-American Bund, William Pelley of the Silver Shirts, and Deatherage of the Knights of White Camellia, had all "warmly endorsed the Dies committee and . . . urged its continuation." He objected to the "leniency" which Dies had shown toward fascists. Coffee indicated numerous editorials and a list of five hundred leaders of American thought who had asked Congress to disband the Dies committee. He thought the activities of the committee menaced good relations between the U.S.A. and the U.S.S.R. Only two out of nineteen reporters polled by the *New York Daily News* thought the committee hearings "fair"; and Wendell Willkie assailed the committee for using methods which were "undermining the democratic process."

One hundred prominent members of the bar had said:

That the Dies committee, while giving lip service to impartiality and fair play and proclaiming its devotion to Americanism and American institutions, used its hearings, the forum provided by Congress, for the dissemination of irresponsible slanders against honest public servants and private individuals and against public-spirited organizations, on testimony consisting of surmise, conjecture, unfounded opinion, unsupported conclusions, and unwarranted deductions, without any attempt at verifications or confirmation, which no self-respecting, fact-finding agency anywhere would consider—a proceeding wholly unworthy of the committee of the legislative body of a great and free Republic. [Findings from a study made of the Dies committee in 1939 and signed by over 100 attorneys, including Frank P. Walsh of New York City, Prof. Louis L. Jaffe, of Buffalo, Prof. D. James Farage, of Carlisle, Pa., etc.]

Coffee concluded:

Mr. Speaker, I submit that the Dies committee, on the face of the record, has shown itself not to be entitled to continuation. I submit that the committee has demonstrated itself to be the foe of groups the Government is trying to unite in the war effort; the tool of big business; the disrupter of relations with our military Allies; the creator of internal confusion, hub-bub, and disunity; the implacable antagonist of the New Deal; the avoider of fair and judicial committee procedure; the exemplar of marked solicitude in its treatment of American Fascists; the grantor of the committee forum as a platform from which Jew-baiters, crackpots, and totalitarians identified with Fascist organizations spouted their nauseating nostra. These, and many other attributes, omissions, and commissions of the committee, make it, in my judgment, deserving of a quiet and not too well heralded funeral.[28]

Representative Thomas, a committee member, declared the Dies committee was the one agency of government which fought subversive and bureaucratic groups without cease. The committee could have accomplished more if obstacles had not been placed in its way by the executive department. "At no time," said Representative Thomas, "did we get so much as a blessing from the White House." Moreover, the committee had been handicapped by lack of funds. The nation was endangered by Spanish Falangists, he said, who were doing work in America formerly performed by the German-American Bund. Moreover, "the Dies committee," he said, "may turn out to be the last remaining safeguard against the dictatorship of the proletariat in America."

Representative Eliot said that the committee's record was "one of big promises and little or no performance" against fascism; the committee had not touched George Sylvester Viereck.

Mail had been coming in, Eliot said, in the ratio of 1,000 to 1 against the Dies committee, including letters from American Legion posts. Referring to Dies' speech of a week before, in which Dies said that Eliot must learn "to love and respect every Member of the House," and in which Dies had referred to his own father's term in the House, Representative Eliot explained that it took time to become acquainted with "everybody in the House" and mentioned that his own great-grandfather had served in the House ninety years before.[29]

Leland M. Ford of California thought the increased activity of subversive groups made the Dies committee even more necessary than under ordinary circumstances. He praised the Dies committee for "one of the finest jobs that has ever been done by any committee" and concluded:

Mr. Dies, I commend you, I congratulate you and your committee of real, courageous, red-blooded Americans for the splendid work you have done; I am surprised to know that any man in this House would ever come out and take up the other side of this question. I may be prejudiced, but I cannot see anything but the American side on your side of this question.[30]

Representative Weiss, who had favored past resolutions supporting the Dies committee, thought the American people did not now favor a committee which spent its time "blasting" our Russian ally. Weiss thanked God that the Russians were "on our side" in this war "whatever they believe in and stand for." The Dies committee had spent a large sum of money "without one piece of concrete, constructive legislation submitted to Congress." Weiss called attention to the fact that although after Pearl Harbor Martin Dies had claimed, "If the Department of State had permitted us to investigate the Japs, Pearl Harbor would have been averted," Dies had declared a few weeks before Pearl Harbor (October 24, 1941), in a speech which he made in New Orleans to the Association of Commerce, "The Japanese policy was just a bluff—and not too good a bluff at that. A lot of Americans like myself would like to see them bring their coal burners out for a good licking, but they won't."

The vote was 331 yeas, 46 nays, 54 not voting, and 26 pairs. The Dies committee had been renewed again.[31]

Extending his remarks in connection with the Dies committee debate, Thomas of New Jersey called attention to the committee's 45 volumes of hearings, reports, and other publications, and 821 letters from government agencies requesting or acknowledging information from the committee. He also listed nine fascist organizations which had disappeared because of exposure by the committee.[32] On March 31, 1942, Voorhis expressed disappointment that Dies still continued his attack on our Russian ally. When Dies wrote an open letter to Vice-President Henry Wallace impugning the patriotism of certain Board of Economic Welfare members, Wallace had declared that the "doubts and anger which this and similar statements of Mr. Dies tend to arouse in the public mind might as well come from Goebbels, himself, as far as their practical effect is concerned." Wallace had expressed hope that "Mr. Dies and

241

others of his kind with an intense itch for publicity, will use their talents to help the United Nations win this war rather than stir up discord among patriotic Americans." [33] Voorhis indicated that Dies' letter to Vice-President Wallace had been released to the press by Mr. Dies without the knowledge of other committee members. To this, Voorhis objected "vigorously." [34]

That attacks on Russia, and on the Board of Economic Warfare, headed by Vice-President Wallace, had led American newspapers to be much more critical of the Dies committee than previously, was noted by Coffee of Washington on April 16, 1942. He also called attention to the committee's failure to act against Father Coughlin, against whom the Department of Justice and the Post Office Department had, finally, taken drastic action. Fascist publications in the United States continued "unimpeded and unmolested by the Dies committee," said Coffee. In fact, the warmest support of the Dies committee came from fascist sources.[35] Coffee cited an editorial in the final issue of *Social Justice*, before it was barred from the mails, urging readers, "In your appreciation of the work accomplished by Mr. Dies, employ some of your leisure moments to write him a letter of encouragement. In fact a million letters brought to his desk would be answer to those who are bent on destroying him. . . ." The Axis radio was broadcasting Dies' charges against the Board of Economic Warfare to the whole world before many Americans had read them in their newspapers, so "eager" was the Axis to "capitalize" on Dies' charges. Coffee wondered how long the House would continue "this amazing committee." [36]

Congressman O'Connor of Montana wanted to reduce the appropriation for the Dies committee from $110,000 to $35,000. This would honor the financial commitments made by the committee to date, and thereafter, O'Connor thought, it would be highly desirable if the committee were "quiet" for the remainder of the war. Although Dies requested $300,000, the Accounts Committee recommended only $110,000; this brought appropriations for the committee to $495,000 since January 9, 1938, the largest appropriation any House committee had ever received. Printing costs involved an additional expenditure of approximately $80,000.

DIES DEFENDS HIS COMMITTEE

Marcantonio charged Dies with "untrue" statements concerning the extent of the dependence of the Department of Justice on the Dies committee for the information necessary to convict German agents in this country. Goebbels would rejoice if Dies and his chief investigator, J. B. Matthews, who received $7,200 salary per year, were authorized to continue their activities and to make statements which Berlin could use for propaganda purposes. Goebbels would regret it if the appropriation for the Dies committee were defeated. In the *Fiery Cross* of January 27, 1942, the Imperial Wizard of the Ku Klux Klan had said, "The [Dies] committee has rendered a great service to our country," Marcantonio concluded.

Representative Cox rose to the defense of the committee, declaring that its intentions were good and suggesting that if those who were working for a new order in the United States would "cease their efforts to make over the country," it might be possible to suspend the investigations of the Dies committee. When, at the end of the debate, the vote was taken on the appropriation, there were 291 yeas, 64 nays, 1 present, and 75 not voting.[37]

On June 2, 1942, Congressman Rich rose to condemn the magazine *In Fact* which had said the congressmen voted in support of Dies, although they knew he was a "faker," because they were afraid of their home town newspapers. Said Rich: "The Communists and radicals are trying to overthrow our form of government—and they are making too much progress to suit me. I am for getting them out of the country and doing it quickly." [38] Eliot of Massachusetts called attention to an editorial in the *New York Times*, describing the Dies committee's attack on the Union for Democratic Action as "silly" rather than "patriotic." [39] On July 9, Dies acknowledged the error of his committee in naming David Vaughn, of the Board of Economic Warfare, as a sponsor of the League for Peace and Democracy.[40] This false charge against Vaughn had led to a $75,000 lawsuit against Martin Dies personally, which was discontinued

243

when Dies apologized and agreed to pay the $611 due to Vaughn's counsel. When Dies asked Congress to pay this bill, Representative Celler of New York insisted that Dies pay it himself, because it was due to his own "carelessness and error." [41] Dies was distressed by attacks upon him by the *Daily Worker,* official Communist newspaper. Dies said the *Daily Worker* was "utterly unethical" and he could see no reason why it should be extended the privileges of the Press Gallery since it was "an agent of a foreign principal." [42]

Voorhis reported to the House, on September 3, 1943, summarizing Dies committee action on the Pelley case.[43] Mason followed on September 7 with a report on federal employees who were members of "subversive" organizations. This report, signed by Dies, listed what were considered to be subversive organizations by the Attorney General's office. This list included the Communist party, the American League Against War and Fascism, the American League for Peace and Democracy, American Peace Mobilization, American Youth Congress, League of American Writers, National Committee for the Defense of Political Prisoners, National Committee for People's Rights, National Federation for Constitutional Liberties, National Negro Congress, Washington Cooperative Bookshop, and the Washington Committee for Democratic Action. All—except the first, which was clearly the real thing—were alleged to be Communist-front organizations. In light of this list Dies could not understand the Justice Department's opposition to the Dies committee's efforts to find out which federal employees were active in such organizations, or why it had called Dies' investigation of the matter "a sort of inquisitional procedure." [44] On September 27, 1942, Representative Osmers called attention to an editorial in the *New York Journal* acknowledging public endorsement of the Dies committee in the decisive defeat administered to Thomas H. Eliot, foe of the Dies committee, in the Massachusetts primary election.[45]

On September 24, 1942, Martin Dies rose again "to a question of personal privilege." The provocation was a pamphlet published by the National Federation for Constitutional Liberties, which charged that the tactics of the Dies committee were those of Goebbels, that the committee had "shielded" Axis agents and "jeopardized national unity." Then, too, there was a declaration by the Federal Bureau of Investigation describing one of Dies' attacks as "fake." Dies charged that the F.B.I. investigation of federal employees had been restricted by the Justice Department. He read into the record "strictly confidential" memoranda of the Attorney General's office relative to the eleven organizations described by Dies as Communist-front organizations, which "confirmed . . . in strong language" all of the "findings" which Dies had revealed earlier. Among these organizations was the National Federation for Constitutional Liberties which "had the effrontery to write to the Attorney General and demand a grand jury investigation of [the Dies] committee." Dies pointed out that the National Federation for Constitutional Liberties got most of its money from the Robert Marshall Foundation. Robert Marshall had at one time been a government official and had left a sum of $1,535,000 in his will "to be used for the education of the people of the United States . . . [in] production for use and not for profit. . . ." This fund had taken the place of the Garland Fund in financing Communist-front organizations, said Dies. And one of those who disbursed Robert Marshall Foundation money was Gardner Jackson.

Dies described as a "malicious lie" the charge that his committee had not "vigorously exposed" Axis agents in the United States. The committee had exposed "every leader of every Fascist and Nazi organization" two years before. And there had been an investigation of anti-Semitism. Dies said that he had fought the Ku Klux Klan in Texas when it was "the dominating power" in that state—and he had supported Alfred E. Smith in 1928. He declared himself in no sense anti-Semitic. For the Negro people he felt "deep affection." In fact, said Dies, "I have always been identified with every movement designed to preserve the constitutional basis of this country." America, he said is "the home of all of us—Gentiles, Jews, Negroes." We could survive only "through cooperation and a spirit of tolerance and good will." But, said Dies, "I deplore the fact that throughout the South today subversive elements are attempting to convince the Negro that he should be placed on social equality with the white people; that now is the time for him to assert his rights." He also deplored "that any attempt [was] being made to spread hatred and misunderstandings between different races and religions in America." Such attempts served Adolf Hitler's purpose. During the four years that Dies had been chairman of the Dies committee, he declared, "not one word of intolerance can be attributed to me. Wherever I have been I have preached the fundamental doctrine of American tolerance."

"Our main job today," said Dies, "is to win this war, and, of equal importance, to preserve democracy. All of us admire the heroism and valor of the Russian people, and we want to see Russia win her fight against Germany. But we do not wish to embrace communism." And we do not wish to permit "destructive elements in our midst to use vast sums of money for the purpose of blackening the names of honest and patriotic men." If there was to be unity, the executive department would have to "meet [the Dies committee] half way" and would have to "cooperate" with the Dies committee. In these days, said Dies, "President Roosevelt needs us all—he needs Martin Dies of Texas." During the period of national emergency the members of the committee had made no speeches or statements "for a long time," in an effort to co-operate with the executive department of the government. The executive department should reciprocate. The committee had been "grossly misrepresented" by people who wanted to stop the Dies committee. And why? The misrepresentation, said Dies, came from people who wanted to be freed from the restraints which the committee had imposed upon them.[46]

"A QUESTION OF PERSONAL PRIVILEGE"

When the fourth report of the Dies committee was submitted to the House on January 2, 1943, it included a minority report by Voorhis. He had not signed the majority report because, although it was submitted to all members of the committee before it was submitted to Congress, it had not been prepared, corrected, or considered by the committee collectively. Voorhis thought the report should have placed more emphasis on those Nazi and Fascist activities in the United States which were weakening America's war effort.

Representative Mason, also a member of the committee, explained that the Dies committee had suspended public hearings, probably for the duration of the war, in order to avoid the danger of premature disclosures. Mason called attention to the fact that the C.I.O. had joined the list of those organizations opposed to the committee. Hamilton Fish, firm supporter of the Dies committee, declared that approximately two-thirds of those who had voted against the last extension of the committee had been defeated in the recent elections.[47]

On February 1, Martin Dies was on his feet in the House, rising again "to a question of personal privilege." One might almost conclude that "personal privilege" had become a habit with Dies by 1943. Dies read to the House an excerpt from a pamphlet prepared by the National Lawyers Guild which declared, "Martin Dies and his committee is the secret weapon with which Adolph Hitler hopes to soften up our Nation for military conquest." On the basis of this, Dies was recognized for an hour. Not considering an hour sufficient time to deal with a charge of such gravity, Dies asked for an additional thirty minutes; this request was also granted without objection. As a matter of fact, he spoke for two full hours.

There was a great military struggle going on, said Dies, but there was another phase of the conflict which was almost equally important. That phase was ideological. On the one hand there were "those great and eternal beliefs and philosophies" characteristic of "nineteenth century liberalism" which stood for "the protection of individual rights." This philosophy was challenged, said Dies, by communism in one country, by fascism in another, by Nazis in a third, and by bureaucracy in a fourth. Communism, fascism, nazism and bureaucracy, he said, were "essentially the same" in underlying principle. All four favored centralization and all four subordinated the individual to the state. Democratic progress, on the other hand, had been identified with decentralization. In the United States itself there had recently been a tendency toward bureaucracy and centralized government. The legislative branch of the government might gradually be subverted by the executive. At last "we have the totalitarian scheme of bureaucracy which means government by bureaucratic edict, which is the first step toward dictatorship, which creates conditions under which dictatorship is inevitable." An "insidious" effort was now being made to discredit Congress; there could be no surer way to destroy American democracy.

An effort had been made, said Dies, "to pin the Nazi and Fascist label upon all those who do not agree to certain principles or certain policies of the present [Roosevelt] administration." An effort had been made to "smear" him, too, he said, by magazines like *The New Republic,* member of a "coalition of antiparliamentarianism" and author of a "vicious document" entitled *A Congress To Win the War.* Dies was disturbed over the fact that if a congressman "wanted to sue *The New Republic* for the irreparable damage which he suffered in consequence of the magazine's admitted falsehoods," he would be unable to do so because the magazine's stock was "owned by a foreign corporation," adding that this foreign-owned corporation attempted to advise Americans on the kind of Congress they should elect. (The fact is that *The New Republic* is owned and published by a corporation organized under the laws of New York State, all its officers and directors are residents of New York, and it can be, and has been, sued for libel.)

Mr. Dies went on to say that *The New Republic* and other associated groups had one common objective: "to discredit Congress in order that their program of internationalism will not be hampered after the war by a strong and alert Congress." These groups attacked congressmen "as obstructionists and Fascists in an effort to undermine the people's faith in Congress." Moreover, these groups were in close association with Government officials, e.g., with Gardner Jackson, whom Dies apparently disliked.

Dies reserved special condemnation for Marshall Field, whom he accused of contributing large sums of money to "known pro-Communist and purge organizations." Asking himself whether Marshall Field was "sincerely a liberal," Dies came

248

to the conclusion that Field, like Julius Caesar, sought to "out-demagogue the worst demagogues." It is "sheer hypocrisy" for men like Marshall Field "to pose as defenders of the poor and then to denounce Members of Congress, the overwhelming majority of whom are not wealthy," reasoned Mr. Dies. It disturbed Dies that rich men in America had used their wealth to give the impression that there were men in the House who "secretly want the Axis Powers to win." Dies' son had volunteered; his nephew was in Africa. Yet here in America were "so-called proponents of liberalism who would reverse nineteenth-century liberalism and who would make of it an entirely different philosophy than it was always understood to be." These men would centralize government instead of fighting against centralization. "We are rapidly approaching a period in America when the real power and function of government will be exercised . . . by bureaucracy," and not by Congress.

Why do people attack me? asked Dies rhetorically. Those who had been investigated must know that he was not anti-Semitic, anti-Catholic, or anti-Negro. He had come to the defense of all these groups in his own state of Texas, even in the days when the Ku Klux Klan was predominant there. He could not be justly attacked on his war record, because he had "a record of 100 per cent support of war measures." Why had Drew Pearson, the National Lawyers Guild, Walter Winchell, and the C.I.O. all attacked him at one and the same time? Dies found "a well-organized attempt to build up in this country a united front of radicals—a united front of Communists, crackpots, Socialists, men of different shades of totalitarian beliefs," and an effort by this group to bring the Negro population under its influence. "Constantly," said Dies, "the Negroes are told that now is the time for them to achieve that degree of social equality to which they are entitled." And what did the radical united front hope to gain by arousing racial antagonism in this way? "We in our country live in peace with the Negro; we respect him, for he has contributed much to the progress of our country," said Dies. Moreover, had not Dies "said to the American people that the great majority of the Negroes are loyal, patriotic American citizens?"

Dies found the reason for attacks against himself and against the South in the fact that "there are people in this country who do not believe in America and who have never believed in it." Such people used "democracy" as a cloak for totalitarianism; they wanted centralized government, economic regimentation, government by bureaus. But they would not be willing to stop with economic regimentation. They would interfere with our religious and personal rights as well. These people were fanatical and drunk with power. "The history of the world has always shown that free enterprise is the basic foundation of all democracy. When people are regimented economically, then the next step is to regiment them politically and religiously." Dies was aroused over the effort of certain individuals to weed out of Congress all those who did not share their own particular views. "I speak," he said, "with all the sincerity in my heart." The bureaucrats, reaching for power and more power, already were so deeply entrenched in power that they did not show "even ordinary courtesy" to congressmen. Congressmen had to "come crawling on their knees to them in order to get jobs for needy constituents," said Dies. Bureaucracy, he declared, "is as deadly and poisonous as any form of fascism there is and is as destructive of the freedom and the liberty of the American Nation as anything could possibly be."

How was it that these bureaucrats could get positions in Washington "with fat salaries," when they could be "elected" to no job whatever? "I consider it my duty to my boy and to the boys of my friends and to the people of my district during this critical hour to be perfectly frank," said Dies. He was going to "make crystal clear just what we mean by irresponsible, unrepresentative, crackpot, radical bureaucrats." Dies thereupon called attention to Frederick L. Schuman, chief political analyst of the Federal Communications Commission, who received a salary of $5,600 a year. Dies was shocked. Why, the district judge of Dies's home district received less than that. Ninety-five per cent of the lawyers in his home district received less than that! "As for the farmers, why, Mr. Speaker, out of all the farmers in my district there are not half a dozen who get $1,000 a year after they have worked in sleet and wind and rain and in the heat of the midday sun, after they have battled insects and drought and everything else. To come out with $1,000 would make them feel like 'economic royalists.' " (Dies did not mention his own Congressional salary, or compare his service to America with the service rendered by Frederick L. Schuman, who is one of the great scholars, analysts, and writers of our time.) Dies called Schuman a man of "Communist affiliations" and "violent political views." He charged that Schuman had signed a statement calling upon professional people to "join in the revolutionary struggle against capitalism under the leadership of the Communist Party." He pictured the embarrassment of a congressman trying to explain to a father or mother who "had just received word that their dearly beloved son has given his life in defense of America" why he had appointed to the federal bureaucracy a man like Schuman, "who does not believe in the system these boys fought and died to preserve." Reaching a new high, Dies exclaimed:

In my own little town, three of the boys who grew up with my boys, who used to play on my front porch and in my yard, have all made the supreme sacrifice. For what? For bureaucracy, for totalitarianism, for socialism, for crackpotism? No, Mr. Speaker; for the American way of life and the American Constitution.

Then there was Goodwin B. Watson, chief broadcast analyst of the Federal Communications Commission, receiving a salary of $6,500 a year. This man, said Dies, had Communist views and was affiliated with Communist-front organizations. Watson, among other things, had "lumped Couéism, pyorrhea, and Congress together as . . . great jokes of the age." William E. Dodd, Junior, was another "radical bureaucrat" who should be removed from federal employment. We should not harbor radicals in federal employment merely because communist Russia is fighting on our side in the war, explained Dies, adding:

As for me, Mr. Speaker, I care not what kind of a government Russia has. I did not care what kind of a government Germany has,

251

if Germany had not sought to impose that kind of government upon the peoples of other lands and upon my own land. I am not a maudlin internationalist who believes that I or my Government can go all over the world and make people democratic, whether they want to be democratic or not. I do not mean by that that I do share the views of extreme nationalism that has been a curse of many countries. I do not believe in extreme internationalism or extreme nationalism, but I do believe that every true American must put his own Country's interests above that of every other country in the world.

While Dies would not deprive people in America of the right to believe in communism, if they chose to do so, "because that is an inherent right of every citizen," he considered it right to tell such people that they had "no right to take the hard-earned tax money of ... loyal, patriotic people ... and ... give it to people who are on record against the very Government that is supporting them."

(This is typical Dies logic. People have a right to think as they choose; but if they do not think as Dies himself does about the desirability of retaining "nineteenth-century liberalism," Dies would deny them the opportunity to participate in government, even if appointed in a legal way by duly elected representatives of the people. His position implies that it is more "patriotic" to favor a continuance of what Dies calls "nineteenth-century liberalism" than it is to favor the enactment, by strictly constitutional means, of legislation intended to modify nineteenth-century practices to twentieth-century needs. Dies fortifies his basic intolerance for anything new or different in America by pretending that anyone who favors change in our present system is a "radical" or "Communist." To say that no one may join an organization without assuming the attributes of the least desirable member of the group is to condemn organized effort on the part of all individuals who desire to see modifications in the status quo. Such a theory leaves the status quo in complete possession of the field, with no one daring to employ organizational activity in favor of better conditions, through fear that if he does, he may become contaminated by association with the attributes of some "undesirable" person. If Dies took this theory seriously in his own conduct, he would be compelled to barricade himself in Orange, Texas, there being no other way to retain the patriotic odor which adorns him. It would be interesting to place Mr. Martin Dies and Mrs. Elizabeth Dilling in a room and see which came out first! But this theory of association cannot be taken seriously, except as a propaganda device in the hands of a demagogue. That Dies does not apply the rule of association to himself is seen in the ease with which he has associated with both communists and fascists in connection with the hearings of his committee, and with men of diverse views in Congress, without apparently having lost the slightest scintilla of that native intellectual virginity which has characterized him from first to last in his Congressional career.)

Dies ran through a long list of "radicals" occupying important posts in Washington and indicated that many of them had not only condemned the capitalistic system but had expressed themselves in favor of a Marxist philosophy of economics. Among those listed as objectionable were Paul R. Porter, chief of the shipbuilding branch of the War Production Board, at a salary of $8,000 a year; John Herling, business consultant in the Office of Co-ordinator of Inter-American Affairs, at $5,600 a year; Paul F. Brissenden, consultant of the shipbuilding stabilization committee of the War Production Board, at $8,000 a year; David J. Saposs, assistant to the chief of the labor division of the War Production Board, at $8,000 a year; Maurice Parmelee, economist for the Railroad Retirement Board, at a salary of $4,600; Harold Loeb, senior economist in building materials for the War Production Board, at $4,600 a year; Sam Schmerler, Social Security policy consultant, at $3,800 a year; Emil Jack Lever, head labor adviser in the War Production Board, at $6,500 a year; Tom Tippitt, chief of the rent section of O.P.A., at a salary of $5,600; Henry G. Alsberg, senior feature writer for the Office of War Information, at $4,600; David Karr, assistant chief of the foreign language division of the Office of War Information, at $4,600 a year; Guiseppi Facci, David Wahl, Hugh Miller, Walter Gellhorn, Jack Fahy, Nathaniel Weyl, Robert Morss Lovett, Merle

Vincent, Gardner Jackson, Alice Barrows, William Pickens, Arthur F. Goldschmidt, Leonard Emil Mins, Henry T. Hunt, Mary McLeod Bethune, Harry C. Lamberton, T. A. Bisson, Katherine Kellock, Jay Deiss, Milton V. Freeman, George Slaff, A. C. Shire and Edward Scheuenmann. Dies declared that he could "stand on the floor of the House day in and day out and read ... the records of men who have no place in our Government." And the plain people of America did not want men like these to hold important federal positions, he said.

Speaking of the National Lawyers Guild, which attacked him and his committee as Adolf Hitler's secret weapon, Dies declared it "a shrewd tactic for those who really do not believe in democracy to wrap the cloak of democracy and liberalism around themselves and to pretend to go forth to battle for democracy when the thing that they believe in is the very thing that has brought curse and destruction to the republics of other countries and other ages." And they pretend that those who expose them are fascists. People had wanted Dies to brand people as Communists because they had "progressive" views, and as fascist because they were "conservative." But, said Dies, "there is no law against a man's being intolerant, as much as we deplore intolerance [sic]." In America a man might legally denounce the South; he might also denounce Jews. But in America we must all support the Bill of Rights, "the chief cornerstone upon which this Republic was established."

At the conclusion of Dies's address, Rogers of California rose, and, obtaining recognition, said he wanted it to be known that he (Rogers) disagreed "with the sentiments expressed, the flamboyant manner of expression, and the use of this great public forum as a means of what we in Hollywood would call personal publicity." [48]

A week later Dies delivered a detailed attack on William Pickens, the one Negro among the thirty-eight persons he had named in his February first speech, and charged that Pickens belonged to twenty-one different Communist-front organizations, and should not be employed by the Government. [49]

Representative Voorhis later expressed the opinion that

no one could seriously injure Congress if Congress itself were "constructive, farsighted, determined, and unafraid." He did not consider it "un-American" for citizens to oppose those congressmen with whom they disagreed. Voorhis expressed agreement with Dies that no Communist should be permitted to hold governmental office, but Dies had gone further and wanted to eliminate everyone whom Dies himself categorized as "crackpot." Dies' speech was "an expression of the point of view of the gentleman from Texas personally," said Voorhis, and was in no sense an expression of the Committee on Un-American Activities. Katherine Kellock, F. C. McKee, Paul Porter, and Guiseppi Facci, named by Dies in his speech of the preceding Monday, were not Communists by the farthest stretch of the imagination. Nevertheless, said Voorhis, the House had come within seven votes of denying the right to work for the government to the thirty-eight people mentioned by Dies "without any charge having been lodged against them, except that in the judgment of one member they fall into the vague category of 'crackpots.'" In that group were actually "one man now serving overseas in the Army of his country, one serving in Africa with the Red Cross," three who had been out of government service "for months," "a man chosen by the votes of the Army, Navy, and Maritime Commission, to head the work of stabilizing...the shipbuilding industry," another man who had voted for Herbert Hoover in 1932 as well as in 1928, and "a woman highly recommended by a priest of the Catholic Church."

Voorhis insisted that "things like this, mistakes like this, ought not to be laid in the lap of the House until the most mature consideration has been given them, not by one Member but by a whole committee working on problems of this sort." It was as easy to prepare a list of "crackpot" conservatives as to prepare a list of "crackpot" radicals, and "if we are going in for lists of crackpots we ought to be even-handed about the matter." Confusing political disagreement with disloyalty to the country played into the hands of the extremists, making it possible for them to draw many people into their orbits of influence who would not have been attracted by either extreme if a clear distinction had been drawn between fascists and conservatives, on the one hand, and Communists and progressives, on the other. In America political minorities had a right "to exist and express their opinions" in favor of either "very much more conservative policies than those being pursued by the Government or very much more progressive policies than those being pursued by the Government." "If people are going to define a Communist in some big category of people who somehow seem to be too far to the left, then inevitably the corresponding definition of fascist moves over to include people who in some other people's judgment are too far to the right."

Voorhis did not consider it within the province of the Dies committee "to sit in judgment on the political view of any loyal American, be he reactionary or radical." He wanted the committee to concentrate on Axis propaganda and on those activities in America which were helpful to the enemy. He was much opposed to bringing charges against persons "without either substantial documentary evidence or an opportunity to be heard." Under the circumstances, Voorhis declared, he found it increasingly difficult to serve on the Dies committee.[50]

Marcantonio declared that 1,250 prominent Americans had signed a petition against continuance of the committee. The C.I.O., hundreds of A.F. of L. locals, and several conservative newspapers urged its discontinuance. On the other hand, George Sylvester Viereck, Fritz Kuhn, Gerald L. K. Smith, and Ku Klux Klan Imperial Wizard Colescott wanted the committee continued. J. B. Matthews, chief investigator for the Dies committee at $7,500 per year, had written articles for Kontra-Komintern, one of Hitler's propaganda sheets. The Dies committee had a filing cabinet listing as "subversive" one person out of every 130 in the United States.

The Department of Justice of the United States had in 1943 charged thirty-four individuals, forty-four organizations, and forty-two publications with being conspirators against the nation. Practically all of these had "completely escaped the attention of Mr. Dies and his committee." "In other words," said Representative Sadowski of New York, interrupting Marcantonio, "that great mountain from the plains of Texas labored and labored, and finally produced a mouse." The gentleman from Texas, continued Marcantonio, had completely missed the one big domestic conspiracy against our national safety. Dies had been "too busy" fighting Communists, labor, liberals, progressives, New Dealers, the Administration, and the Soviet Union, to investigate the subversive activities of Axis agents or domestic fascists. "While Americans are gloriously fighting at Guadalcanal and North Africa and the Red Army is smashing the enemy at Stalingrad and Rostov, Hitler and Mr. Dies are still crusading against communism." The Dies committee was following the anti-Comintern line, which had permitted Hitler to undermine democracy in Germany and Europe; Dies had "missed the real foe" and fallen victim to Hitler's favorite propaganda device, said Marcantonio.[51]

On February 9, 1943, Representative Scanlon expressed opposition to continuing the Dies committee because (1) the money spent did not promote winning the war, but actually created disunity, and (2) the committee had not acted with justice and fair play. He opposed tarring men with subversion unless there was substantiating evidence to prove their guilt "beyond reasonable doubt."[52] Representative Sabath opposed continuance of the Dies committee because Dies had forgotten that we were at war with Germany and Japan, and not with Russia. Moreover, Dies had "branded either inferentially or directly as communistic" many organizations which Sabath denied were any more communistic than he (Sabath) was a "Nazi ideologist."[53]

Legislation to extend and to increase the membership of the committee was debated in the House on February 8, 1943. Mason wanted a new lease of life for the committee. Clark of North Carolina thought that it was "unreasonable" and "foolish" to continue it at a time when the entire might of the nation was mobilized against our national enemies and the F.B.I. had been granted $39,000,000 to "spend in investigating anything that is un-American." Thomas of New Jersey called attention to the committee's "unparalleled experience" in dealing with subversive groups. Sadowski of Michigan said that whereas in 1938 he had received letters and telegrams "from practically everybody" in support of the Dies committee, now there was universal opposition to it. "One would think we were at war with Russia instead of with Germany," said O'Connor of Montana, who noted "an ancient and fishlike smell about the way the committee [had] been directing its efforts."

Eberharter of Pennsylvania, who in 1938 had said that the committee would be "fair, just, and impartial, both in its investigation and its findings," now declared that it had "created suspicion, distrust, and disunity all over the United States," had "embarrassed the State Department," and had "had a bad effect upon our diplomatic relations with other countries." Gale of Minnesota said that many congressmen were afraid to vote against the Dies committee for fear that such a vote would be interpreted as a vote for communism. The victims of the Dies committee were not accused of treason; their crime was in being liberals. They were "not accused of incompetence in office, inefficiency, or corruption, but of holding different opinions." The word "un-American" meant Communists today; tomorrow it might mean Jews, Catholics, isolationists, or even Republicans.

Baldwin of New York said his family had left England in 1638 to avoid the sort of thing the Dies committee represented in America today. He opposed the committee also because it put our military intelligence services in the position of trying to shoot a bird "over a green dog that flushes birds so soon that most of them get away." Weiss of Pennsylvania wanted to "quiet Martin—for the duration." In time of war, Weiss preferred "the F.B.I. with its subtle, careful, well-planned, organized, manner of dealing with sabotage and espionage, and subversive and un-American acts against the Government, rather than the headline-seeking, advance-notice dangerous tactics of the Dies committee."

Dies rose to charge that those who were opposed to his committee had throughout its history engaged "in personal abuse and in denunciation of the most vicious kind." In the tone of one bearing scars which he had suffered in the courageous defense of his country, Dies referred to those who denounced him in these words:

It is not me alone that they denounce. They also denounce a majority of the Members of the House. I say to you, Mr. Speaker, and I say to this House, continue the committee, but only on one condition, that we will do our duty, the administration, the C.I.O., and other foes not withstanding, and if this Congress and if this country does not want a fearless and courageous investigation, if you do not want this committee to expose these evils that threaten this country, then, Mr. Speaker, I submit, the investigation should be voted down and the committee discontinued.

From a propaganda standpoint Dies's speech was a work of art. He did not attempt to answer the arguments of his critics. He simply declared that the opposition had engaged in personal abuse and vicious denunciation. In other words, he did not defend his committee; he attacked those who opposed it. He fought not for himself but for the House and its prerogatives. In the name of "duty," "fearlessness," and "courage" Dies would, if Congress insisted, carry on his heroic crusade against the "evils that threaten this country." He did not say exactly what those evils were, but it was obvious that he thought he knew what they were.

Voorhis said that he would vote against the committee's continuance, and that under such circumstances he did not expect to be named a member of the committee in the future. Fish declared there was now more reason than ever to continue the Dies committee, inasmuch as "the administration and those in authority, including President Roosevelt, [had] appointed Communists, Reds, and Fellow Travelers to key positions [and had not] ousted them when they were exposed by the Dies committee." One-third of those who had voted against the Dies committee the preceding year were defeated at the polls, said Fish on February 8. (On January 12, Fish had said approximately two-thirds were defeated.)

When the vote was taken, there were 302 yeas, 94 nays and 38 not voting; consequently the resolution was passed.[54] But this was more opposition than had ever been registered previously.

Discussion of the Dies committee continued. On February 15, 1943, Shafer of Michigan called attention to an editorial in the *Pittsburgh Post-Gazette* entitled "Mr. Dies's Popularity," which explained the perennial extensions granted Dies' committee as a tribute to Dies' eternal vigilance against the Washington bureaucrats.[55] The same day which brought these words of fulsome praise for Dies and his committee also brought a communication from Jerry Voorhis submitting his resignation from the committee.[56]

On February 18, Representative Celler again objected to the House of Representatives' paying the legal expenses incurred by David Vaughn in a libel suit against Dies. Dies explained that the accusation made against Vaughn of the Board of Economic Warfare had been made in error, through confusing him with another David Vaughn. The House appropriated $75,000 for Dies committee expenses.[57] The same day brought four new appointments to the committee, Courtney of Tennessee, Costello of California, Eberharter of Pennsylvania, and Mundt of South Dakota.[58] The other members of the committee were Chairman Dies of Texas, Thomas of New Jersey, Starnes of Alabama, and Mason of Illinois. The committee, previously consisting of three Republicans and four Democrats, now consisted of three Republicans and five Democrats.[59]

On February 25, Representative Mason introduced into the record a speech which Martin Dies had delivered over the radio. In this speech Dies explained that while America carried on the fight across the seas, Congress had an obligation to make sure that when our fighting men return, they will find that "constitutional government and the American way of life for which they fought are still intact and unimpaired, and that awaiting them will be jobs and opportunities for advancement under a system of free enterprise which is the basis of our democracy." Federal bureaucrats were taking over more and more governmental functions. "Socialistic planners in the bureaus" were trying to put across "their socialistic schemes" on "an unsuspecting country." Some of these people were trying to undermine the profit system by getting jobs inside the government.[60]

One week later Representative Rankin called the attention of the House to a subsequent radio speech by Dies in which Dies said the "campaign of lies" against him was because of the effectiveness of the committee's work. In four and one-half years it had driven out of existence more than one hundred Axis organizations, had "ferreted out and unmasked" more than one hundred Communist-front organizations of which 60 per cent had been forced out of existence.[61]

On March 15, 1943, McMurray of Wisconsin entered in the record a reply to Dies' radio addresses by Reinhold Niebuhr, professor of applied Christianity at Union Theological Seminary. Niebuhr asserted that the Dies committee had "never seriously investigated anything," that "the primary interest of Mr. Dies and a majority of his committee is to embarrass the Roosevelt administration." Speaking of Dies in particular, Niebuhr commented, "In his perverse ignorance he regards all the necessary measures of Government for the control of economic life in wartime as bureaucracy: and in his simple mind bureaucracy is identical with fascism." In concluding, Niebuhr said, "Mr. Dies himself is unimportant, but his committee incarnates for the moment a peril to democracy. The people of America must understand this peril and the Congress must summon up the courage to destroy it." [62]

When Dies discovered a letter written by the National Sharecroppers Week, an organization whose sponsors, he said, included Harold L. Ickes, Mrs. Eleanor Roosevelt, and Archibald MacLeish, he went on the warpath, declaring it "inconceivable" that a Cabinet officer, or a President's wife, would sponsor an organization which spread "such outrageous lies." The letter said that there were "hundreds of thousands of sharecroppers and tenant farmer families who live bleak, despairing lives in our own South." Dies wanted to know why there was no mention in the letter of sharecroppers in other parts of the country, and no word "about the people who live in the slums and alleys of our great cities." Of the sharecroppers in the South the letter had said, "They are no longer free, for they have lost the land which gave them freedom and security. And through the poll

261

tax they have lost their right to vote in defense of their interests." This language displeased Dies. The poll tax in the South did not keep people from voting in elections. Moreover, asserting as had this organization, that people in the South were enslaved, played right into the hands of the Axis propagandists, said Dies. The poverty of the South was due to discrimination against it in the interests of other sections of the country. Southerners resented the effort of Northerners to exploit the poverty of the South "for political purposes." Why did Northerners not concern themselves more with the slums in Northern cities? Perhaps they are "more concerned about the Negro vote in the North than they are about the welfare of the Negro in the South."

"Has it never occurred to these professional uplifters to be fair and just in their treatment of the South and to avoid exaggeration of conditions which all of us deplore?" asked Dies. "If the Government will treat us as it does every other section of the country we can raise our standard of living and solve our own problems." [63]

DIES FINDS "SUBVERSIVES" ON THE FEDERAL PAYROLL

Dies appeared in a new and strange role on March 31, 1943, when he opposed certain "language" in the War Security Act which would penalize "acquiring, compiling, obtaining access to, or transmitting any data calculated to inform the enemy with respect to the war effort of the United States." He objected to this "language" on the ground that it was so general that it might be made to include "anything on earth." For example, "the war effort" might mean "practically everything that the people of the United States are now engaged in." The meaning of the act would depend too largely on the people who administered it, said Dies; he had his doubts about some of them.

"Nearly a year ago," said Mr. Dies, "I sent a letter to the Vice-President of the United States respectfully and politely calling his attention to the fact that there were certain individuals on the Board of Economic Warfare who had subversive records." What happened? Dies continued, "The Vice-President of the United States construed my letter as information that would aid the enemy." In fact, Vice-President Wallace "went so

262

far as to say publicly in the press that if I had been on Hitler's payroll I could not aid the Axis cause more effectively." This episode indicated, said Dies, that there were men who "disagreed" with Dies, and also with "the findings" of his committee. "There is, therefore, a great difference of opinion with respect to many of these matters," concluded our hero. He was "disturbed" because someone in the Department of Justice might consider Dies himself an enemy agent. Consequently, he wanted the terms of the bill more specifically defined.

Dies continued: "Mr. Speaker, I want to point out that if we adopt such general and loose language, it could be used by people in the administration who dislike me or dislike some other Member of Congress for the purpose of intimidating the member of Congress in the discharge of his duty." (Yet he had used "general and loose language" to intimidate people whom he disliked, and prevented people from exercising their full rights and duties as citizens to organize and discuss problems of social moment, when their conclusions and programs of social action were different from those of Martin Dies.) Dies denied that he was more frequently and favorably quoted than any other American on the Axis radio. He wanted the "language" of the War Security Act changed "so that people who are exercising their constitutional rights may do so without fear of intimidation."

It was particularly necessary to use precise language in times of hysteria; in such times "loose" language was "extremely dangerous." Therefore Dies wished Congress to "insist that language be used that will protect all of our people in the exercise of their God-given rights to honestly criticize what is wrong and to do their duty without fear of intimidation." [64] (This last statement completes the paradox; Dies had gone around the full circle and had himself set forth the argument which other congressmen had failed to make against Dies himself with equal force and vigor. One wonders why no congressman saw the identity of the two instances and put the shoe on Dies' foot.)

On April 1, 1943, Dies inserted in the record a report that 654 federal employees had been dismissed from their posts because of "suspected disloyalty." [65] On April 7, reporting on the

263

examination of certain federal employees by his committee, he said "you could never accomplish anything" in matters of this kind if you required a committee "to prove beyond a reasonable doubt that a man is subversive or even to prove that he is a Communist." No one had ever been able to secure a complete membership list of the Communist party, because members thereof perjure themselves. But Dies said he had "conclusive proof" that there were about 165,000 members who paid dues to the Communist party. Since subversion and communism could not be proved "beyond a reasonable doubt," Dies advocated that the government should not employ anyone who "knowingly or carelessly affiliates or associates with a subversive organization." It was strange, thought Dies, that the government would instantly discharge any employee who was a Nazi, yet the Communist party "is just as revolutionary, just as disloyal and unpatriotic as the German-American Bund." (Dies said this sixteen months after Pearl Harbor.)

We repeat Dies' statement about proof: "It seems to me," he said, "that if you ... require any committee to prove beyond a reasonable doubt that a man is subversive or even to prove that he is a Communist ... you could never accomplish anything." Dies said that it was "a question of what degree of proof you want." It was his own opinion that when there was clear evidence that an employee had "openly associated and affiliated with a subversive organization, whether ... Nazi, Communist, or Fascist," had given expression to "utterances in which he ... denounced our form of government," he ought to be "stricken from the payroll without any question." If the same rules were applied and the same degree of proof required in these cases as when a man was being tried for crime, said Dies, "there will be no way to strike these people from the payroll because ... Communists perjure themselves." Dies did not mention that in a trial for the commission of a crime, the defendant is not required to convict himself by his own testimony. Dies, therefore, was arguing that so-called "subversive belief or organizational membership" was worse than any other crime, and justified denial of judicial protection for the individual accused. Dies maintained that if a Federal appointee "has knowingly or carelessly used his name and his influence to promote, to support, and to strengthen subversive movements in this country that fact, and that fact alone, ought to be sufficient to disqualify him from the Government service." The only question, then, was whether these organizations were actually subversive. Both the Department of Justice and the Dies committee, after independent inquiry, had found that they were, said Dies.[66] (Of course, if organizations are actually subversive they should not be permitted to exist. There is no actual proof that many of the organizations libeled by Dies are really subversive. If they were, they could be driven out of existence by legislation and judicial procedure. Dies uses the word "subversive" as a club with which to destroy progressive individuals who have, at some time or other, been members of progressive organizations which Mr. Dies dislikes and which he would destroy if he could because their social ideals are different from his own. Neither Dies nor the Department of Justice have shown that these so-called "subversive" or "Communist-front" organizations have actually denounced our form of government. Dies confuses "our form of government" with capitalism, which is not even mentioned in the Constitution of the United States. And our form of government has changed considerably since 1789 when it was first instituted, and there is no reason to believe that it will not undergo further change and modification. Democracy thrives on diversity rather than on uniformity. There is no one man or group of men blessed by God with the privilege to determine what is good for the rest of us and to tell us what we are to think and not to think. Under the democratic system, we are free to believe whatever we like, to advocate any change we desire in government by constitutional means, and to belong to any organizations we like. These organizations require no further justification than that they please us who are their members, and that they operate within the law and under the Constitution of the United States.)

Dies maintained that the federal employees whom he wished removed from office on the ground that they were "subversive" would not receive 2 per cent of the votes if they were required to run for public office.[67] (This, too, is utterly irrelevant, incompetent, and immaterial. Under the American system of government relatively few men are elected to office; these elected representatives appoint others, and there are many provisions supporting the effort to have them appointed on the basis of merit [the ability to do the work assigned them] rather than on any political basis. Dies appears to be unaware that under the American system of government the executive department is independent of the legislative; nor has he noticed, apparently, that the President of the United States is elected on a wider and more inclusive vote-getting basis than even Mr. Dies. If J. B. Matthews, Dies' director of research, does not have to run for office, there is no reason why the President's appointees should be required to do so. In the case of appointed officials, merit is judged on the basis of the quantity and quality of the work performed, not on the basis of vote-getting capacity. Dies, however, is an elected official, and as such is judged by his ability to get votes and, fortunately for him, not on the basis of the quality of his work.)

On April 9, 1943, Dies announced his introduction of two bills. One bill was to make any person ineligible for employment by the federal government "who affiliates himself or associates with" any organization found to be subversive by the Dies committee, or the Interdepartmental Committee, or the Attorney General. (This would make it possible for the Dies committee to remove any federal employee.) The other bill provided for the forfeiture of citizenship by any person "who affiliates himself in the future with any organization subject to foreign control which engages in political activity." [68] (This could be interpreted in such a way as to deprive all Catholics of citizenship.)

On May 27, 1943, Representative Mason denied a rumor that the Dies committee would be discontinued because the Comintern had been abandoned. Mason said that the Dies committee still had to counterbalance the work done by the Comintern during a twenty-year period. [69]

In the summer of 1943 Harold Ickes, Secretary of the Interior, announced that the wealth of the United States was much greater than popularly supposed, because ordinary estimates of the nation's wealth had not included our vast mineral resources. Ickes found that the nation's wealth totaled $12,023,000,000,000, or $89,000 for every man, woman, and child in the United States. Discovering an article in the newspapers setting forth this estimate, Dies subjected Ickes to ridicule. There was no longer any need to be "seriously concerned" over our "colossal" war debt, said Dies. Our "great financier, genius, statesman, humanitarian, liberal, reformer, and chicken raiser," Harold Ickes, has shown us how niggardly Congress has been in appropriations. "I am not only happy for the Nation and for my financially distressed colleagues in the House, but it is only human that I feel a sense of personal relief to know that I, my wife, and three children are now worth $445,000." He was glad, he said, that in "this dark and troubled hour" there had appeared "a stupendous intellect and a $12,000,000,000,000 heart to bring hope, consolation, and encouragement to suffering humanity." Dies suggested that, in light of this new estimate, it might be possible for Vice-President Wallace to step up his plan from a quart of milk daily for everybody everywhere to twelve gallons of milk each day for each and every person in the whole wide world.[70]

ANTI-CLIMAX

When, in 1943, the Dies committee was increased from seven to eight members, when Voorhis resigned, and Congressman Mundt, Courtney, Costello, and Eberharter were added, the rule of the Dies, Starnes, Thomas, and Mason majority was weakened. Dies was in anti-climax. The committee has lost its former flavor. The fire was gone, momentarily.

Who were the new men added to the committee? One was a Republican; three were Democrats. The Republican was Karl E. Mundt of South Dakota. He was born in South Dakota in 1900. Mundt is married. After getting his B.A. degree from Carleton College in 1923, he received an M.A. degree from Columbia University in 1927. Mundt started his career as a high school teacher of speech and social science, later became a school superintendent, and still later was chairman of the speech department and instructor of social sciences at Eastern State Teachers College, Madison, S.D., 1927 to 1936. During this latter period he devoted part time to the insurance and loan business, and since 1936 has been secretary of the Mundt Loan and Investment Company in Madison, S.D. He has served in Congress since 1939. He is a Mason, a Methodist, and a Kiwanian.[71]

Wirt Courtney of Tennessee, John M. Costello of California and Herman P. Eberharter of Pennsylvania are Democrats.

Courtney was born in Tennessee in 1889. He attended Vanderbilt University and studied abroad, is married and has four children. He is a lawyer and has been circuit judge, and a brigadier general in the Tennessee National Guard. He is a Mason, Elk, Shriner, and Episcopalian. He has been in Congress since 1939.[72]

Costello was born in California in 1903. He is a graduate of Loyola University, and is unmarried, has practiced law, taught school, and been a bank president. He has been in Congress since 1935, is an Elk and a member of the Knights of Columbus.[73]

Eberharter was born in Pennsylvania in 1892. He is a graduate of Duquesne University and is a lawyer, is married and has two sons. Eberharter is a Catholic. He served in World War I and has served in Congress since 1937.[74]

These four men have changed the nature of the Dies committee. Mundt is an educator, with a background in social science; Courtney, Costello, and Eberharter are lawyers, who have shown an interest in hearing testimony to determine what the facts actually are.[75] On December 17, 1943, Committeeman Mason resigned from the Dies committee. Representative Fred E. Busbey of Chicago, a Republican, was appointed. Despite these changes the committee remains a menace to American civil liberties. The increase of the membership from seven to eight and the recent resignation of Noah Mason are more than offset by the loss of Jerry Voorhis. The statement by the new member, Representative Busbey, that he has been "an authority on subversive activities for more than 20 years"[76] leads one to believe that the void left by Mason's withdrawal has been more than adequately filled. Moreover, Dies, Thomas, and Starnes are still on the committee, and they, together with Busbey, constitute half of its membership.

Nor does that give an adequate picture of the actual balance of power. Martin Dies is still chairman of the committee. The Dies committee has been engaged in character assassination. So long as a section of the committee is able to use the hearings and reports as a sounding board for its peculiar political, social, economic, and religious beliefs, and so long as the conservative and the reactionary press give free publicity to these expressions, so long will the Dies committee constitute a threat to American democracy.

11 PORTENTS: WHAT OF THE FUTURE?

B Y THE END OF 1943 the Dies committee had spent $570,000 of public funds. It lacked money to cover its December payroll of $6,000 for its nineteen employees.[1] There were those who anticipated the end of the committee, which might have been announced with a euphonious headline, "DIES DIES." But the committee is still very much alive. In January, 1944, the House committee on accounts approved a resolution to appropriate an additional $75,000 for the Dies committee.[2]

Nor was Dies long in regaining the headlines. Shortly after progressive groups exposed the "Peace Now" movement Dies dubbed it "treasonous," declaring its activities "calculated to interfere with the successful prosecution of the war." [3] Dies had discovered something. And this time, as usual, he had followed public opinion; observing a trend in public opinion, he responded to it and attained momentary popularity. But shortly thereafter Dies was back at his old game of labor-baiting.

Sidney Hillman, chairman of the Political Action Committee of the Congress of Industrial Organizations, announced that the Dies committee had asked for access to the committee's records. A Dies investigator had gone to the bank in which the C.I.O. committee's funds were deposited and asked to examine its accounts. In other words, Dies was again using his so-called "investigating committee" *not* for the purpose of investigating "un-American activities" but as a shield behind which to attack a labor group which has consistently supported progressive labor legislation and the domestic policies of the New Deal. Dies is grooming himself to play the same insidious role in the election of 1944 which he has played in the elections of 1938, 1940, and 1942. As chairman of a "bi-partisan" committee dominated by reactionaries of both old-line parties, financed at public expense, blessed with Congressional immunity on the theory that his committee is investigating un-American activities, Dies will use the committee as an agency to influence the outcome of a national election.

It is clear that the C.I.O. is not to be easily scared. "It is high time," Hillman said, "that someone in America challenged Martin Dies' abuse of Congressional power." Hillman flatly refused to turn over the records, documents and files of his committee. Declaring that the C.I.O. committee represents five million patriotic American men and women, Hillman challenged the authority of Dies to carry on any such investigation under the terms of the resolution authorizing the Dies committee to investigate "un-American activities." C.I.O. records and books have been examined by the Federal Bureau of Investigation and by the Attorney General; Hillman would gladly turn them over to any Congressional committee vested with proper power; but he would not turn them over to the Dies committee.

Hillman accused Dies of starting a "fishing expedition in fields outside his committee's jurisdiction in order to defeat the legitimate political aspirations of millions of workers and their families, farm groups, small businessmen and genuinely progressive elements who wish to maintain and expand the American way of life. The C.I.O. executive added these significant words:

Why does Martin Dies seek out our committee at this time? Why does Martin Dies attempt to stifle the political rights of Americans? Can it be that he fears them?

The C.I.O. Political Action Committee will resist by every legitimate means the efforts of Martin Dies to thwart the civil and political rights of the American people.[4]

In Hillman, Dies has found a foe who can give him blow for blow.

On March 9, 1944, Dies rose once more in the House to a point of personal privilege.[5] He declared the *Beaumont Enterprise,* largest newspaper in his own congressional district,

271

contained an article on March 6, in which Martin Popper, executive secretary of the Lawyers Guild, demanded abolition of the Dies committee on the ground that it functioned not as an agent of Congress but as an American equivalent of Hitler's anti-Comintern. Popper said, "When Dies' activities are joined to the anti-Semitic, anti-Negro tirades of his close collaborator, Congressman Rankin, and to Congressman Howard Smith's efforts to destroy the functioning of decisive war agencies—" At this point, Dies' reading of the newspaper article was interrupted by the Speaker of the House who declared Dies entitled to personal privilege. After Dies read part of a letter sent to congressmen by the political action committee of the C.I.O. charging that Dies had "earned and received the blessing and praise" of the friends of fascism, he was granted the floor for one hour.

What did he say? "Malicious charges" were being circulated throughout the entire United States "not only against me but against the majority of the Members of this House." There was, said Dies, "a well-organized, concerted, and highly financed campaign to smear the majority of the Members of the Congress of the United States." (It was Dies' old trick of trying to make it appear that an attack on Dies, and others like him, was an attack on a majority of Congress.) Dies objected to the publicity given *Sabotage* and *Under Cover* by certain radio commentators and newspapers. He declared certain persons had gone into his own state of Texas and, pretending to review these books, launched "a vicious attack against me, questioning my patriotism and my sincerity."

Dies said that his committee had been accused of "spreading fascism in the United States," of being anti-Semitic and anti-Negro. Harry Bridges had said, "There are more Hitler agents to the square inch in Congress than there are to the square mile in Detroit"; this was but an instance of the propaganda being spread by "communist-controlled" groups. It was all part of a "sinister" plan to undermine the confidence of the American people in their parliamentary system of government. In fact, "scurrilous attacks [were] made by hundreds of so-called labor leaders in the C.I.O. and by heads of some of these so-called progressive organizations upon the Congress of the United States."

Dies declared the Lawyers Guild controlled by the Communist party and that Martin Popper, its national executive secretary, had a "Communist record," having belonged at one time to "the seditious and potentially treasonable American Peace Mobilization group." Furthermore, Robert W. Kenney, national president of the Lawyers Guild, was once a member of the national committee of "the seditious and potentially treasonable" American League for Peace and Democracy. Dies asserted that leaders of the C.I.O. political action committee had also been "moving spirits" in "the seditious and potentially treasonable American Peace Mobilization group."

Dies quoted Mussolini's definition of fascism as "everything for the state, nothing outside the state, and nothing against the State; in other words, a highly centralized government." He declared that while the C.I.O. political action group had long favored a corporate state it now attacked those who like himself had "consistently resisted the totalitarian trend toward bureaucratic government." He attacked John Roy Carlson, author of *Under Cover,* as one who "sought to smear me [Dies]," and charged that Carlson was foreign born and had used aliases. He argued that inasmuch as Carlson admittedly belonged to some of the organizations which he sought to expose, Carlson was guilty of the sins of the organizations to which he belonged and responsible for views contained in the literature he distributed for these organizations. (Dies' own investigators had engaged in under cover activities without incurring any moral liability in Dies' judgment, but when Carlson employed the same methods he was held morally responsible by Dies for everything which he had said as a spy within these organizations while seeking inside information on pro-Nazi groups.) Dies wanted Carlson tried with the 33 alleged seditionists being prosecuted by the Department of Justice. When Representative Celler pointed out the absurdity of Dies' position in charging Carlson with subversion because he had played fascist to expose fascist groups, Dies quickly changed his ground and objected not to Carlson's activities or motivation, but to the fact that his book had been used by reviewers in "small communities" like his own to smear members of Congress.

Trying to prove that he had no anti-Semitic bias, Dies read questions which he had addressed to a witness trying to show that it was absurd to base racial prejudice on the objection which one might have to certain persons who happened to belong to minority groups. (Nevertheless, this is precisely the pattern of Dies' own reasoning when he attributes objectionable characteristics to an entire organization because it contains individuals whose economic and governmental ideas he dislikes.)

Declaring that Walter Winchell had said over the radio that Joseph Kamp, an alleged pro-Fascist, had access to the files of the Dies committee, Dies denied this and other statements made by Winchell. He said he had requested Winchell and the Blue Network to give him an opportunity to submit conclusive proof of the falsity of these charges. Later, the Blue Network wrote Dies a letter refusing his request that Winchell's program be cancelled and Dies be allotted Winchell's time on the air. Dies considered it "only just and correct" that he be given a chance to reply to and answer charges brought against him before the audience to whom Winchell had addressed his charges. The Blue Network wrote Dies that an examination of Winchell's references to Dies indicated they were "sometimes complimentary . . . and never exceed the limits of reasonable criticism accorded any citizen in commenting on the activities of prominent public officials." Dies was shocked at the Blue Network's refusal to grant him an opportunity to speak over a nationwide hook-up in answer to Winchell. "Think of that," exclaimed Dies. (It seems not to have occurred to Dies that under the cloak of congressional immunity he had himself injured the reputations of many individuals without providing them an opportunity to answer him either in Congress or before his own committee. What if Dies had no recourse against Winchell's charges except to appear before Winchell and answer questions which Winchell cared to ask him; nevertheless, that was the only recourse granted many against whom Dies made false charges.)

Dies charged that Michael Sayers and Albert E. Kahn had

plagiarized material from Dies' committee reports in writing their book *Sabotage*,[6] adding:

Nowhere in the annals of our history has there ever been a more dastardly attempt to defame and smear public servants than this current attempt on the part of Under Cover, Sabotage, and certain radio commentators and the political action committee.

Now, let me develop for a moment this extensive plot to destroy the parliamentary system. I wish to deal at some length with the political action committee. What I shall say is substantiated by conclusive proof, and I defy anyone to take issue with the statements I shall make.

Dies asserted that recent attacks on his committee and the effort to make it appear "pro-Fascist" had come from Communist-dominated organizations which sought to defeat "Members of this House whose only crime in their eyes was that they had refused to be subservient to the domination of the Communist leadership." The program of action for the 1944 elections, followed by Philip Murray and Sidney Hillman, was, unwittingly perhaps, part and parcel of Browder's program and had the support of Communists in the C.I.O. movement. Dies concluded:

Mr. Speaker, I do not have the time to go into this question in detail, but as I have previously indicated, the report which I trust our committee will soon issue contains conclusive proof showing how the Communists have seized control of this Political Action Committee, how they are now using it and the vast funds which they are raising not only for the purpose of electing people friendly to them, but more insidiously to create the widespread impression that in the Congress of the United States a majority of its members are Fascists and sympathetic with Hitler. It would seem to me, Mr. Speaker, that minority groups who enjoy the protection of the American Constitution would be very careful not to engage in the same type of intolerance and hatred that characterized their own suffering in Europe, that they would be careful to set an example of tolerance, that they would not associate with any movement or any group designed to engage in the same strategy, the same tactics that led to the defeat of democracy in Europe and the rise of totalitarianism.

275

At the end of Dies' one-hour speech, Representative Fish asked unanimous consent for Dies to continue another half hour, but to this there was objection.

However, on March 16 Dies was back again,[7] this time with an Associated Press quotation from Walter Winchell, saying "Dies is the kind of man who does not like any kind of criticism. Some time ago he asked Drew Pearson to please ask Walter Winchell to lay off him. When I told Pearson to tell him to go to hell I expected him to use the *Congressional Record* to even matters." Dies said this statement was "utterly false" and that it convinced him that Winchell is "not concerned with the truth and that he deliberately and intentionally spreads falsehoods over the airways." In fact, "it must be obvious to every fairminded citizen that he is not interested in ascertaining the truth." Dies said he had received "thousands of letters from people everywhere" who wanted to "give concrete proof" before his committee of the "deliberate falsehoods" used by Winchell in his radio broadcasts. For example, one man had made a study of Winchell's broadcasts over a period of time and found 60 per cent of their content deliberate falsehood. Continuing, Dies read a letter he had written to the Blue Network charging its refusal to let him speak made it "increasingly apparent" that the Blue Network was "a party to this scheme to malign and smear and discredit American public officials and American citizens as a part of an insidious propaganda program that you are carrying on over the airways of the United States."

Thereupon, Representative Dickstein declared Walter Winchell "an outstanding American" helpful in exposing the same sort of un-American activities which Dies had exposed. Dickstein thought there must be some misunderstanding or confusion concerning Winchell's efforts. Dies replied that in spite of his efforts to be fair, Winchell had given the press "a statement as vicious, and insulting, and as indicative of arrogance ...if it does not exceed [that of] Father Coughlin." Catholic leaders had striven "to restrict and restrain" Coughlin. Now there was "another man evidently drunk with the praise and the power he thinks he enjoys, who believes he can imitate the methods and technique of Father Coughlin and use the radios of this country for the purpose of spreading deliberate falsehoods." There had been a time, said Dies, when Winchell had opposed the Communists, but more recently he had endorsed *Sabotage* as "one of the finest books ever published in the United States," when that book contained material "stolen" from reports of the Dies committee "for the purpose of smearing and discrediting me and the committee I have the honor to head." Dies continued:

Mr. Chairman, I do not say that Mr. Winchell should not have the right to criticize me as a public official. Long ago I ceased to be sensitive about anything that anybody said about me. I am not contending that we should abridge freedom of speech. I do not propose that the broadcasting companies of this country censor the fair truthful statements of commentators. What I am trying to say is that when a man uses the airways for the purpose of promoting hatred, whether that hatred is directed against the Jewish people, the Catholic people, or other people in the United States, he is imitating the dangerous technique of Hitlerism, fascism, and all other forms of totalitarianism.

Dies declared his own analysis of Winchell's scripts showed that Winchell had an "insidious way in which he seeks to create false impressions." The "propaganda" method employed by Winchell, was, said Mr. Dies, "similar in every respect to the method used by Goebbels and the propagandists of Germany." Dies added:

It is inconsistent, Mr. Chairman, for anyone to brand and condemn intolerance, then be guilty of it himself. If we condemn intolerance we must set an example of tolerance ourselves. It is as wrong to condemn people of one race as it is to condemn people of another race. Yet here is a man who because he is intoxicated with the flattery and applause that greets him at Miami, Fla., has grown so bold that he does not hesitate to tell public officials who have never criticized him, who in all of their statements have been dignified and respectful, "Go to hell." Now that is a fine way to meet an issue.

Mr. Chairman, remember that I did not condemn Mr. Winchell when I spoke the other day. I merely answered the statements that he had made over the radio about me and the committee I serve as chairman. I said nothing that could have reflected upon him; yet with that arrogance, that confident belief that because he has the radio facilities of the country at his disposal, he can use innuendoes, inferences, and falsehoods to destroy public officials and the committees of this Congress. It is a repetition of the Coughlin incident in almost every detail. I want to say that bigger men than he have sought to discredit this committee. Smarter and more clever propagandists have sought to smear us, and they have not succeeded. If Mr. Winchell could see the thousands of letters that are pouring into my office, he would realize that he has just gone too far. The people of this country are sick and tired of radio commentators of any stripe who use the airways for the purpose of promoting hatred and spreading falsehoods.

As usual, Dies maintained that Dies is right—others are wrong—and Dies is tolerant—others intolerant. The success of Dies despite opposition and criticism does not prove, however, that he is serving the best interests of America. Hitler has been in power longer than Dies. The fact that the Nazis went on persecuting people in spite of the fact that "bigger men" than their victims had sought to discredit the Nazis, does not prove that the Nazi program was right; moreover, it does not prove that the Nazis will be able to continue forever their program of rule or ruin. Hitler's time will come, and so will that of his American analogues.

Meanwhile, it seems likely that as long as Dies is protected by congressional immunity and supported at public expense, he will go on calling individuals communistic, malicious, and unfair, when they have the temerity to criticize him, that he will go on destroying American civil liberties, while pretending to protect them, that he will go on praising tolerance while he is himself grossly intolerant of all those who do not accept his own peculiar brand of "Americanism."

To meet Dies' demand for radio time in which to answer Winchell, the latter's sponsor provided a fifteen-minute period immediately following Winchell's broadcast on Sunday, March 26. Obviously, Dies has "muscled his way" onto a Blue Network broadcast. Meanwhile, pending the broadcast, Winchell made no new charges over the air.[8] However, in a newspaper, appearing the day before the broadcast, Winchell asked Dies fifteen questions on his record and on the performance of his committee. These questions implied that Dies was much too considerate of Charles E. Coughlin, Gerald L. K. Smith, Gerald Winrod, and others, winning the acclaim of native American fascists; that he had smeared loyal governmental employees, attacked progressive Americans, lifted material from the Congressional Library and other sources in an exposé of Japanese propaganda; that he had made American taxpayers pay the cost of a lawsuit resulting from Dies' own irresponsible charges; and, finally, that Dies had one of the worst attendance records of any member of Congress.[9]

In his broadcast on March 26, Winchell read what he called "A Reporter's Report to the Nation" in which he explained that "the power of Congress to subpoena is not the right of an individual Congressman to hold court," and challenged Dies to "lay aside his immunity (long enough) so that [Winchell could] challenge him" before "any open American court" of justice. Winchell insisted that "the men of the American Revolution" had given him, in the Bill of Rights, the "right to criticize the Government of the United States and the official acts of any of its servants." [10]

If Winchell thought Dies would attempt to answer his fifteen questions in the fifteen-minute period allotted the congressman, he was disappointed. Dies called him the "tool" of a "smear Bund" backed by powerful and well-organized interests. He promised that his committee would tell the American people "who is supplying the brains and who is paying the bills." Dies charged Winchell with building up a large radio audience as "a peddler of bedroom keyhole scandal to the American people" and that he sandwiched political propaganda in between items of scandal. He said Winchell was "used as a transmission belt pouring political propaganda into millions of ears with damaging statements, half-truths, innuendo, and indirection." Winchell not only impugned the loyalty of public men; he was part of a "movement to undermine the authority and destroy the prestige of Congress in the interest of setting up an all-powerful Central Executive. . . . This would not be serious if Mr. Winchell were the only Charley McCarthy in the smear Bund,"said Dies. "He is, however, only one of many. Who are they? Who is behind them? The American people would like to know and I promise you that Congress will soon find out." [11]

The reader of this book will recognize immediately that Dies' broadcast in "answer" to Winchell was Dies' usual answer when he is attacked. He does not attempt to answer the charges that are brought against him—he attacks those who make the charges on the ground that they are attempting to undermine the confidence of the American people in Congress-as-an-institution. There is no instance on record in which Dies has been attacked by a private citizen, has acknowledged that the attack was on *him*, and has sought to answer it on a reasonable basis. The attack, he invariably finds, is not on him but is, on the contrary, "an attack on this great body of which I am an humble Member," whereupon he launches into an attack on his critic and, taking full advantage of congressional immunity, is able to outdistance in name-calling and innuendo any private citizen bound by the prevailing laws against libel and slander. Dies is careful not to waive his immunity; [12] consequently, he appears to excellent advantage against those not armed with any corresponding immunity. And it is safe to predict that Dies will continue to use these tactics as long as he has the power to use them. The times and the places, the names and the faces, may change, but as long as Dies has power he will play Goliath against every David who he suspects is unarmed.

Perhaps the most amusing passage in Dies' entire broadcast was his cry, "My crime is my own refusal to join in the conspiracy of character assassination by using the power of our Committee to smear loyal citizens." [13]

Three days later the Dies Committee on Un-American Activities issued a 215-page "special" report, comparable to the "special" report issued on June 25, 1942—another election year —and directed against the Union for Democratic Action. The current report, issued March 29, 1944, was an attack on the

Political Action Committee of the C.I.O. The report was signed by Dies, Starnes, Thomas, Busby, Mundt, and Costello. (Two are southern Democrats; three are Republicans; and the one northern Democrat is a banker.) The report was not signed by Eberharter or Courtney, both northern Democrats. The report stated that Sidney Hillman had taken the place of Earl Browder as leader of the Communists in the United States because "the political views and philosophy of the Communist party and of the C.I.O. Political Action Committee coincide in every way." The Communist party, it was stated, had dissolved in order to "throw [its] entire weight" behind the political action committee in the 1944 election. Eighteen out of forty-nine men on the C.I.O. executive board were said to be Communists, and a "majority" of the C.I.O. unions, affiliated with the Political Action Committee, were said to have "strongly entrenched" Communist leadership. While it was not asserted that Hillman was a Communist, it was indicated he had entered into a "sinister" coalition with the Communists for political action. Speaking of the $2,000,000 which the C.I.O. expected to spend during the election, the Dies majority said, "Inasmuch as many members of the CIO who do not share Hillman's views are compelled by Government coercion to belong to its affiliated unions, such members are subjected to a form of tyrannical taxation without representation."

The Dies committee asserted that it did not "challenge for one moment the right of organized labor to engage in political campaigns." It would be "irresponsible and untruthful," it continued, to charge that it "would deny to organized labor any of its lawful rights." *But* that did not "'deter" the committee, it explained, "from exposing the subversive activities of the Communists who have, in line with their current strategy, decided to work through the CIO Political Action Committee." The political action group of the C.I.O. estimated the voting strength of its unions and their families at 14,000,000, and this group hoped to organize 28,000,000 voters. While these figures indicated a large amount of "wishful thinking" to Dies, they also indicated the "political ambitions" of the Philip Murray-Sidney Hillman-C.I.O. coalition, according to the report.[14]

Sidney Hillman, chairman of the National Political Action Committee of the C.I.O., when informed of these charges, stated that Dies had not investigated the political action group, but had "delved into the recesses of a warped mind and come up with the same shopworn smears which he has been peddling to the American people for the past eight years in an effort to stir up national disunity." Hillman charged Dies' attack was based on fear that unity within the labor movement "will drive Mr. Dies and others of his stripe from the American political scene." He declared the C.I.O. an organization of 5,500,000 "patriotic men and women" and its leadership "immune to this kind of scurrility." When Dies said members of the Political Action Committee were "fronts" or "stooges" for the Communist party, Dies "lies, and he knows he lies," said Hillman.

He predicted that Dies' effort to divide the progressive forces in America would fail, that attention could not longer be diverted from "the real issues" to "false and phony issues." Dies' methods, though successful in the past, would no longer work. Hillman felt the outcome of the primary election of the American Labor Party in New York City the day before Dies had issued his "special" committee report, in which Hillman's slate had emerged victorious, demonstrated that. "The American people can no longer be swayed by the hysterical cry of communism, which is Mr. Dies' only stock in trade. Voters in other states will give the same answer to Mr. Dies in November. That is what he fears. That is why he uses his committee to spread lies, disunity and hatred throughout the nation in a desperate effort to protect the political hides of himself and his allies." [15]

What did Hillman have in mind? Here are a few facts.[16] The Second Congressional District of Texas, which Dies is "supposed to represent," is half the size of New York State and includes 11 counties and 330,000 people. Texas is a poll-tax state and in the last election Dies received votes of only 5 per cent of the people in this district. The war has increased industrial activity in Dies' district, and although William Green, president of the American Federation of Labor, has endorsed Dies for re-election in 1944,[17] members of the A.F. of L. unions are joining with members of C.I.O. unions in an effort to get the voters to pay their poll taxes so that they will be able to vote this fall. The payment of poll taxes in Dies' district has already risen 25 per cent; the payment of poll taxes by Negroes in his district has risen approximately 40 per cent. And the same day Dies was "exposing" the C.I.O. in Washington an election in a large industrial plant in his home district voted overwhelmingly to affiliate with the C.I.O. There *may* be a connection.

The basic conception on which the Dies committee rests is "un-American."

It has usurped the authority of the Congress, the executive, and the judiciary; has refused witnesses the right of examination by their own counsel, has accepted as evidence material which would be thrown out of any court in the land, and has precipitated a witch hunt which hampers the free expression of ideas so necessary to our form of democracy.

Moreover, it has failed completely to discover the really "un-American" forces. Despite frequent requests by democratic groups, Dies has not exposed the fascist organizations, both foreign and native American, which exist in this country. The little space devoted to fascist activities in the hearings and reports has uncovered only material of common knowledge or has uncovered it only after its possible usefulness in combating these activities has passed. Instead the committee has devoted its time to insulting our ally, the Soviet Union.

Finally, the Dies committee is interfering with the successful prosecution of the war for the main issue—democratic victory over fascism. In this war the entire population must devote itself to the task of defeating the enemy. The Congress of the United States is not apart from the people it represents. When our people place the defeat of Germany and Japan as the all-important task facing the nation, Congress should recognize that goal as the problem of greatest importance. The Special Committee on Un-American Activities, appointed by Congress, has a similar responsibility to subordinate everything to the prosecution of the war. But the Dies committee has ignored the constitutional relationship between Congress and the American people. It has contributed nothing to the defeat of fascism. It has continued to proceed as though Pearl Harbor had never occurred. Not only has it sought to divide the patriotic forces within our country working for the defeat of the Axis; it has also done much to create distrust among the Allies. Such activities by a committee which has its basis in the will of the American people is a luxury which could ill be afforded in time of peace. Now, when the country is engaged in a war for national survival, the Dies committee is a threat to the actual existence of our American democracy.

While the rest of the democratic world fights the Axis, Dies is fighting a one-man campaign against an American ally. Dies has done everything in his power to arouse distrust of our Soviet ally. From the inception of his investigation Dies maintained that Russia was the main enemy, and in spite of the fact that his committee had no substantial evidence whatever in support of that contention, Dies has held to his previous opinion with the greatest tenacity. Dies is unable to distinguish between the German and Russian systems of government—if anything, Dies considers the latter more dangerous.

It would be a reflection on the intelligence of the United States if, after spending $570,000 on an "investigation" which has already lasted five years, the American people continued to employ a detective who does not know even yet who the criminal is. An extension of the Dies committee would be a reflection on our sincerity in giving assurances to Russia that we will do our share to win the war against fascism.

World peace in the future cannot be maintained by a return either to "nineteenth-century liberalism" or to a world of competing national imperialisms. Isolationism has been tested in the laboratory of world history and been found wanting. If the world wishes to avoid a repetition of the events leading to the present conflagration, it must not pursue the policies of imperialism, isolation, and appeasement of the past. Rather, the conferences of Moscow and Teheran must be used as the basis for continued co-operation between the nations of the world. The American people cannot permit the decisions of Roosevelt, Stalin and Churchill to be voided by the divisive influence of men like Martin Dies. The American people cannot permit a reactionary like Martin Dies to hinder the triumph of the United Nations over the forces of fascism.

If men are to be persecuted and organizations killed because they have ideas "from across the sea," what will happen to the churches in America, which accept the Christian-Hebraic tradition? What will happen to capitalism, which accepts many of the economic theories proclaimed by Adam Smith? What will happen to American science, industrialism, and nationalism, drawn in considerable measure from foreign sources? What will happen in music, art, and literature? What will we do with the English language? And what will we do about democracy, derived from the Greek city states, the Christian-Hebraic tradition, the English and French revolutions and other foreign sources? If it were actually "foreign" influence which concerned Martin Dies, he would have to extend his investigation to cover every aspect of American life. But it is not the foreign aspect of the so-called "front" organizations which concerns Dies; rather it is the fact that these organizations have been striving to promote purposes which are foreign to his own desires.

If national isolation were carried to the extreme which Dies seems to espouse in the political and economic areas, we should find ourselves confronted with a situation reminiscent of a scene in *Meet the People* which may be paraphrased as follows:

Two cannibals are sitting on a log, engaging in deep philosophical discourse. Bongo, the first cannibal, says that he wants to take the bone out of his nose. Thereupon, Wowsy, the second cannibal, explains that taking the bone out of his nose would be not only "improper" but "a case of indecent exposure." Becoming even more "radical," Bongo says that he does not want to eat any more people; Wowsy immediately accuses him of getting his ideas from across the river and explains that the only worth-while ideas are those which have developed on their own side of the river. Then Bongo says that he does not want to kill any more people; Wowsy answers that Bongo has been reading again, reading books written by people from across the river, and explains to Bongo "the obvious fact" that not to kill people would be "unnatural." "The natural thing is to kill people; that's why our tribe has been doing it all these years." Then, Wowsy, turning to Bongo and speaking to him in a tone of deep compassion, pleads, "Bongo, your mother is getting to be an old woman now, and it won't be very long until we'll be pushing her off the cliff. You don't want your mother to spend her last years knowing that her son has been a failure. Why, Bongo, you only had two small skulls over in your back yard the last time I was over at your place!" Bongo replies that he does not identify skull-gathering with success. Aroused by this "indifference to success," Wowsy accuses Bongo of having "subversive" ideas, and explains to him, "If people didn't have the incentive which is provided by the right to gather skulls, people wouldn't do any work at all. Human nature is like that, and you can't change human nature." Then Bongo, apparently immune to "logical thought," expresses the opinion that it would be better to eat vegetables rather than to eat human flesh. He says that he "doesn't like the idea" of eating men whom he has seen living a few days before, particularly men of his own age group. This is too much for Wowsy. In indignation he tells Bongo that he has "taken up with a lot of foreign isms." "What you ought to do, Bongo," Wowsy warns him, "is to limit your thinking to the one and only true ism, and that ism, needless to say, is cannibalism, now and forever."

The Dies committee was designed to do a job which could not be done legally but which had to be done under the cloak of legality for fear of offending public sensibilities. In 1938 the depression had lasted for almost a decade and the great masses of the American people were becoming increasingly restless. The leaders of American business wanted to put an end to sit-down strikes. The Republicans and the anti-New Deal Democrats were anxious to cripple the New Deal and all other organized movements that challenged the economic or political status quo. American big business and the reactionaries of both major political parties were much in need of a person to do to the "radical" movement in America what Hitler had done to it in Germany.

Dies was the man for the part; he had all of the vanity and swagger which Charlie Chaplin depicted in *The Great Dictator*.

Moreover, he did not have enough ability to become seriously dangerous to either the political or the economic reactionaries who fostered him. As has been said, "He is just a great big boy from Texas."

Everything worked out beautifully. Dies shortly became the beau ideal of every reactionary group in America. There were ample funds at his disposal, and there was lots of publicity for Chairman Dies himself. The Dies committee is a pressure group, organized and financed by Congress, to accomplish by unfavorable publicity, ostracism, and intimidation what could not have been achieved by legislative or judicial means under the American system of government. Legally, no man in America can be punished for what he thinks; he can be punished only for an illegal act of which the courts find him guilty. He is granted the right to be heard in his own defense and, in the absence of proof to the contrary, is assumed to be innocent. But in America in recent years there have been some beliefs so distasteful to certain economic interests that those who have held these beliefs have been persecuted in spite of the Bill of Rights. Men can be destroyed by ostracism, intimidation, unemployment, and violence, as well as by being sent to jail. These other equally destructive forces were turned loose against dissident groups and individuals to accomplish results which could not be achieved by constitutional or judicial means.

The Dies committee has been a "front organization" for reactionaries in both major political parties. Through this committee they have destroyed many organizations and countless individuals whose sole offense has been their rejection of certain beliefs accepted as fundamental by the reactionary united front. To charge individuals and organizations with having foreign ideas is no cause for action against anyone under our American Constitution, even if the charge is true. Under the American Constitution a man can believe anything he wants to believe; he is judged by his acts, and the legality of his acts is determined by a court of law, not by a kangaroo court in which the decision is rendered before the defendant has been given an opportunity to be heard in his own defense.

Dies' committee was authorized by law "to investigate." But

287

instead of confining itself to that purpose, it acted as a pressure group outside the law insofar as its victims were concerned. Because of the Congressional immunity it enjoyed, the committee was able to render decisions without the evidence required by criminal or civil courts. Dies was able to classify organizations and individuals as "subversive," "un-American," "Communist," or "Communist-front," not only without sufficient evidence but also without fear of legal reprisals. Allegedly representing a "congressional investigation," he was able to make charges which would have been libelous if they had come from any other source. Certain American newspapers, including a chain owned by a very old gentleman in California and a large daily in the Mid-West which describes itself as "the world's greatest," published Dies' declarations as if they were as authoritative and final as the Ten Commandments. These newspapers acted as storm troopers for Dies in the assassination of groups and individuals. The individual is helpless in the presence of such abuse and slander. Consequently, as a result of Dies' attack, men lost their jobs and their reputations. They were the victims of a pressure group supported at public expense and enjoying the prestige and immunity of government.

Dies is very sure of himself—up to now. His strength is as the strength of ten because he is so sure of the purity of his intentions and the righteousness of his acts. In fact, Dies is so sure of himself that he has volunteered to "educate" the American people. It used to be considered the role of the public to educate its congressmen. But that is not Dies' idea. His job is to awaken and educate *us*. It is for us to follow the leader. What leader? Our leader, Martin Dies. *Heil Dies!*

NOTES

CHAPTER 1

1. *Liberty Magazine*, February 10, 1940, p. 42, "More Snakes Than I Can Kill," by Martin Dies.

2. Raymond Gram Swing, *Forerunners of American Fascism*, Julian Messner, Inc., New York, 1935, p. 14.

3. John Dewey: *Logic, the Theory of Inquiry*, Henry Holt and Company, New York, 1938, *passim;* William H. Kilpatrick, *The Educational Frontier*, D. Appleton-Century Company, New York, Chap. XI.

4, 5. Institute of Propaganda Analysis, *Propaganda Analysis*, Volume 1, Number 2, Nov. 1937, pp. 5-8.

CHAPTER 2

1. *Who's Who in America*, 1918-1919, p. 744; *The Congressional Record*, 65th Congress, 3rd session, p. 5031, March 4, 1919; *Who's Who in America*, 1938-1939, p. 749; William Edwards, "Crusader for America," *Chicago Sunday Tribune*, March 17, 1914.

2. *The Congressional Record*, 61st Congress, 1st session, pp. 294-296, March 25, 1909.

(Hereafter, reference to *The Congressional Record* like the above will be abbreviated as follows: C.R., 61, 1, pp. 294-296, March 25, 1909.)

3. C.R., 61, 1, pp. 586, 587, March 26, 1909.

4. C.R., 61, 1, pp. 2048-2057, February 10, 1910.

5. C.R., 61, 3, pp. 3211, 3212, February 23, 1911.

6. C.R., 63, 3, p. 2111, January 22, 1915.

7. C.R., 64, 1, p. 1691, January 28, 1916.

8. C.R., 64, 1, p. 1695, January 28, 1916.

9. C.R., 64, 1, p. 9307, June 6, 1916.

10. C.R., 64, 1, pp. 9342, 9343, June 7, 1916.

11. C.R., 64, 1, p. 1695, January 28, 1916.

12. C.R., 64, 1, pp. 9342, 9343, June 7, 1916.

13. C.R., 65, 3, p. 3397, February 14, 1919.
14. *Ibid.*, pp. 3473-3476, June 11, 1917.
15. *Ibid.*, pp. 4044, 4045, June 21, 1917.
16. C.R., 65, 3, p. 2841, February 6, 1919.
17. *Ibid.*, p. 2844, February 2, 1915.
18. *Ibid.*, p. 2845, February 6, 1919.
19. C.R., 63, 1, pp. 2319, 2331, 2333, July 5, 1913.
20. C.R., 64, 2, pp. 4192, 4193, February 24, 1917.
21. C.R., 62, 2, p. 5564, April 29, 1912.
22. *Ibid.*, pp. 6988, 6989, May 22, 1912.
23. *Ibid.*, p. 2989, March 7, 1912.
24. *Ibid.*, pp. 5564, 5565, April 29, 1912.
25. C.R., 65, 3, pp. 2829, 2830, February 6, 1919.
26. C.R., 62, 2, pp. 5564, 5565, April 29, 1912.
27. C.R., 63, 1, pp. 2450, 2453, July 15, 1913; C.R., 65, 3, p. 2846, February 6, 1919.
28. C.R., 63, 2, Appendix, p. 603, May 9, 1914.
29. C.R., 63, 1, pp. 4003, 4004, August 30, 1913.
30. C.R., 63, 3, p. 2415, January 27, 1915.
31. *Ibid.*, p. 3597, February 11, 1915.
32. *Ibid.*, pp. 1430-1432, January 12, 1915.
33. *Ibid.*, p. 2352, January 26, 1915.
34. C.R., 63, 2, Appendix, p. 606, May 9, 1917.
35. C.R., 65, 2, p. 2544, February 22, 1918.
36. C.R., 65, 3, pp. 5031-5032, March 4, 1919.

CHAPTER 3

1. The *Chicago Daily News Almanac and Year Book* (Chicago, 1936), p. 174.
2. *The Congressional Record,* Index, 1931-1940, *passim.*
3. C.R., 72, 1, pp. 732-737, December 17, 1931.
4. *Ibid.*, pp. 2290-2296, January 19, 1932.
5. C.R., 75, 1, pp. 5667, 5677, 5682, June 14, 1937.
6. C.R., 72, 1, pp. 2290-2296, January 19, 1932.
7. C.R., 75, 1, p. 5603, June 11, 1937.
8. *Ibid.*, p. 5667, June 14, 1937.
9. *Ibid.*, pp. 5901, 5936, 5937, 5946, June 17, 1937.
10. C.R., 72, 1, pp. 482-483, December 14, 1931.
11. *Ibid.*, p. 8, December 17, 1931.
12. *Ibid.*, pp. 2290-2296, January 19, 1932.
13. C.R., 74, 1, pp. 7319, 7320, May 10, 1935.
14. C.R., 72, 1, pp. 2290-2296, January 19, 1932.
15. C.R., 75, 2, pp. 196-199, November 19, 1937.
16. C.R., 72, 1, p. 736, December 17, 1931.

17. C.R., 75, 1, p. 5603, June 11, 1937.
18. *Ibid.*, p. 5667, June 14, 1937.
19. *Ibid.*, pp. 3692-3694, April 21, 1937.
20. *Ibid.*, pp. 5667, 5677-5682, June 14, 1937.
21. C.R., 72, 1, p. 8, December 17, 1931.
22. C.R., 75, 1, pp. 2637, 2638, March 23, 1937.
23. *Ibid.*, pp. 8623-8625, August 10, 1937.
24. C.R., 75, 2, pp. 1387-1389, December 13, 1937.
25. C.R., 75, 3, pp. 7275-7278, May 23, 1938.
26. C.R., 72, 1, pp. 1736, 1822, 1823, 1958, January 12, 1932.
27. *Ibid.*, p. 6352, March 17, 1932.
28. C.R., 73, 1, pp. 488, 498, March 15, 1933.
29. C.R., 73, 2, pp. 4845-4849, March 19, 1934.
30. C.R., 75, 1, p. 3779, April 23, 1937.
31. C.R., 73, 2, pp. 11800, 11801, June 15, 1934.
32. C.R., 75, 1, p. 5069, May 27, 1937.
33. *Ibid.*, pp. 5620, 5621, June 11, 1937.
34. C.R., 74, 1, pp. 2124-2127, March 18, 1935.
35. C.R., 72, 2, pp. 119, 120, December 7, 1932.
36. C.R., 72, 1, pp. 845-847, December 18, 1931.
37. C.R., 74, 2, pp. 1367, 1368, February 3, 1936.
38. *Ibid.*, p. 3532, March 10, 1936.
39. C.R., 75, 3, pp. 3335, 3336, March 14, 1938.
40. C.R., 72, 1, pp. 2290-2296, January 19, 1932.
41. *Ibid.*, pp. 12098-12104, June 6, 1932.
42. *Ibid.*, p. 159, December 8, 1931.
43. C.R., Index, *passim.*
44. C.R., 72, 1, p. 736, December 17, 1931.
45. C.R., 73, 2, pp. 3736-3740, March 5, 1934.
46. *Ibid.*, pp. 11785-11789, June 15, 1934.
47. C.R., 74, 1, pp. 5849-5853, April 17, 1935.
48. *Ibid.*, pp. 7319-7320, May 10, 1935.
49. *Ibid.*, pp. 7883-7885, May 20, 1935.
50. *Ibid.*, pp. 8458-8461, May 31, 1935.
51. *Ibid.*, p. 10232, June 26, 1935.
52. C.R., 74, 2, pp. 1367-1368, February 3, 1936.
53. *Ibid.*, pp. 3532-3533, March 10, 1936.
54. C.R., 75, 1, pp. 5540 ff., June 10, 1937.
55. C.R., 75, 3, Appendix, p. 1207, March 28, 1938.
56. C.R., 76, 1, p. 2561, March 9, 1939.
57. C.R., 74, 2, pp. 6356, 6357, April 29, 1936.
58. C.R., 75, 3, pp. 4602, 4603, April 1, 1938.
59. *Ibid.*, pp. 5018, 5019, April 7, 1938.
60. C.R., 72, 2, pp. 119, 120, December 7, 1932.
61. C.R., 73, 1, p. 2126, April 21, 1933.

291

62. C.R., 74, 1, p. 429, January 14, 1935.

63. C.R., 74, 2, pp. 3447-3449, March 9, 1936.

64. C.R., 75, 1, p. 2665, March 23, 1937.

65. *Ibid.*, pp. 3299-3300, April 8, 1937.

66. *Ibid.*, p. 2794, March 25, 1937; p. 4896, May 20, 1937; p. 5854, May 17, 1937.

67. *Ibid.*, p. 2665, March 23, 1937.

68. M. Nelson McGeary, *The Development of Congressional Investigative Power* (Columbia University Press, 1940), pp. 15, 16.

69. C.R., 73, 1, p. 493, March 15, 1933.

70. C.R., 75, 2, pp. 196-199, November 19, 1937.

71. C.R., 76, 1, p. 4408, April 18, 1939.

CHAPTER 4

1. C.R., 75, 3, pp. 6562, 6605, May 10, 1938.

2. *Ibid.*, pp. 7367, 7368, May 26, 1938.

3. *Ibid.*, pp. 7567-7586, May 26, 1938.

4. *Ibid.*, pp. 7567-7586, May 26, 1938.

5. *Ibid.*, p. 8392, June 7, 1938.

6-9. *Who's Who in America, 1942-1943.*

10. Hearings Before a Special Committee on Un-American Activities, House of Representatives, pp. 898-899.

11. *Ibid.*, p. 817.

12. *Ibid.*, p. 2799.

13. *Ibid.*, p. 2857.

14. *Ibid.*, p. 2750.

15. *Ibid.*, p. 2792.

16. *Ibid.*, p. 4434.

17. *Ibid.*, p. 4484.

18. *Ibid.*, pp. 2814, 2865, 3366-3367.

19. *Ibid.*, p. 2951.

20. *Ibid.*, p. 4484.

21. *Who's Who in America, 1942-1943.*

CHAPTER 5

1. *Propaganda Analysis,* "Mr. Dies Goes to Town," Vol. III, Number 4, January 15, 1940; Drew Pearson and Robert S. Allen, "The Dies Committee...Is it American?" *Look Magazine,* January 2, 1940; Wesley Price, "We Investigate Dies," *American Magazine,* May, 1940.

2. Hearings Before a Special Committee on Un-American Activities, House of Representatives, pp. 857 ff.

3. *Ibid.*, pp. 7072-7073.

4. *Ibid.*, pp. 6365-6367.
5. *Ibid.*, pp. 7785, 7787-7788.
6. *Ibid.*, pp. 7880, 7890-7891.
7. *Ibid.*, pp. 8093-8094, 8104, 8111-8112.
8. *Ibid.*, pp. 7892-7956 *passim*, 7977, 7980, 7957-8005 *passim*, 6354-6388 *passim*.
9. *Ibid.*, pp. 7719, 8093-8112 *passim*, 6213-6330 *passim*.
10. *Ibid.*, pp. 6264-6265, 6213-6330 *passim*.
11. *Ibid.*, pp. 7052-7055 *passim*.
12. Appendix, Part V, p. 1622; Hearings, pp. 7892-7951.
13. Appendix, Part V, p. 1624; Hearings, pp. 8093-8112.
14. Hearings, pp. 8093-8112.
15. Martin Dies, *The Trojan Horse in America—A Report to the Nation* (Dodd Mead and Co., N. Y., 1940), p. 285.
16. *Ibid.*, p. 292.
17, 18. *Ibid.*, p. 293.
19. *Ibid.*, pp. 349-350.
20. *Ibid.*, p. 363.
21. *Ibid.*, p. 222.
22. *Ibid.*, p. 197.

CHAPTER 6

1. Hearings Before a Special Committee on Un-American Activities, House of Representatives, pp. 1-3, 193, 277, 1223.
2. *Ibid.*, pp. 91, 192, 1240, 1359, 2233, 2671-2673.
3. *Ibid.*, pp. 1240, 1423, 1364, 270.
4. *Ibid.*, pp. 91, 277, 1239, 1714.
5. *Ibid.*, p. 278.
6. *Ibid.*, pp. 417, 418, 424, 425, 426, 427.
7. *Ibid.*, pp. 432, 436-437, 1360.
8. *Ibid.*, pp. 1167, 2642-2643.
9. *Ibid.*, p. 1170.
10. *Ibid.*, pp. 1200, 1201, 1236.
11. *Ibid.*, p. 1223.
12. *Ibid.*, p. 1242.
13. *Ibid.*, p. 1558.
14. *Ibid.*, p. 1603.
15. *Ibid.*, p. 1716.
16. *Ibid.*, p. 1718.
17. *Ibid.*, p. 1738.
18. *Ibid.*, p. 1755.
19. *Ibid.*, pp. 1910-1912, 1916.
20. *Ibid.*, pp. 1919-1921.
21. *Ibid.*, pp. 1921-1927, 1929, 1937-1940, 1950.
22. *Ibid.*, pp. 2019, 2020.
23. *Ibid.*, pp. 1239-1713.
24. *Ibid.*, pp. 192, 193.
25. *Ibid.*, pp. 1694, 1695.
26. *Ibid.*, p. 2025.
27. *Ibid.*, pp. 2055-2059.
28. *Ibid.*, pp. 283, 2059-2060, 2086, 2129, 2409, 2662.
29. *Ibid.*, p. 2237.
30. *Ibid.*, p. 2246.
31. *Ibid.*, p. 2337.
32. *Ibid.*, p. 2339.
33. *Ibid.*, p. 2336.
34, 35. *Ibid.*, pp. 2367, 2374.
36. *Ibid.*, p. 2381.
37. *Ibid.*, p. 2435.

38. *Ibid.,* pp. 2427, 2428.
39, 40. *Ibid.,* pp. 2623, 2624.
41. *Ibid.,* pp. 2638, 2639.
42. *Ibid.,* pp. 2641, 2642.
43. *Ibid.,* pp. 2691, 2692.
44. *Ibid.,* pp. 2708, 2713, 2714.
45. *Ibid.,* pp. 2729-2733.
46. *Ibid.,* p. 2772.
47. *Ibid.,* p. 2777.
48. *Ibid.,* p. 2786.
49. *Ibid.,* p. 2805.
50. *Ibid.,* pp. 2807-2809.
51. *Ibid.,* p. 3011.
52. *Ibid.,* pp. 3016, 3830 ff.
53. *Ibid.,* pp. 3017-3020.
54. *Ibid.,* pp. 3039, 3061.
55. *Ibid.,* pp. 3045, 3062-3064.
56. *Ibid.,* pp. 3217, 3218, 4044.
57. *Ibid.,* pp. 3328, 3329.
58. *Ibid.,* pp. 3342, 3343.
59. *Ibid.,* p. 2814.
60. *Ibid.,* pp. 3366, 3367.

61. *Ibid.,* pp. 3508-3512.
62. *Ibid.,* p. 3520.
63. *Ibid.,* pp. 4110-4114.
64. *Ibid.,* pp. 4212-4213, 4258, 4259.
65. *Ibid.,* p. 4571.
66, 67. *Ibid.,* pp. 4574, 4575.
68. *Ibid.,* pp. 4603, 4604.
69. *Ibid.,* p. 4626.
70. *Ibid.,* p. 4704.
71. *Ibid.,* p. 4716.
72, 73. *Ibid.,* pp. 4719, 4720.
74. *Ibid.,* p. 4746.
75. *Ibid.,* pp. 5173-5175.
76. *Ibid.,* pp. 5177-5179.
77. *Ibid.,* pp. 5202, 5203.
78. *Ibid.,* pp. 5222, 5223.
79. *Ibid.,* p. 5256.
80. *Ibid.,* pp. 6270-6271.
81, 82. *Ibid.,* pp. 6362-6364.
83. *Ibid.,* p. 6366.
84. *Ibid.,* p. 6387.

CHAPTER 7

1. Hearings Before a Special Committee on Un-American Activities, House of Representatives, p. 142.
2. *Ibid.,* pp. 204-209.
3. *Ibid.,* p. 278.
4. *Ibid.,* pp. 376-379.
5. *Ibid.,* p. 423.
6. *Ibid.,* pp. 417-428.
7. *Ibid.,* p. 429.
8. *Ibid.,* p. 450.
9. *Ibid.,* pp. 476-477.
10. *Ibid.,* pp. 872-873.
11. *Ibid.,* pp. 876-877.
12. *Ibid.,* pp. 870-871.
13-16. *Ibid.,* pp. 943-973.
17. *Ibid.,* p. 1240.
18. *Ibid.,* pp. 1291-1299.
19. *Ibid.,* pp. 1327-1332.
20. *Ibid.,* p. 1341.
21. *Ibid.,* p. 1357.

22. *Ibid.,* pp. 1445, 1487, 1504-1510.
23. *Ibid.,* p. 1655.
24. *Ibid.,* p. 2207.
25. *Ibid.,* p. 2231.
26. *Ibid.,* pp. 1717, 1976-1977, 1986-1987.
27. *Ibid.,* pp. 1988-1990.
28. *Ibid.,* pp. 2142, 2143, 2144, 2156.
29. *Ibid.,* pp. 2435-2438.
30. *Ibid.,* pp. 2439-2443.
31. *Ibid.,* p. 2451.
32. *Ibid.,* pp. 2452, 2504, 2505.
33. *Ibid.,* pp. 2523, 2660.
34. *Ibid.,* pp. 3032, 3043-3045.
35. *Ibid.,* p. 4529.

36. *Ibid.*, pp. 4699-4701.
37. *Ibid.*, p. 4696.
38. *Ibid.*, pp. 4714, 4715.
39. *Ibid.*, p. 4745.
40. *Ibid.*, p. 4300.
41. *Ibid.*, pp. 4329-4331.
42. *Ibid.*, pp. 4462, 4463.
43. *Ibid.*, pp. 4496-4499.
44. *Ibid.*, pp. 4863, 4864, 4907.
45. *Ibid.*, pp. 4927-4929.
46. *Ibid.*, pp. 5137, 5140, 5155.
47, 48. *Ibid.*, pp. 6831-6833.
49. *Ibid.*, pp. 6835-6836.
50, 51. *Ibid.*, pp. 6837-6838.
52. *Ibid.*, pp. 6836-6837.
53. *Ibid.*, pp. 6839-6856.
54. *Ibid.*, pp. 6856-6911.
55. *Ibid.*, p. 6911.

CHAPTER 8

1. Statement made in a speech on "The Un-American Front" at Evanston Township High School in Evanston, Illinois, May 11, 1940.
2. 1939 House Report, Seventy-sixth Congress, first session, Report No. 2, January 3, 1939, pp. 1-10.
3. *Ibid.*, pp. 10, 11.
4. *Ibid.*, p. 12.
5. Report 2290, Seventy-first Congress, third session, House of Representatives (U. S. Govt. Printing Office, Washington, D. C., 1930), p. 4.
6. 1939 House Report, Seventy-sixth Congress, first session, Report No. 2, January 3, 1939, p. 12.
7. 1939 House Report, Seventy-sixth Congress, first session, Report No. 2, January 3, 1939, p. 13.
8. *Ibid.*, pp. 13-23.
9. *Ibid.*, pp. 23-28.
10. *Ibid.*, pp. 29-66.
11. *Ibid.*, pp, 68, 69.
12. *Ibid.*, p. 88.
13. *Ibid.*, pp. 91-118.
14. *Ibid.*, pp. 118-122.
15. *Ibid.*, pp. 123, 124.
16. 1940 House Report, Seventy-sixth Congress, third session, Report No. 1476, January 3, 1940, pp. 1-25.
17. Hearings Before a Special Committee on Un-American Activities, House of Representatives, p. 2337.
18. 1941 House Report, Seventy-seventh Congress, first session, Report No. 1, January 3, 1941, pp. 1-25.
19. 1942 House Report, Seventy-seventh Congress, second session, Report No. 2277, June 25, 1942, pp. 1-22.
20. 1942 House Report, Seventy-seventh Congress, second session, Report No. 2277, Part 2, July 7, 1942, pp. 1-7.
21. 1943 House Report, Seventy-seventh Congress, second session, Report No. 2748, January 2, 1943, pp. 1-16.

CHAPTER 9

1. C.R., 76, 1, p. 287, January 12, 1939.
2. *Ibid.*, pp. 17, 38, January 3, 1939.
3. *Ibid.*, p. 1101, February 3, 1939.
4. *Ibid.*, p. 1098, February 3, 1939.
5. *Ibid.*, Appendix, pp. 485-487, February 3, 1939.
6. *Ibid.*, Appendix, pp. 385-387, February 1, 1939.
7. *Ibid.*, pp. 1098-1129, February 3, 1939.
8. *Ibid.*, p. 1176, February 6, 1939.
9. *Ibid.*, p. 1228, February 8, 1939.
10. *Ibid.*, p. 11210, August 5, 1939.
11. C.R., 76, 2, pp. 1033-1035, October 27, 1939.
12. *Ibid.*, Appendix, pp. 634-636, October 31, 1939.
13. *Ibid.*, p. 1278, November 1, 1939.
14. *Ibid.*, Appendix, pp. 678-680, November 2, 1939.
15. C.R., 76, 3, pp. 572-605, January 23, 1940.
16. *Ibid.*, pp. 604-605.
17. *Ibid.*, pp. 572, 605, January 23, 1940.
18. *Ibid.*, p. 593.
19. *Ibid.*, pp. 571-572.
20. *Ibid.*, pp. 585-586.
21. *Ibid.*, pp. 575, 592.
22. *Ibid.*, p. 600.
23. *Ibid.*, p. 584.
24. *Ibid.*, pp. 568-605, *passim*.
25. *Ibid.*, pp. 572, 573; p. 602.
26. *Ibid.*, p. 574.
27. *Ibid.*, p. 584.
28, 29. *Ibid.*, p. 578.
30. *Ibid.*, p. 584.
31, 32. *Ibid.*, pp. 579, 580.
33. *Ibid.*, p. 591.
34. *Ibid.*, pp. 593-598.
35. *Ibid.*, pp. 600, 601.
36. *Ibid.*, p. 574.
37. *Ibid.*, pp. 576, 580.
38. *Ibid.*, p. 577.
39. *Ibid.*, p. 579.
40. *Ibid.*, p. 581.
41. *Ibid.*, p. 581.
42. *Ibid.*, p. 585.
43. *Ibid.*, p. 585.
44. *Ibid.*, p. 593.

45. *Ibid.*, pp. 602, 603.
46. *Ibid.*, pp. 817, 824, 946, 952-956, 1123.
47. *Ibid.*, p. 958, February 1, 1940.
48. *Ibid.*, pp. 1201, 1202, February 7, 1940.
49. *Ibid.*, pp. 1528, 1529, February 15, 1940.
50. *Ibid.*, pp. 1987, 1988, February 26, 1940.
51. *Ibid.*, pp. 3694, 3695, March 29, 1940.
52. *Ibid.*, pp. 3856, 3857, April 2, 1940.
53. *Ibid.*, pp. 4153-4160, April 8, 1940.
54. *Ibid.*, pp. 6171, 6203, 6295-6304, May 17, 1940.
55. *Ibid.*, pp. 8540-8542, June 18, 1940.
56. *Ibid.*, p. 8668, June 19, 1940.
57. *Ibid.*, pp. 13768-13771, November 28, 1940.
58. *Ibid.*, Appendix, p. A172, January 19, 1940.
59. *Ibid.*, p. 13534, October 10, 1940.
60. *Ibid.*, p. 13898, December 12, 1940.
61. *Ibid.*, pp. 13912-13913, December 12, 1940.
62. C.R., 77, 1, pp. 215-218, January 21, 1941.
63. *Ibid.*, pp. 571-572, February 5, 1941.
64. *Ibid.*, Appendix, pp. A422, A423, February 5, 1941.
65. *Ibid.*, pp. 886-889, February 11, 1941.
66. *Ibid.*, p. 889, February 11, 1941.
67. *Ibid.*, p. 890, February 11, 1941.
68. *Ibid.*, p. 891, February 11, 1941.
69. *Ibid.*, pp. 887, 891-892, February 11, 1941.
70. *Ibid.*, pp. 892-898, February 11, 1941.
71. *Ibid.*, pp. 898-900, February 11, 1941.
72. *Ibid.*, pp. 916, 917, February 11, 1941.
73. *Ibid.*, p. 919, February 12, 1941.
74. *Ibid.*, pp. 1397-1399, February 25, 1941.
75. *Ibid.*, pp. 2354, 2355, March 19, 1941.
76. *Ibid.*, Appendix, pp. A1276-A1277, March 20, 1941; pp. A1301 A1303, March 21, 1941.
77. *Ibid.*, Appendix, pp. A1352-A1353, March 24, 1941.
78. *Ibid.*, Appendix, pp. A1369-A1370, March 25, 1941.
79. *Ibid.*, Appendix, pp. A1442-A1443, March 27, 1941; pp. A1423-A1424, March 26, 1941; pp. A1508-A1510, March 31, 1941; *Ibid.*, p. 2574, March 26, 1941.
80. *Ibid.*, pp. 6926, 6927, August 8, 1941.
81. *Ibid.*, pp. 7037, 7038, August 12, 1941.
82. *Ibid.*, p. 7543, September 25, 1941.
83. *Ibid.*, p. 7543, September 25, 1941.
84. *Ibid.*, Appendix, pp. A4507-A4508, October 2, 1941.
85. *Ibid.*, p. 9008, November 19, 1941.
86. *Ibid.*, pp. 9122-9125, November 25, 1941.

87. *Ibid.*, pp. 9144-9145, November 26, 1941.
88. *Ibid.*, pp. 9201-9203, November 28, 1941.
89. *Ibid.*, pp. 9323-9328, December 2, 1941.
90. *Ibid.*, p. 9379, December 3, 1941.
91. *Ibid.*, pp. 9381-9382, December 3, 1941.
92. *Ibid.*, pp. 10051-10057, 10061-10062, December 19, 1941; p. 10075, December 20, 1941.

CHAPTER 10

1. C.R., 77, 2, pp. 407-410, January 15, 1942.
2. *Ibid.*, p. 510, January 21, 1942.
3. *Ibid.*, p. 589, January 23, 1942.
4. *Ibid.*, pp. 799-806, January 28, 1942.
5. *Ibid.*, p. 1924, March 4, 1942.
6. *Ibid.*, p. 692, January 26, 1942.
7. *Ibid.*, Appendix, p. A595, February 10, 1942.
8, 9. *Ibid.*, pp. 1430-1434, February 18, 1942.
10. *Ibid.*, pp. 1920-1926, March 4, 1942.
11. *Ibid.*, p. 2030, March 6, 1942.
12. *Ibid.*, Appendix, p. A505, February 12, 1942.
13. *Ibid.*, Appendix, pp. A760-A761, February 27, 1942.
14. *Ibid.*, Appendix, pp. A891-A892, March 7, 1942.
15. *Ibid.*, Appendix, pp. A923, A924, March 9, 1942.
16. *Ibid.*, Appendix, pp. A928-A929, March 10, 1942.
17. *Ibid.*, Appendix, p. A482, February 10, 1942.
18. *Ibid.*, Appendix, pp. A619-A620, February 18, 1942.
19. *Ibid.*, Appendix, pp. A708-A709, February 25, 1942.
20. *Ibid.*, Appendix, pp. A737, A738, February 26, 1942.
21. *Ibid.*, Appendix, pp. A724-A727, February 24, 1942.
22. *Ibid.*, pp. 2055-2064, March 7, 1942.
23. *Ibid.*, pp. 2064-2067, March 7, 1942.
24. *Ibid.*, p. 2111, March 9, 1942.
25. *Ibid.*, p. 2212, March 10, 1942.
26. *Ibid.*, p. 2282, March 11, 1942; *Ibid.*, Appendix, pp. A1084-A1085, March 18, 1942.
27. *Ibid.*, pp. 2282-2286, March 11, 1942.
28. *Ibid.*, pp. 2287-2292, March 11, 1942.
29, 30. *Ibid.*, pp. 2292-2295, March 11, 1942.
31. *Ibid.*, pp. 2296-2297, March 11, 1942.
32. *Ibid.*, Appendix, pp. A950-A953, March 11, 1942.
33. *Ibid.*, Appendix, p. A1282, March 31, 1942; *Ibid.*, p. 3143, March 28, 1942; *Ibid.*, pp. 3204-3206, March 30, 1942.
34. *Ibid.*, pp. 3213-3217, March 30, 1942; p. 3287, April 2, 1942.

35. *Ibid.*, pp. 1426, 1427, April 16, 1942; pp. 1465-1467, April 20, 1942; pp. 1448, 1449, April 20, 1942.
36. *Ibid.*, pp. 3617-3619, April 21, 1942.
37. *Ibid.*, pp. 3753-3758, April 28, 1942.
38. *Ibid.*, p. 4789, June 2, 1942.
39. *Ibid.*, Appendix, pp. A2525-A2526, June 29, 1942.
40. *Ibid.*, Appendix, A2676-A2677, July 9, 1942.
41. *Ibid.*, Appendix, p. A3035, July 15, 1942.
42. *Ibid.*, Appendix, pp. A3015-A3016, August 3, 1942.
43. *Ibid.*, pp. 3212-3214, September 3, 1942.
44. *Ibid.*, Appendix, pp. A3231-A3233, September 7, 1942.
45. *Ibid.*, Appendix, A3427-A3428, September 24, 1942.
46. *Ibid.*, pp. 7441-7458, September 24, 1942.
47. C.R., 78, 1, Vol. 89, No. 5, pp. 138-140, January 12, 1943.
48. *Ibid.*, No. 16, pp. 504-516, February 1, 1943.
49. *Ibid.*, No. 21, pp. 738-745, February 8, 1943.
50. *Ibid.*, No. 21, pp. 759-762, February 8, 1943.
51. *Ibid.*, No. 21, pp. 762-767, February 8, 1943.
52. *Ibid.*, No. 23, Appendix, pp. A541-A542, February 9, 1943.
53. *Ibid.*, No. 23, Appendix, pp. A548-A549, February 10, 1943.
54. *Ibid.*, No. 23, pp. 836-849, February 10, 1943.
55. *Ibid.*, No. 25, Appendix, pp. A607-A608, February 15, 1943.
56. *Ibid.*, p. 1042, February 16, 1943.
57. *Ibid.*, pp. 1144-1146, February 18, 1943.
58. *Ibid.*, No. 28, p. 1165, February 18, 1943.
59. *Ibid.*, No. 63, p. 3087, April 7, 1943.
60. *Ibid.*, No. 33, Appendix, pp. A847-A849, February 25, 1943.
61. *Ibid.*, No. 40, Appendix, pp. A1094-A1095, March 8, 1943.
62. *Ibid.*, No. 45, Appendix, pp. A1262-A1263, March 15, 1943.
63. *Ibid.*, No. 52, Appendix, pp. A1503-1504, March 24, 1943.
64. *Ibid.*, No. 58, pp. 2833-2840, March 31, 1943.
65. *Ibid.*, No. 59, Appendix, A1684-A1685, April 1, 1943.
66. *Ibid.*, No. 63, pp. 3066-3068, April 7, 1943.
67. *Ibid.*, p. 3088, April 7, 1943.
68. *Ibid.*, No. 65, p. 3248, April 9, 1943.
69. *Ibid.*, No. 97, Appendix, p. A2812, May 27, 1943; p. 4987, May 27, 1943.
70. *Ibid.*, No. 125, p. 7112, July 2, 1943.
71-74. *Who's Who in America*, 1942-1943.
75. Hearings, Vol. XV, *passim*.
76. *Chicago Sun*, December 18, 1943.

1. *Chicago Sun*, December 18, 1943.

2. *Ibid.*, January 26, 1944.

3. *Chicago Tribune*, February 17, 1944; *Chicago Sun*, February 17, 1944.

4. *New York Times*, February 19, 1944; *Chicago Daily News*, February 19, 1944.

5. C.R., 78, 2, Vol. 90, No. 45, pp. 2470 ff., March 9, 1944.

6. *PM*, March 20, 1944, p. 5.

7. C.R., 78, 2, Vol. 90, No. 50, pp. 2728, 2729, March 16, 1944.

8. *PM*, March 21, 1944; *Ibid.*, March 24, 1944.

9. *Ibid.*, March 26, 1944.

10. *New York Mirror*, March 27, 1944, Walter Winchell, "A Reporter's Report to the Nation."

11. *New York Times*, March 27, 1944; *New York Herald Tribune*, March 27, 1944; *New York Sun*, March 27, 1944; *PM*, March 27, 1944; *New York Journal-American*, March 27, 1944; *New York World Telegram*, March 27, 1944.

12, 13. *New York Post*, March 22, 1944, quoting *The Post* (Washington, D. C.).

14, 15. *New York Times*, March 30, 1944; *New York Herald Tribune*, March 30, 1944.

16. *PM*, April 2, 1944.

17. *The New Republic*, March 6, 1944, p. 301.

INDEX

Dies, Martin: aided by John Nance Garner, 31; answers Representative Dickstein, 208 ff.; attacks C.I.O. Political Action Committee, 270 ff., 280 ff.; attacks Lawyers Guild, 271 ff.; attacks *Sabotage* and *Under Cover*, 272 ff.; attacks Walter Winchell, 274 ff.; biographical data, 65 f.; on bureaucracy, 39, 247 ff.; capitalism helped by, 9; challenges democracy, 7 ff., 9 f.; chip off old block, 31; claims to have educated American people, 151; concerned over government employees, 102 f.; condemns bureaucracy (centralization and internationalism; praises 19th century liberalism), 247 ff.; condemns class, racial and religious hatred, 103 ff., 108; condemns "Giants of Concentrated Wealth," 33, 34; condemns New Deal, 93 f.; contradicts earlier position, 8 ff., 32 f.; defends his committee: (in 1939), 180 f., (in 1941), 208 ff., (in 1942), 258 f.; defines "Americanism," 5, 140 f.; defines Communism, 142 f; defines un-Americanism, 143 f; on depression and unemployment, 40 f.; discusses communism and criminality, 218 ff.; discusses democracy, 38 f.; discusses freedom of speech, 111, 277; discusses "isms," 47 ff.; discusses labor legislation, 218 ff.; discusses liberalism, tolerance, 56 f., 186, 277; discusses methods of communism, 47 ff; discusses revolution of our times, 33 f.; discusses whispering campaign, 108; and early investigations, 54 ff.; explains fall of France, 210 f.; expresses his own views, Chapter 6 *passim;* favors conservation, 44; finds subversives on federal payroll, 262 ff.; how he examines a witness, 73 ff.; on immigration and the "alien menace," 49 ff.; on immigration and unemployment, 50; on individualism, 36 ff.; investigates education, Chapter VII, *passim;* on isolation and unemployment, 50; on isolation and national defense, 44 ff., 202; on labor, 41 f.; makes omnibus speech to Congress, 217 ff.; member of Rules Committee, 31; might have averted Pearl Harbor, 223 f.; on monetary legislation, 42 ff.; president of cloak-room Demagog Club, 199; pretends attacks on him are attacks on Congress, 272, 274, 278, 280; and the President,

53 f.; proclaims new Monroe Doctrine, 203; radical views of, 8 f., 33 f.; radio address by, 184 f.; reduces tolerance, 3 f.; refers to his father, 30, 180 f., 184, 228 f.; requires little evidence, 91 ff.; in retreat, Chapter X; rises to a point of personal privilege, 227 ff., 244 ff., 247 ff., 271 ff.; said Japanese were bluffing, 241; says communism, nazi-ism, and fascism are fundamentally alike, 80 ff., 147, 200, 211, 214; says fundamental causes of communism and nazi-ism should be examined, 115; says Lindbergh is not a Fascist, 114; sees things as black or white, 155 f.; and sit-down strikes, 55 f; solution to immigration problem, 51 f.; solution to refugee problem, 52; speaks for resolution authorizing his investigation, 62 ff.; speaks on Trojan Horse in America (1940), 199 ff., 208; states form of German government not of concern to American people, 45, 148 f.; threat to America, Part III, 171; under fire, Chapter IX, *passim,* 173 ff.; uses pressure device, 150, 270; uses propaganda tricks, 13 ff., 69 f., 86 ff., 156 f., 252 f., 259, 272, 274; uses weasel words, 149 f.; warns against Communist fifth column, 112, 201, 203, 220 ff., 223; warns the President, 213 ff.

Dies, Martin, Sr.: called himself "an honest demagogue," 29 f.; called himself a reformer, 22; called Samuel Untermeyer "Hebrew brother," 21; condemns socialism, 26 ff.; congressional career of, Chapter II; contrasts attributes of man and woman, 24; discusses causes of war, 20 f.; discussion of democracy, 18 f.; disliked investigations, 21 f.; farewell address of, 28 ff.; favored demagoguery, 23; favored white supremacy, 17, 22; opposed conservation, 23; opposed foreign immigration, 17 f.; opposed militarism, 19 f.; opposed woman suffrage, 23 ff.; son's references to, 32; supports World War I, 21

Dilling, Mrs. Elizabeth, 177, 253
Dingell, Rep. John D., 177
Disabled American Veterans of the World War, 63
Dobrzyniski, Zygmund, 122
Dodd, William E., Jr., 251
Dolsen, James H., 199
Douglas, Melvin, 158 f.

Douglas, Prof. Paul H., 121, 128. 183, 190
Dubrowski, Dr. D. H., 131
Dutt, R. Palme, 131

Eberharter, Herman P., 258, 268, 281; appointed to Dies committee, 260
Edelman, John W., 158 f.
Education, Chapter VII
Educational Movements of Today by Walter Albion Squires, D.D., 125
Einstein, Albert, 121, 190
Eliot, Rep., 212, 225 ff., 228, 229, 231 ff., 237, 240, 243 f.
Emergency Peace Committee, 122
Export-Import Bank of Washington, D. C., 197

Facci, Guiseppi, 253, 255
Fahy, Jack, 253
Farage, Prof. D. James, 239
Farmers' Educational and Co-operative Union, Local No. 68, of Pennsylvania, 63
Fascism: contrasted to Americanism, 142 ff.; defined, 7 f.; referred to, 165, 220, 229, 247, 261, 277
Fascist, 7 f., 168, 200, 208, 226, 229, 233, 238, 239, 241, 245, 248, 274, 275, 279
Fascist party, 104
Federal and government employees, 184, 262 ff.; and radicalism, 102, 104, 250 ff., 252 f., 262 ff.
Federal Bureau of Investigation, 206, 226, 245, 257, 259, 271
Federal Communications Commission, 216, 225, 231, 250 f.
Federal Council of Churches of Christ in America, 63
Federal Writers' Project, 106
Fellow traveler, reference to, 13, 80, 113 f., 185; defined, 145; discussed, 259
Fellowship of Reconciliation, 72
Fenlon, Prof., 119 f.
Field, Marshall, 248 f.
Fiery Cross, 243
Fifth Column, 199 ff., 206, 220 f., 222 f., 225, 227, 228, 231 f.
Fischer, Louis, 158 f.
Fish, Rep. Hamilton, 143, 175 f., 198, 207, 247, 259, 276
Fitzgerald, Vinson L., 121
Flanagan, Mrs. Hallie, 67
Fleischer, Mr., 83 f.
Fly, James Lawrence, 215, 225, 231
Foreign governments, character of, no concern of America, 45, 148 f., 251 f.

Foreign relations, American involvement in, opposed, 18, 45 f.
Foreign sources of American culture, 285 f.
Ford, Henry, 197, 238
Ford, Rep. Leland M., 214, 240 f.
Forsyth, Margaret, 158 f.
France, 107, 203, 210 f., 213 f.
Frank, Waldo, 158 f.
Frankfield, Phillip, 199
Franklin, Jay, 186 f.
Fraternal Patriotic Americans, Inc., 63
Frazier-Lundeen bill, 124
Free enterprise, 216 f., 250
Freeman, Milton V., 254
Frey, John P., 101, 116 f.
Friends of Soviet Russia, 131, 159 ff.
Front organizations, 48, 80, 103, 113 f., 119, 147, 201, 226, 232, 245, 251, 254, 261, 265, 285, 287

Gale, Rep. Richard P., 258
Gallup Poll, 188
Gannet, Lewis, 158 f.
Garland Fund, 245
Garner, John Nance, 31
Gellhorn, Walter, 253
George Washington University, 118
German-Americans, 112
German-American Bund, 105, 147, 197, 201, 203, 211, 220, 238, 240, 264
German-American League for Culture, 63
Germany, *see* Axis.
Geyer, Rep., 192 f.
Giants of concentrated wealth, 34 ff.
Gilbert, 197
Gitlow, Benjamin, 128 f.
Glass, Sen. Carter, 225, 232
Goebbels, Herr, 241, 243, 245, 277
Goldschmidt, Arthur F., 254
Goodrich, Trudy, 76
Goodsell, Prof. Wyllistine, 190
Graham, Frank P., 153 f.
Granger, Lester B., 158 f.
Great Britain, 117, 203, 208, 213
Green, William, 52, 188, 232, 282

Hall, Rep. Leonard W., 204
Hand, Prof. Harold C., 123
Hardman, J. B. S., 158 f.
Harrison, Charles Yale, 158 f.
Harrison, Sen. Pat, 75
Hart, Merwin K., 205
Hartmann, Dr. George, 131, 134 f., 136
Harvard University, 118, 129
Hays, Arthur Garfield, 178
Healey, Rep. Arthur D., 65, 174 f., 184

Hearings before the Dies Committee, Chapter V, *passim;* appendix volumes, 91 f.; destroyed organizations by unfavorable publicity, 113; quantity of, 70; reports not dependent on, 138 f.; samples of, Chapter V, *passim*
Hecht, Harold, 75 f.
Heights Jewish Club, Inc., of New York City, 63
Henderson, Leon, 216, 222
Henson, Mr., 78 f.
Henson, Francis, 158 f.
Herberg, Will, 158 f.
Herling, John, 253
Hicks, Granville, 118, 129 f., 160 f.
Hillman, Sidney, 270, 271, 275, 281, 282
Himwich, Harold E., 160 f.
Hinckley, William, 90
Hitler, 38, 45, 146, 150, 181, 197, 200, 202 f., 206, 213, 219, 222, 227, 233, 238, 246, 247, 254, 257, 272, 277, 278, 286
Hoffman, Rep. Clare E., 227, 236
Holmes, Justice, 190
Hook, Rep., 176, 193, 197, 198, 208, 212
Hoover, Herbert, 40, 255
Hopkins, Harry, 68
Howard University, 124
Howe, Chester, 120
Hughes, Chief Justice Charles Evans, 232
Hull, Cordell, 52
Human rights, 140 ff.
Hunt, Henry T., 254

Ickes, Harold F., 93, 100, 105, 196, 208, 232, 261 f., 266 f.
Immigration, discussed by Dies, 49 ff.; relationship of unemployment to, 50 f.; solution to, by Dies, 51 f.
Imperialism, 284
Individualism, 36 ff.
In Fact, 243
Institute of Propaganda Analysis, 13
Interdepartmental Committee, 266
International Labor Defense, 159 ff.
International Publishers, 131
International Typographical Union, 63
International Workers Order, 63, 159 ff.
Investigations, early attitude toward, 54 ff.
Investigators, the, Chapter IV, *passim,* 267 ff.; found what they sought, 138 f.

Isaacs, Stanley, 160 f.
Isolation, favored by Dies, 44 ff.
Isolationism, 284
Isolationists, 258
Isms, early views on, 47 ff.
Italy, 4

Jackson, Gardner, 160 f., 217 f., 245, 248, 254
Jackson, Robert, 93, 232
Jaffe, Prof. Louis L., 239
Japanese, The, 167, 169, 221, 223, 225, 227, 228, 231 f., 237, 241, 257, 279, 283
Jemison, Alice Lee, 124 ff.
Jewish War Veterans of the United States, 63
Jews and anti-Semitism, 6, 51, 81, 108, 109 f., 112, 167, 177, 183, 208, 240, 245, 249, 254, 258, 272, 274
Johnson, Alvin S., 126
Johnson, Mary, 226
Johnson, Mordecai W., 124
Junior Chamber of Commerce, 226
Justice Department, 167 f., 178, 204, 206, 220, 223, 227 f., 242, 243, 244, 245, 256, 263, 265 f., 271, 273

Kaen, A. S., 123
Kahn, Albert E., 274 f.
Kamp, Joseph, 274
Katz, Vera, 120
Karr, David, 253
Kefauver, Dean Grayson N., 123, 190
Keller, Rep., 174 f., 191
Kellock, Katherine, 254 f.
Kenney, Robert W., 273
Kenyon, Dorothy, 160 f.
Kidd, A. M., 123
Kingdon, Frank, 160 f.
Kirchen, J. L., 123
Kirchwey, Freda, 160 f.
Knowles, Harper L., 99, 101, 123 f., 124
Knowles, Shepard, 174
Knox, Sec. of Navy Frank, 228, 232
Kontra-Komintern, 256 f.
Ku Klux Klan, 177, 238, 243, 245, 256
Kuhn, Fritz, 112, 195 f., 238, 256

Labor, 41 f., 86, 96, 107, 150 f., 181, 189, 191, 218 ff., 257, 270, 271, 272, 273, 281, 282
Labor Department, 99, 145
Labor unions, 111, 147, 181
Ladies of the Grand Army of the Republic, 63
LaFollette, Senator Robert M., 99
La Guardia, Mayor Fiorella, 232

Time Magazine, 165
Tippett, Tom, 253
Toby Edison Memorial Club of Newark, N. J., 64
Tolerance: Dies reduces limits of, 3, 5; discussed, 175, 182; praised by Dies, 57, 245 f., 277
Totalitarianism: essence of, 3, 166, 250 ff.; defined by Dies, 155 f.
Totten, Ashley P., 160 f.
Trachtenberg, Alexander, 131
Transport Workers of America, 84 ff., 92 f.
Trojan Horse in America, the, 91 f.; Anti-New Deal campaign document, 93 f.; Dies speaks on, in Congress, 199 ff., 204, 208
True, James, 177
Tugwell, R. G., 128

Un-Americanism, 143 f., 146, 226, 235, 258, 283 f.
Under Cover, 272, 273, 275
Unemployment, 40 f.
Union for Democratic Action, 156 ff., 243, 280
Union Theological Seminary, 261
United American Mechanics, Inc., the General Executive Boards, State Councils of Junior Order of, 63
United Automobile Workers, 106
United Spanish War Veterans, 64
United Nations, 285
United States Housing Authority, 197
United War Veterans Council, 64
University of California, 123, 190
University of Chicago, 190
University of Minnesota, 131
University of Moscow, 126

Van Doren, Carl, 131
Vassar College, 190
Vaughn, David, 243 f, 260
Veterans of Foreign Wars of the United States, 64, 117, 188
Viereck, George Sylvester, 240, 256
Vincent, Merle, 253 f.
Voltaire, 67
Voorhis, Rep. Jerry, 70 f., Chapter V, *passim*, 76 ff., 132 f., 134, 137, 153, 155, 157 ff., 162 ff., 166 ff., 177 f., 182 ff., 198, 204, 212, 236, 237, 241, 242, 244, 246 f., 254 ff., 260, 267, 268; affirms right of criticism, 162 ff., 255 f.; cramps Dies' style, 155; resigns from committee, 260; wants committee procedures changed, 182, 191 f.

Wahl, David, 253
Wallace, Henry A., 93, 232, 241, 242, 262 f., 267
Walsh, Frank P., 239
War, winning of, the main issue, 164 f., 246
War Production Board, 253
War Security Act, 262 f.
Ward, Harry F., 87 ff., 113
Washburne, Carleton, 124 ff.
Washington Committee for Democratic Action, 159 ff., 168, 244
Washington Committee to Aid China, 168
Washington Star, 227
Washington Cooperative Bookshop, 168, 244
Watson, Dr. Goodwin, 122, 216, 218, 251
Wayne University, 120
Weinstein, Jacob, 160 f.
Weiss, Representative Samuel A., 241, 258
Welsh, Edward, 160 f.
Wiggins, Lee Manning, 160 f.
Williams, Howard Y., 160 f.
Winrod, Gerald B., 177, 230, 279
Washington Evening Star, 187
Washington Post, 173, 187, 194 f.
Washington Times-Herald, 165
Weyl, Nathaniel, 253
Wheeler-Hill, Mr. James, 197
Whipple, T. K., 123
White Camellia, Knights of, 226, 239
Who's Who in America, 65
Williams, Aubrey, 105
Willkie, Wendell, 218, 226; condemns methods of Dies committee, 239
Wilson, Major Hampden, surveys education for Dies committee, 131 ff.
Wilson, President Woodrow, 21, 23, 31
Winchell, Walter, 249, 274, 275, 276, 277, 278, 279, 280
Wolff, Milton. 80 ff.
Woll, Matthew, 125
Woodward, Mrs. Ellen, 67 f., 106 f.
Workers Alliance, 76, 159 ff.
Works Progress Administration, 106, 193, 213
World Youth Congress, 119

York, (Pa.) *Gazette and Daily*, 233
Young Women's Christian Association, the National Board of, 188